MORE WITH LESS

MORE WITH LESS

PAUL MacCREADY

AND THE DREAM

OF EFFICIENT

FLIGHT

PAUL CIOTTI

ENCOUNTER BOOKS
SAN FRANCISCO

First edition published in 2002 by Encounter Books, an activity of Encounter for Culture and Education, Inc., a nonprofit tax exempt corporation.

Encounter Books website address: www.encounterbooks.com

Manufactured in the United States and printed on acid-free paper.

The paper used in this publication meets the minimum requirements of ANSI/NISO Z39.48-1992 (R 1997)(*Permanence of Paper*).

FIRST EDITION

Library of Congress Cataloging-in-Publication Data

Ciotti, Paul.
    More with less : Paul MacCready and the dream of efficient flight / Paul Ciotti.—1st ed.
    p. cm.
    Includes bibliographical references and index.
    ISBN 1-893554-50-3 (alk. paper)
    1. MacCready, Paul B.   2. Aeronautical engineers—United States—
Biography.   3. Human Powered aircraft.   4. Mechanical efficiency.   I. Title.
TL540.M227 C56 2002
629.13'0092—dc21
[B]

2002072464

10   9   8   7   6   5   4   3   2   1

In the summer of 1976, the Pasadena aerodynamicist Paul MacCready loaded his family into a van and began driving across the country on a much-needed summer vacation. By the time he got to Kansas he was driving with his head out the window to watch circling hawks and vultures. It completely changed his life. Thus began the Golden Age of Paul MacCready.

Contents

List of Illustrations

ONE

From Rodent-Powered Aircraft to Stratospheric Satellites

ONE FREEZING DAWN IN NOVEMBER 1988 at Edwards Air Force Base, in the high desert sixty miles northeast of Los Angeles, a group of reporters found themselves standing near the runway looking at a huge, long, ungainly flying wing. Called the Centurion, it was proportioned more like a stepladder than an aircraft. There was no fuselage or tail, only fourteen electric motors with awkward, fat propellers spaced along a 247-foot Mylar-covered wing. The transparent, drooping wing didn't seem capable of supporting its own weight. A resolute hawk could rip it to shreds.

When the ground controller first applied power, the windmill-like props began to turn so languorously that it was hard to believe they could have any effect at all. But against all odds the plane began to roll. As it gained speed the wingtips flexed upward with a kind of stately majesty, not unlike some great mythical bird slowly unfolding its wings or a massive ocean liner edging away from the pier. Gradually it rose from the runway, in the words of *Los Angeles Times* reporter Bob Jones, "never exceeding the speed of a man riding on a bicycle." From a distance it strummed psychic chords about huge silent objects hanging motionless in the sky. As the wing passed over their heads, the watching reporters cheered.

Designed and built by Paul MacCready's company, AeroVironment, the Centurion was designed to run on solar cells during the daytime and fuel cells at night. The commercial version, called the Helios, would stay up as long as six months at a time, flying in small slow circles high over a city. Earlier versions of the aircraft, called the Pathfinder, had reached 80,000 feet—higher than rain, hail, the jet stream or weather. Once in commercial operation, said AeroVironment, the Helios would serve as a "stratospheric satellite," doing everything a communications satellite does but do it from an altitude of 13 miles instead of 22,236 miles.

Because Helios used off-the-shelf components, it would be straightforward to build. As it ran on solar power, fuel costs would be zero. With the propeller shaft being the only moving part, the electric motors would be maintenance-free. The Helios would fly at around 60,000 feet, an altitude low enough that it wouldn't need space-hardened (cosmic ray resistant) electronics. People could communicate with it via light mobile phones and portable computers. Unlike satellites, whose technology couldn't be updated during their six-to-ten-year lifespan, the Helios could return to earth for new technology retrofits every six months. Wireless broadband Internet service would be available to home users at a small fraction of the estimated $1,000 hookup fee for private fiber-optic connections.

Because the Helios was so big and unwieldy, the fleet would be based in a place like Hawaii where the weather was mild and the winds were light. After takeoff, the planes would slowly climb to altitude and then spend days or even weeks flying to their destinations. Being made of sections, each of which was capable of flying independently, the Helios wing performed less like a single structure than a flight of planes in line-abreast formation. In turbulence it flexed and rippled rather than broke. It rode the wind the way an inflatable air mattress rides the incoming surf.

Whether such a plane could ever replace land-based cell phone technology or rapidly improving low-earth-orbit satellite communication systems was a question whose answer was literally up in the air. But the fact that such a plane had been designed to fly autonomously for six months at a time entirely on solar power (backed up by fuel cells at night) was both a marvel in itself and a tribute to the vision of its designers.

The Helios had its unplanned origins in the efforts of a small group of largely unknown southern California modelers, builders and visionaries, working independently on their own whims, hobbies and obsessions over more than four decades. Back in the summer of 1976 a then-unknown meteorologist and businessman named Paul MacCready pulled some of them together to spend what he thought would be a few weekends building a man-powered plane to try to win an aeronautical engineering prize that had gone unclaimed for the previous seventeen years. Although that prize proved surprisingly difficult to win, ultimately taking this group nearly a year in

Even as a boy, MacCready liked big models.

spite of MacCready's radically different approach, that first success led quickly to an even greater one: a man-powered plane that flew across the English Channel in June of 1979. MacCready soon followed that with a solar-powered plane that flew from Paris to London; an 18-foot flying model of a pterodactyl that flew under its own power for a Smithsonian-sponsored IMAX film in January 1986; a solar-powered car that won a race across Australia in July of 1987; and the still-in-development Helios "eternal" plane.

As MacCready's growing company proved itself capable of carrying out these increasingly difficult projects without his constant oversight, MacCready increasingly began to divorce himself from the company to follow his own sometimes highly eccentric interests, such as strap-on leg braces (called "Technalegs") that would, he said, enable athletes to run 90-minute marathons and 3-minute miles. Within his own company he became an increasingly enigmatic figure, showing up not so much to talk business as to focus on technical details, find just the right size of motor or scrounge for spare parts. He worked on all sorts of ideas: pocket gyms; ornithopters (flapping-wing planes); remote-controlled, battery-powered, camera-equipped model planes; cars with legs; battery-assisted bikes; Pogo Stick–powered boats; robotic cockroaches and, for an educational project, a rodent-powered model plane.

The funny thing was, the cutting-edge planes and vehicles that made MacCready an internationally famous figure, hailed for his genius and creativity, were, with the exception of the Helios, not so much practical machines as concrete metaphors for a personal philosophy that he called "doing more with much less." Although this wasn't a notion original to him, MacCready had become the most visible spokesman for a kind of philosophical yearning that had been around as long as man himself: an innate attraction to efficiency.

TWO

The Moral Case for Efficiency

WHEN I WAS YOUNGER I had a bedtime fantasy: Before I fell asleep in my cozy bed I pictured myself gliding through the frozen north woods at night in an electric-powered snowmobile of my own design. Under a bubble canopy, I was warm and comfortable in a leather-padded reclining seat. As Bach or Vivaldi played softly on my stereo speakers, my instrument panel glowed a gentle green and the front skis quietly hissed through the snow. While I threaded my way slowly and silently through snow-covered trees, miles from civilization or the hope of outside aid, my cozy and efficient little machine kept me safe and warm even as I was enveloped by the stark beauty of the frozen woods and the icy indifference of the eternal stars.

I have no idea what a psychiatrist might make of my dream, but the desire to use low-powered technology to get closer to nature is hardly a unique one. Many people passionately prefer canoes to motorboats, bicycles to motorcycles and skis to snowmobiles. They aren't deliberately obstinate or hostile to technology, and their preferences aren't necessarily related to fears of global warming, ozone holes or a shrinking oil supply. Such people are trying not so much to save the world as be fully a part of it. They aren't driven by politics but rather by an inner sense that some kinds of efficiency just feel natural and right.

In some quarters, efficiency has a terrible reputation, conjuring up images of relentless assembly lines, aesthetically unconscious engineers and an ugly, antihuman worldview, lacking compassion, sensitivity or soul. But there is reason to believe that there is a moral component to efficiency, and that the yearning for it can bring out the best in human beings, not the worst, and that the idea of efficiency is not only some horrible construct imposed on us by technology or profit-obsessed corporations, but actually something that is embedded in our genes and thus one of our most enduringly human traits.

Certainly it appears to be present in the genes of some other species. As MacCready himself has noted, nature doesn't tolerate failed experiments. Mistakes get culled in a single generation—the misfits leave no progeny. On the other hand, supremely efficient species, such as the wandering albatross, can survive quite nicely in hostile environments like Roaring Forties, an almost-mythic world of gale-force winds and towering waves, nearly unimpeded by the presence of land, in the far South Atlantic and Pacific. Such fierce storms sweep over the albatross rookeries that the chicks survive only by clinging to their nests with beaks and feet, while the adults ride out the storms over the ocean in the air. Far from suffering in the wind and waves, they use their tapering 11-foot wings to extract energy from wind gradients (sharp variations in velocity with altitude). By shuttling back and forth in the wind gradient an albatross can stay aloft all day virtually without flapping its wings at all. "Once it gets to ten meters," observes MacCready, "its work is done for the day." A smaller relation, the black-footed albatross, routinely shuttles back and forth between Hawaii and the waters off San Francisco in search of food for its young, sleeping on the wing.

It's not just birds who operate efficiently. John Lighton, a Nevada entomologist who has done pioneering work studying the metabolism of insects, says there is a good reason ants are so ubiquitous: for them, the cost of walking is very low. Even so, harvester ants seeking food never venture more than about a hundred yards from the nest, instinctively realizing that beyond this point it takes more energy to get the food home than they get out of it.

Nowadays, when virtually anyone, including the old, obese, lame or pregnant, can get on an airplane and fly nonstop from Los Angeles to London, it's easy to forget that for the first 2.5 million years of human existence, man walked where he needed to go, and for much of that time, walking was the most efficient way—and often the only way—to get anywhere. Humans walked out of Africa, into Europe, across Asia, and over the Bering Strait down through North America to the very tip of South America. As biologist Bernd Heinrich explains in *Racing the Antelope,* early man was an "endurance predator." While many animals had better physiology for running, such as longer, leaner legs or proportionally larger hearts, few animals had man's hypertrophied sweating response, which gave him far superior endurance in midday hunts on the African savannas.

Because early man (a descendant of what Heinrich calls "bipedal savanna hunting apes" from 6 million b.c.) was highly mobile, he was able easily to move from Africa to the northern European steppes to prey on the large herds of caribou, bison and woolly mammoths. Before the climate warmed up at the end of the last ice age, causing the big northern herds to disappear and forcing man to switch to agriculture, humans lived primarily off protein. They had strength and stamina. The hunting territory of a band of prehistoric men was 500 to 1,500 square miles, far larger than that of any other primate and the same size as that of wolf packs, often considered the widest-ranging land predator.

On the chase, all of man's advantages came into play: his sweat glands kept him cool; the hair on his head protected him from the heat of the sun; his erect, two-legged stance enabled him to keep his prey in sight; and his superior intelligence enabled him to envision his ultimate success, even when his prey had disappeared over the next rise. "Other things being equal, those hunters who had the most love of nature would be the ones who sought all of its allures," writes Heinrich. "They were the ones who persisted the longest on the trail. They derived pleasure from being out, exploring, and traveling afar. When they felt fatigue and pain, they did not stop, because their dream carried them still forward. They were our ancestors."

As a superpredator, man was unsurpassed. When it came to calories expended per pound of body weight per mile, a man on foot was fifty times more efficient than a mouse, five times more efficient than a rabbit, twice as efficient as a dog, almost as efficient as a horse and half as efficient as a salmon. When the Navajos wanted an unblemished deer hide for religious ceremonies, Heinrich writes, they chased a deer until it fell from exhaustion, then throttled it with their hands.

Over the eons the genes of the most efficient superpredators were passed down to their descendants, which may explain why their yearnings, passions and, yes, appreciation for efficiency still flow through the veins of humans today. It may also be why so many people instinctively understand the aesthetic and practical advantages of living off the amount of energy the sun gives each of us every day, rather than, as MacCready says, always drawing down the principal—using up fossil fuel, "the stored energy of sunlight captured millions of years ago."

SOME SCIENTISTS HAVE SUCH a visceral distaste for scientific inelegance that they fret and stew over a problem until they end up making a major discovery. The young Albert Einstein, for instance, was so offended at the inability of electromagnetic field theory to explain the dynamo (an electrical generator) satisfactorily that he ended up totally altering our conception of space and time. As science writer Tim Ferris notes in *Coming of Age in the Milky Way,* Einstein wrote his initial paper on relativity ("On the Electrodynamics of Moving Bodies") in part to remedy what he regarded as an aesthetic aberration. Quoting the American historian Henry Adams, Ferris points out that at the beginning of the twentieth century, dynamos weren't just another technology but a "moral force" and a "symbol of infinity." Although dynamos were changing the world right in front of Einstein's eyes (his father and uncle had built them in their back yard), no one, including Albert, fully understood how they worked. Ferris writes,

> Under existing theory, the moving field was to be explained according to one set of rules if viewed from the perspective of a dynamo's rotating magnet, and another if viewed from the stationary electrical coil.... It bothered Einstein as unaesthetic. "The thought that one is dealing here with two fundamentally different cases was for me unbearable," he recalled. "The difference between these two cases could not be a real difference but rather, in my conviction, only a difference in the choice of the reference point."

Stephen Wozniak, the cofounder of Apple Computer, once stayed up to 2 A.M. laying out black Mylar traces for a circuit board for the original Apple II. Unlike Einstein, Wozniak did not solve some great mystery of the universe, feed-throughs being simply places in the circuit board where the printed electrical traces pass under adjoining ones so they won't touch. But to Wozniak, having more feed-throughs than absolutely necessary struck him as inelegant. By rigorously rearranging his design Wozniak reduced the number of feed-throughs from 50 down to 3. "I just wanted to minimize feed-throughs," he said. "It's totally aestheic. Nobody even knows I did it. But I know, and it's just aesthetically perfect to me."

Thomas Hoving, the down-to-earth former head of New York's Metropolitan Museum of Art, once showed a metal object to a group of art students and then asked them whether it was a tool or a work of art. In fact, the object, which was polished metal, lean and flowing and full of subtle curves, turned out to be an obstetrical tool. Similarly, the hull of a racing yacht is fashioned for only one thing—to win races; yet even people who know nothing about sailing can appreciate its symmetrical beauty and fluid lines. Airfoils often display beautiful compound curves, even though the engineers who designed them were only trying to maximize lift and minimize drag.

At a certain level, engineering is aesthetically satisfying to the soul. In a world without constraints, the need for efficiency vanishes, and in many cases so does beauty too. For example, back in the days of the CP/M operating system, many computer programs were written by inspired artists. No one but an artist could write a program that was both very useful and yet small enough to work in the tiny amount of internal memory available at the time. But as better operating systems became available and the cost of memory and storage devices plummeted, personal computer programs went from lean, light gazelles to massive, plodding Clydesdales, lacking both elegance and efficiency. In the process, something important was lost and the result was that few people (including the programmers themselves) thought of programmers as artists anymore.

Although it's hard to feel much sympathy with the modern-day Luddite left when it talks about the terrible social impact of pollution-free fusion power, I've often wondered if cheap, limitless energy would really be the unambiguous good that many power advocates think it will. For just as artists tend to be more creative when they have to work under constraints, so do engineers. Any aeronautical engineer can design a plane that will fly with a 1,000-horsepower engine, but if you tell him he has to design a plane that can fly on the amount of power a single human can continuously produce (one-third horsepower) or on the output of a 47-foot wing panel of solar cells (1,500 watts, the same as a hair dryer), that is when artistry and creativity flourish. Only a few people can do that. Many live in southern California. The best known is Paul MacCready.

THREE

Alpha Males and the Twilight Club

When I first began discussing low-power people and their inventions with Paul MacCready, I found it hard to reconcile his appearance and demeanor with what I already knew of his accomplishments. Although it's not always apparent in casual conversation (he can be low-key almost to the point of vanishing into the wallpaper), MacCready is known worldwide for his efficient, man-powered machines. He's been called the "Dr. Edward Teller" of solar power, a "cold dreamer," and the "poet laureate of flight." He's a friend and confidant of Nobel Prize winners, generals, cutting-edge academicians, entrepreneurs and CEOs. He's a ubiquitous lecturer on creativity, thinking skills and efficiency ("doing more with much less," he calls it) and represented by the same speakers' bureau that handles Jimmy Carter, Jerry Seinfeld, Dan Rather, Tommy Lasorda and Kareem Abdul-Jabbar. His achievements have been recognized by dozens of prestigious organizations, including the Lindbergh Foundation, the National Aeronautics Association and the American Society of Mechanical Engineers, which in 1980 named him "Engineer of the Century." *Time* called him one of the twentieth century's one hundred most creative minds.

Still, for someone hailed by *Esquire* as the most "delightful and creative" engineer of the last hundred years, he's the opposite of hale-fellow-well-met. Perhaps as a result of his childhood dyslexia, he has a hard time with names and faces. Although I had two long exploratory breakfast meetings with him at the California Institute of Technology when I first thought of writing this book, when I ran into him on the stairs of Caltech's Thomas

Hall a few months later, we chatted pleasantly for a couple of minutes before I realized that he didn't know who I was.

Far more than most public figures, MacCready seems to have no interest in asserting dominance or authority. He generally speaks without passion or emphasis, sometimes in a voice so soft and inflection-free that a tape recorder can't pick it up from three feet away. His letters to the editor are so moderate that one wonders why he bothers to write at all. Despite his many successes, he's never been a prima donna or someone to whom deference must be paid. Back in the late 1980s, when he was less jealous of his free time, I read something he had said in the newspaper and gave him a call, and we chatted happily for half an hour. Later he mailed me a book on the same subject. Not only is he unimpressed by flashy appearances, he himself doesn't dress for success, often appearing in casually mismatched outfits, battered sneakers and a plastic digital watch. Sometimes in conversation he toys with his jacket buttons in the manner of a bashful five-year-old. Although in his seventies, he still gets a primal thrill out of windup flapping-wing ornithopters and retains enough boyish enthusiasm to mount a video camera on a remote-control vehicle in order to chase a skunk out from under his house.

"In person, Paul MacCready is a less-than-awe-inspiring figure," wrote Josh Hammer in a 1987 *Los Angeles Times* story.

> He's a slight man, with a pale, birdlike visage and oversized horn-rimmed spectacles perched on a sunburned nose—a classic Walter Mitty character. His voice comes out in a reedy monotone, devoid of the tiniest change in pitch or emotion. He moves awkwardly, carrying traces of the ungainly adolescent who was always picked dead last in schoolyard choose-'em-ups.

But it's a mistake to conclude from his image that MacCready is a negligible personality. "He's always been very competitive by nature, just like Bill Gates," says old friend and former Caltech classmate Henry Jex. "These are people who go to extremes to get something done and they accomplish miracles." MacCready is self-assured, congenitally optimistic, loyal to his friends, physically courageous and at times almost irrationally persistent. He was the U.S. soaring champion three times while still in his twenties and the international champion at age thirty-one. He has climbed Mt. Kilimanjaro, scuba dived with the whale sharks of western Australia and rafted down the Yangtze through the mountains of Tibet. "He's got a new idea every ten seconds," says Chet Kyle, mechanical engineer, efficiency expert and cofounder of the Human Powered Vehicle Association. "Some are great. Some are lousy." The difference between MacCready and other folks with good ideas is that he makes things happen. "He knows how to do things. He can solve problems in the physical world that have baffled other people for decades."

I knew most of this when I attended a dinner where he was the guest speaker a few years ago. Still, it was hard to reconcile his legendary determination, which I had never seen, with his retiring manner, which was always on display.

On this occasion MacCready was speaking to the Twilight Club, a private organization of doctors, lawyers and businessmen who met monthly for drinks, dinner and a talk in the clubhouse of a private Los Angeles golf course. When we took our seats, I found that the elderly gentleman on my right had once been a good friend of Charles Lindbergh's. On my left was the host, a loud, genial man and not overly subtle. When he discovered I was a writer, he asked what I did for my "day job." He also asked what plans I had for my next book.

Like most writers, I have spent most of my life asking other people what they think, so when someone asks me what I think, I tend to go overboard. My next book, I replied, was tentatively entitled *Songs of the Beta Male*. My host had never heard of alpha and beta males, so I briefly explained that these were terms taken from the study of wolf pack behavior. The leader of the pack was the alpha male; he ran the show and had his choice of females. The less commanding wolves (or men) were beta males. With no responsibility to act a part—to seem always confident and fully in charge—they were free to be creative.

Basically, my theory went, alpha males were good at high-status activities, such as making money, running other people's lives and attracting multiple mates; but they couldn't invent things like steam engines, write novels, make mathematical breakthroughs or even draw a really good comic strip. They were far too worried about their social standing to have the insights or the commitment to truth that real creativity demanded. They were more concerned with wearing power suits, dining at posh restaurants and arranging their office furniture to support their sometimes shaky self-image and tenuous control. (This, in fact, was one reason I admired MacCready. He didn't care about any of that stuff.)

MacCready polishing the windshield of an early glider—the Screamin' Wiener.

I had just begun to explain all this to my host when he interrupted to declare, "Everyone in this room is an alpha male."

I don't remember what I said exactly, but I did make a vague demurrer, which seemed to provoke him even more.

"What about Paul MacCready?" he boomed. "Is he an alpha male?"

I should have derailed the question with flattery—"Oh, those categories don't apply to someone like MacCready; people at his level are in a class by themselves"—but I'd had two glasses of wine before dinner and, as is sometimes the case, I was full of myself.

"Well," I said, thinking out loud, "I'd say he's probably more of a beta male but he's a very complex person who ..."

Suddenly MacCready, whom I hadn't even known was listening, spoke up from across the table. "You don't know me well enough to answer that!"

The entire table was looking at me.

"You're right," I said. "I don't."

They say you learn more from your mistakes than your successes. Well, I learned a lot that night, including the fact my beta male theory needed more work and that whatever else one might want to say about MacCready, he was neither humble nor shy.

FOUR

The Case against Elegant Engineering

WHEN I FIRST INTERVIEWED Paul MacCready, I had been following his work for more than two decades. Back in the mid-seventies I'd seen photographs of his pedal-powered Gossamer Albatross seemingly floating on air, highlighted by the setting sun. I'd seen pictures of his solar-powered Sunraycer speeding along the narrow, straight bitumen through the golden sunlight of the Australian outback. I'd watched videos of his battery-powered pterodactyl replica flying through Death Valley. And I'd marveled at videos of the Pathfinder flying wing (predecessor to the Centurion and the high-flying Helios) soaring over the Pacific.

If those weren't examples of elegant engineering, I didn't know what was. So when I first began talking to MacCready, I told him about Stephen Wozniak, Apple Computer's cofounder, who had done some pretty elegant engineering himself. Wozniak, I explained, didn't just get the job done by the quickest, crudest way possible. He wanted it to be beautiful and efficient too. At the highest level, engineering truth and beauty were deeply intertwined.

MacCready wasn't buying it. He thought I was missing the point, mistaking useless elegance for what was really important: true functionality. It was actually Wozniak's entrepreneurially minded partner, Steven Jobs, who, despite his relative lack of technical expertise, was the true "visionary," said MacCready. "There are thousands of Wozniaks around. There is only one Steve Jobs."

Later, as I talked to MacCready's many friends and associates, they all made the same point: the thing that mattered was getting results. MacCready couldn't care less how a job was accomplished or what the prototype looked like. And once he got something working, no matter how crudely, his interest quickly waned. MacCready is "the anti-craftsman," says longtime associate Taras Kiceniuk. "He takes a perverse pride in it, actually."

When I called MacCready's oldest son, Parker, a University of Washington oceanographer, he told me that his father *never* would have stayed up till 2 A.M. like Wozniak to minimize feed-throughs: "His style of engineering is effective engineering, that is, getting the job done, and his motto is, 'if it works, it's beautiful' or 'if it's done, it's beautiful,' not 'if it looks nice, it's beautiful.'"

There is an attractive clarity to the way MacCready thinks. He avoids people who talk better than they perform. He understands that saying something well is not the equivalent of doing something well. If he has an idea in the morning, he likes to have an answer by the afternoon. He has never suffered from what Ray Morgan, former vice president of AeroVironment's Design and Development Division, once called "the plight of the procrastinator." MacCready was notorious around his own company for building complicated Rube-Goldberg-like contraptions with long hardware-store screw bolts sticking out. There was no level of craftsmanship below which he would not sink and no such thing as a prototype too crude. "If you're not making mistakes," he once said, "you're not going fast enough."

That was another thing about MacCready: he couldn't bear the thought of wasting time. When Morgan joined AeroVironment to help him build the sun-powered Solar Challenger, he discovered that MacCready's basic approach was never to put off anything that could be done right now. "He just went out and threw things in the air," says Morgan, a former Lockheed test flight engineer who was used to aerospace's (sometimes maddeningly) methodical approach. "I tried to do things like a preflight check list when we rolled the airplane out of the hangar in the morning. He would say, 'Let's do that after the flight. Let's get it in the air.'"

And, in fact, as Morgan later realized, there was method to MacCready's seeming madness. Although MacCready's planes crashed over and over (from low altitude and low speed), he learned something every time, even if it was only what wouldn't work. In fact, one might argue that it was precisely his high tolerance for failure that had enabled MacCready to win the Kremer Prize for man-powered flight in the first place. "He would try anything," Morgan eventually realized. "His competitors were out there building extremely elaborate aircraft that took 20,000 hours to build. It might be ten years before they got their first flight. MacCready tried to fly [the Gossamer Condor] the first weekend."

FIVE

From King Bladud to the Wright Brothers

HUMAN FLIGHT HAS BEEN ONE of man's perennial yearnings, appearing over and over in myth, religion, literature and dreams. But because early aviators had no knowledge of low-speed, low-power aerodynamics, they simplistically tried to imitate birds by attaching feathers to wing-shaped paddles and strapping them on their arms. Or they would stiffen a cape with wooden rods, hold out their arms and leap from a tower. Bladud, the ninth king of England and the father of King Leir (Lear in Shakespeare), jumped off the temple of Apollo in Trinovantum (London) wearing feather-covered wings and broke his neck. In Rome in A.D. 67, a magician named Simon hit the ground so hard after jumping off a tower that he reportedly splattered Emperor Nero with his blood. In 1178, the "Saracen of Constantinople" advertised that he would jump off a tower and fly around the hippodrome (an oval ring used for horse and chariot races) using a long white robe stiffened with rods. Ridiculed by a huge crowd of onlookers while he waited for the wind to rise, the Saracen jumped off the tower, briefly rose like a bird, then plummeted to his death. Even Leonardo da Vinci designed a flapping-wing device, but being more prudent than most, he never built it.

The difficulty of man-powered flight, it turned out, was intrinsic to human physiology. The heart constitutes only 0.5 percent of a man's total body weight, compared with 8 percent of an eagle's or 22 percent of a hummingbird's, notes Anthony B. Wright in *Daedalus: The Long Odyssey from Myth to Reality.* Furthermore, unlike a sparrow's heart, which beats 800 times per minute, a human heart beats only about 70 times a minute, a rate far too slow to supply the muscles with enough oxygen to allow men to fly.

By the sixteenth century it was becoming increasingly clear that flapping flight from the top of a tower was literally a dead end. On the other hand, it was also obvious that one could make long downhill glides with large, rigid wings, a fair wind and a steep enough hill. In Lucca, an artist by the name of Paolo Guidotti flew a whalebone-and-feather glider 400 yards, stopping only when he hit a roof and broke his thigh.

In 1853, Sir George Cayley secretly built a glider with a vertical rudder and elevators for pitch control and launched his coachman on a 500-yard flight across a valley at the family seat near Scarborough, York. Despite his stunning success, Cayley's coachman promptly resigned, declaiming angrily that he'd been "hired to drive, not to fly."

Two years later, a French sea captain named Le Bris, long enamored of the effortless flight of albatrosses at sea, built an albatross-shaped glider with 46-foot wings and a 13-foot-long body. When he had it towed into the wind behind a horse-drawn wagon, he and his glider rose 300 feet in the air.

In the 1890s, Otto Lilienthal, a multitalented German bird aficionado who made his living manufacturing foghorns and steam engines, built a series of increasingly elegant and efficient foot-launchable gliders out of split willow wands and drum-taut muslin. With their birdlike cambered wings and filigreed trailing edges they looked like something designed by Jules Verne. Lilienthal controlled them with weight shifts, which is to say by vigorously thrusting his legs from side to side. Although some were aghast at his presumption, saying that if God had intended man to fly he would have given him wings, the hard-nosed Lilienthal rather took the view that if God *hadn't* intended man to fly he wouldn't have given him a brain.

Lilienthal began his flights from a large pile of dirt left over from excavations for a nearby canal. Visiting reporters were astonished by his control and daring. When the wind was blowing up the dirt hill strongly enough, he could take off, gain altitude and remain stationary with respect to the ground, all the while advising news cameramen below how best to frame their photographs. Altogether he made two thousand flights, some up to a quarter-mile long. Crickets would climb aboard his glider in the grass and then chirp frantically once he took to the air.

Glowing accounts of his flights came to the attention of Wilbur Wright, who had read news reports of Lilienthal in his father's library while recovering from a hockey injury. Despite their reputation as dour midwestern bicycle mechanics, Wilbur and his brother Orville were actually quite rigorous engineers who, after mastering all the available knowledge about flight, built a wind tunnel, systematically gathered information on airfoil shapes, and soon were flying gliders themselves. Unlike Lilienthal, however, who had written a book entitled *Bird Flight As the Foundation of Flight,* the Wright Brothers owed nothing to birds. Right from the start they referred to their aircraft as a "flying machine."

In 1903, having sufficiently mastered unpowered gliding flight to take the next step, they mounted a home-built 12 hp gasoline engine on their glider, flipped a coin to see who would go first, and launched a plane on its own power, thus sending mankind's age-old, inchoate yearning to fly off in an entirely new direction.

Their invention changed the world. The advantages of powered flight were so obvious that suddenly no one cared about the spiritual benefits of low-powered, unpowered or birdlike flight anymore. In the rush to capitalize on the commercial and military applications of powered aircraft, the 12 hp motor used by the Wright Brothers quickly became a 50 hp, 100 hp and, by the eve of World War II, a 1,000 hp engine. Progress in aviation was defined as bigger, higher, faster. After the war, aeronautical engineers never looked back, putting all their efforts into faster jet fighters and bigger passenger jets. The only attention that aeronautical engineers paid to birds, MacCready once said, was "how to keep them out of jet engines and how to clean their droppings off airplane wings." It wasn't until the dawn of commercial supersonic flight that it became clear that airplane flight might also have some natural limits too.

Although few people remember it now, at the same time that John Kennedy was promising to land a man on the moon, he also announced another goal: to build a supersonic transport (SST) to compete with the Concorde, a technologically advanced French-and-British-developed plane which, when it went into service, would cruise at 60,000 feet and fly so fast (1,350 mph) that frictional heating would make it grow 6 to 10 inches in flight. It would cross the Atlantic in 3 hours and 45 minutes.

At the time it seemed inconceivable that a country that would shortly land a man on the moon wouldn't want to build an SST as well. But the more deeply engineers, environmentalists and politicians looked into the matter, the more problems they saw. The SST's engine exhaust would help deplete the ozone layer, allowing more ultraviolet radiation to reach the earth's surface and thus increasing the incidence of skin cancer. The heavy SST's massive sonic booms would leave a trail of cracked plaster and shattered windows wherever it flew.

Most important perhaps, the people who would benefit most from expensive, high-speed, long-range aircraft would be urban elites traveling between the East Coast and the West Coast, while the people who would bear the brunt of such flights would be the working- and middle-class residents of flyover country, some 65 million of whom, a Stanford Research Institute study showed, would be subjected to an average of ten sonic booms a day.

As aviation writer T. A. Heppenheimer wrote in *Turbulent Skies,* the FAA decided to test public tolerance for sonic booms by using an F-104 jet fighter to create eight of them a day on a regular schedule over Oklahoma City, a place with an Air Force base and a population inclined to support aviation despite occasional drawbacks. Initial public reaction was quite positive, with a secretary reporting that she used the 7:00 A.M. sonic boom to wake her up and the 7:20 A.M. boom as a signal to get out of the shower. Construction workers used the 11:00 A.M. boom as their signal for a coffee break. But as the sonic booms continued day after day, even the easygoing midwesterners of Oklahoma City began to resent them. Forty-nine hundred people filed damage claims (mostly for cracked plaster), and two highrise buildings suffered a total of 147 cracked windows.

At this point it dawned on public officials that if even a small fighter plane could cause this much damage, they had a serious political problem on their hands. The notion of making working-class Americans suffer through much bigger sonic booms just so the bicoastal elite could cut a couple of hours off their cross-country flights raised the specter of class antagonism. Despite anguished cries from Congress and the aerospace industry that SST opponents were "trying to stamp out technology," the United States finally decided that the SST wasn't such a great idea after all, and banned the British-French Concorde from flying supersonically over its territory. This ban, coupled with the Concorde's absurdly high fuel consumption—twice that of a Boeing 747, which carries four times as many people—helped guarantee that only twelve Concordes ever entered commercial service.

In the following decades it became clear to both airline executives and aeronautical engineers that faster was not necessarily better. In 2000, the big European plane manufacturer Airbus Industrie announced that its next major project wouldn't be a faster airliner, but a wide-body, twin-deck superjumbo jet (the Airbus A380) to compete with the Boeing 747. This plane would fly at almost exactly the same subsonic speed (560 mph) as the 747, but carry 555 passengers (versus 366) in three classes, and have two passenger decks, gyms, showers, shops, a bar, a children's play area and perhaps even private staterooms so people could sleep en route. In short, an economic upper limit on aircraft speed and altitude had apparently been reached, and it was, in the words of T. A. Heppenheimer, "short of the sound barrier and well below the ozone layer."

WHILE IT WAS BECOMING OBVIOUS that there were formidable barriers to the notion of bigger, faster, higher in the airline industry, man's alleged destiny to explore the stars was bumping up against limits too. When Neil Armstrong stepped out of the lunar lander and onto the moon's surface he was the first man to stand there and look back at a fragile earth shining blue and white against an eternal black universe and know that, except for himself and his two companion astronauts, the small globe contained every human being that ever lived, all their dreams, their hopes for their children, their culture, their cities, their myths, their gods and every strand of their DNA.

Given his perspective, one might have thought that Armstrong would have found something to say that was so insightful and dead-on true as to change forever the way we think of ourselves and our place in the universe. But instead, when he stepped off that ladder and onto the moon, what he gave us was some minor word play about a big step for mankind.

Some people were so disappointed by the astronaut's commonplace observations that they suggested that the United States consider sending up a poet to better convey the full spiritual meaning of the event. But the problem wasn't really that the astronauts were emotional flat-liners—Apollo astronauts such as Edgar Mitchell were in fact quite lyrical about the emotional impact of seeing "our small blue-and-white planet floating there" in the "deep black and velvety cosmos"—the problem was the mission itself. Despite what everyone had always thought, the moon wasn't the beginning of man's conquest of the stars; it was the end of his conquest of earth.

A thousand years ago the earth seemed so vast as to be infinite. Most people worked the land and lived in small agricultural villages of no more than a few dozen families, connected to the outside world primarily by footpaths through the fields and forests. Unlike their wide-ranging hunter-gatherer ancestors, they spent their entire lives without ever going so far as thirty miles from home. It was a timeless, unchanging world where man was insignificant, dangers ubiquitous and nature incomprehensibly immense. In Germany's Black Forest it was possible to travel for hundreds of miles without stepping out from under the tree canopy. When Marco Polo traveled to China in the thirteenth century he walked through deserted Indian villages where man-eating tigers had killed so many residents that the remaining population had fled for their lives. Whole continents remained to be discovered. And the world wasn't remotely safe.

Although unexplored areas shrank rapidly in the twentieth century, the notion that parts of the world were yet to be explored persisted through the 1950s. That's when I grew up, watching old black-and-white movies like *Lost World* on late-night television and thrilling to the notion that somewhere there still were uncharted islands or remote plateaus filled with prehistoric beasts. But by the time I'd reached my teens, the dream was no longer tenable even for an impressionable kid. Thanks to long-range jets and increasingly ubiquitous satellite coverage, wild places on the planet had vanished overnight.

Man's technology had tamed the earth so quickly that by the end of the twentieth century, with the possible exception of the waters around Antarctica, it was hard to think of a place where people depended entirely on their own resources without the possibility of outside aid. Not only were there no more unexplored continents or undiscovered islands; what remained of the wilderness was fast becoming a vacation destination. The 1987 movie *Never Cry Wolf,* based on the book by Farley Mowat, tells the story of a neophyte biologist (played by the marvelous Charles Martin Smith) studying wolves in the Canadian north. Except for occasional visits from nomadic Eskimos, the biologist is entirely alone on the tundra, hundreds of miles from civilization. At the end of the movie, he is standing alone in the vast northern expanse when suddenly a multicolored football lands at his feet. Incredulous, he pops his head over a rise and spots a helicopter sitting on the lake shore, a tea party in progress and a real estate developer grandly making plans for a tourist resort.

Today the last remaining frontier is space. It's stupendous, awesome and cosmic in scale, with never-ending ramifications for the way we think of ourselves and the future of mankind. But contrary to what space buffs and science fiction writers so frequently imply, it's also completely inaccessible. Unless physicists find an esoteric way to overcome interstellar distances with some radical technology as yet unknown to science, no one is going to make an interstellar voyage within the lifetime of anyone now alive (or their great-great-grandchildren either). To travel to the nearest sunlike star, Alpha Centauri, would take 16,300 years at 180,000 mph, the fastest speed envisioned by current technology. This is eight hundred generations, more than twice as long as all of recorded history.

"Okay," you might say, "we don't have to go to Alpha Centauri. We'll start off building a moon base and then we'll explore the other planets."

The moon, as it turns out, is neither very interesting nor especially valuable; otherwise we would have returned long ago. As for the planets, they're too hot, too cold or totally uninhabitable bags of gas. Mars, with its vast reserves of frozen water, is the only other remotely viable planet for human habitation. Unfortunately for the astronauts, a round-trip mission to Mars could take as long as three years under some most-efficient-trip scenarios, which could very well be a lot longer than the human body can readily tolerate the hazards of space. In a weightless environment, immune systems falter; astronauts lose calcium; their bones deteriorate; they develop kidney stones; their hearts (perhaps due to the lower demands of pumping in space) lose as much as one-third of their muscle mass. Once astronauts leave the earth's protective magnetic field, some space medicine experts maintain, high-intensity radiation will riddle their bodies, breaking their DNA strands, causing microscopic brain incisions and, if the flight continues long enough, apathy, memory loss and mutations. Even after only a few months in a space station, astronauts frequently have to be carried off the shuttle on stretchers. If NASA were to follow OSHA workplace rules, claims *New Yorker* writer Jerome Groopman, it couldn't legally send a man to Mars for fear of exceeding OSHA radiation guidelines by more than ten times.

PROGRESS IS LIKE WATER FLOWING over uneven ground: when it finds itself blocked in one direction, it quickly finds another. Even as it was becoming clear that there was no economic sense in flying faster than the speed of sound, and that travel to the stars, if possible at all, was centuries away, a small group of people began clustering at the opposite end of the scale— the low-power, inexpensive-technology region. As they saw it, an over-reliance on expensive, complex, high-powered technology had taken man further away from all the reasons he had wanted to fly in the first place: to feel the wind in his face, soar like an eagle, meander over the trees, look down on the villages and flit about with the sparrows.

"After World War II many thousands of people learned flying and the advanced era of personal flying came of age," said Jack Lambie, an early southern California hang-gliding pioneer. "But now that everyone who wanted to was flying, there was a sense of disappointment. The kind of flying we were doing wasn't exactly what many of us had in mind. Grinding around in a light plane talking to [an air traffic control] center or the tower every few minutes ... wasn't it." Where, he asked, was the intense awareness, the union with the atmosphere, a sense of being "a molecule of air"?

Even Charles Lindbergh, for whom aviation did so much, eventually came to rethink the long-term effects of his famous flight. When one of his sons spoke to him of going into aviation, Lindbergh pointed out that aviation's golden age was long over; the thrill was gone. He recommended that the young man try another field instead. The only people who still cared about the kind of low, slow, unfettered flight exhibited by birds were the odd low-power efficiency freak, the hang-gliding pioneers, the sailplane pilots and ambitious, driven introverts like the youthful Paul MacCready.

SIX

Building Self-Confidence

MACCREADY GREW UP AS THE youngest child and only son of an affluent New Haven physician. "I had two sisters, but they were six and seven years older," MacCready would later say. "As far as my father was concerned, I was an only child."

Even as a child Paul never suffered from any lack of confidence. When he was eight, his father, who kept a summer cottage on Long Island Sound, bought him a 10-foot dinghy, which he took out the following morning, tacking two miles out into the sound before anyone even knew he was gone. He liked to play on the rocky shore of a nearby peninsula, exploring the creeks and tide pools. "We found one of these giant caterpillars, a moth that had giant false eyes on the front and a tongue that stuck out," MacCready recalled. He began catching moths and butterflies, looking up their scientific names in Comstock's moth book and mounting his own collection. Before long he knew more than the adults around him, a development which gave him confidence and, he believes, expanded his mental powers. "At puberty," says MacCready, "you've got more neurons than at any other time. Your brain functioning is at its peak. Then the acid wash of puberty fixes the mind like a photographic plate."

Initially MacCready assumed he would be a doctor like his dad. But around age ten he discovered model planes and thereafter they became his whole world. He didn't just build them, wrote Morton Grosser in *Gossamer Odyssey,* he dreamed them, designed them, flew them and covered the family Ping Pong table with partially assembled gliders and gas-powered model planes. He kept flies and beetles captive in the refrigerator to slow them down enough so he could glue them onto his planes as motors. He built helicopters, autogyros and planes that took off from water. He made ornithopters (flapping-wing planes) and microlight, rubber-band-powered models with three-foot wingspans that were so light, delicate and impossibly slow-flying that they looked more like fish swimming in aquariums than planes flying through the air.

"My father was very supportive and took me out to model airplane meets and bought model airplane engines for me as I was getting into that hobby," MacCready told Kenneth Brown in *Inventors at Work.* "But he was a strong, pushy type in a way that I often found offensive. He was so goal-oriented that he occasionally tried to get me to cheat and push my way along, which didn't fit my personality and made it a bit awkward."

Besides, when it came to winning, MacCready hardly needed to cheat. When he was fourteen, he built an autogyro that stayed aloft for thirteen minutes, setting a world record. During the next couple of years he became junior champion in six different categories and, in 1941, the overall junior national champion. The following year, *Model Airplane News,* the sport's journal of record, called the young MacCready "by far the most versatile model flier" it had ever seen. He wasn't just interested in winning, the magazine declared. He also wanted to create new designs. "I built more models than any kid in the country," MacCready would later say.

In later years MacCready would recall that he didn't win because he was a better craftsman than everyone else—technically, he knew, he was in the middle of the pack. His big advantage was his attitude. As he saw it, his ambitions had no limits. The future was wide open. His father's unending support and strong drive helped. But he also had dyslexia, a handicap that required him to put out maximum effort just to stay even. He found it hard to memorize poetry. When doing math or physics he would write a number and quickly double-check it, only to discover he'd written something else. At other times he would open his history book and after the first sentence his mind would be "a thousand miles away." He spent most of his class time daydreaming. He learned by carefully doing his homework, not through anything that occurred in class. "In high school, I was the smallest kid in the class," MacCready says.

That was just the rate I grew physically. Also I was not well coordinated. I never have been. I never will be. I was also a bit shy. I probably wished I was a football hero type in school but I wasn't. I think

Top, MacCready explains mountain lee waves to Interavia
writer Scholer Bangs in 1949.
Above, Soaring the Sierra Wave in his Orlik (eaglet),
MacCready felt "all alone in a mighty unfriendly world."

I got more psychological benefit building model airplanes, getting off to contests in other states, getting lots of experiences. As I look back, boy, am I glad I wasn't a football hero type.... Small, uncoordinated, shy—thank goodness I had that.

MacCready's self-confidence paid him big dividends early on. He soloed in a light plane when he was sixteen. In 1943 he finished prep school and enrolled at Yale and joined the Navy aviation training program. Two years later, after the war had ended, MacCready's future father-in-law, Parker Leonard, took him to the soaring center at Elmira, New York, where the highly regarded sailplane pilot John Robinson gave him a ride in a TG-3 glider.

That first flight in what MacCready called "this large, awkward, silent beast" resulted in an instant addiction. Soaring, he quickly discovered, wasn't at all like flying a small plane, where you just turned the craft in the direction you wanted to go and, barring some disaster, the engine took you there. In a sailplane, getting where you wanted to go was a function of physics, meteorology and pilot sophistication. Your time aloft was directly proportional to your knowledge, skill and, at times, your courage too. For Mac-Cready, who had all three of these qualities in abundance, this was another field to be first in. More than that, it was a sport, one which, because it was so dependent on atmospheric conditions, automatically turned everyone who devoted himself to it into a natural scientist. During a soaring contest in 1947, MacCready landed in a farmer's field in the Texas Panhandle. The farmer took him home, let him use the telephone to call his retrieval crew and gave him his last pork chop for dinner. MacCready was deeply moved. He had thought the farmer would have seen him as a "privileged kid indulging in a trivial and expensive sport." Instead, the farmer thanked him for being involved in such an important field as science and technology. More than fifty years later, in 1999, MacCready told a group of soaring enthusiasts that he's still trying to live up to that farmer's expectations.

In 1948, at age twenty-two, MacCready won his first national soaring title. He was a graduate student in meteorology and aeronautics at Caltech, living in the San Marino home of Glenn Bowlus, brother of Hawley Bowlus, a renowned sailplane designer who also invented the Airstream trailer, supervised the construction of the *Spirit of St. Louis* for the Ryan Aeronautical Company and taught Charles Lindbergh's wife, Anne Morrow, to fly sailplanes. At Caltech, MacCready became a disciple of Irving Langmuir, a

Nobel laureate in chemistry and a pioneer in weather modification. "I just followed him around, interacting with him," MacCready later recalled. "A lot of enthusiasm rubbed off, a feeling of there are no barriers, you just charge ahead. It doesn't matter whether you know anything about that subject."

In December of 1948, Scholer Bangs, a reporter for the French aviation magazine *Interavia,* came to Pasadena to interview MacCready about wave soaring. Seeing that MacCready's room was full of war surplus oxygen masks, recording barographs, heavy flying clothes, batteries, altimeters, air temperature gauges, accelerators and variometers, Bangs quickly realized that MacCready had something more in mind than just a little mountain wave soaring. "It looks like you're getting ready for a date with a cloud," he said.

Bangs was referring to Moazagotl clouds, high-altitude lens-shaped clouds formed by powerful stationary atmospheric waves. Unlike normal clouds, these don't drift with the wind (leading some people to insist they are massive UFOs). In California, they are produced by a meteorological condition—poorly understood at the time—that occurs with great intensity over the Owens Valley east of the Sierra Nevada near the town of Bishop. As MacCready explained to Bangs that winter day in 1948, he hoped to set world sailplane records in both altitude and distance, taking off from Bishop, soaring to 45,000 feet on the stationary Sierra Wave (the source of the Moazagotl clouds), and then, if all went well, flying perhaps 1,000 miles to the Midwest on successive downwind wave oscillations.

The Sierra Wave (also known as the Bishop Wave) was an extremely powerful meteorological condition generated when strong prevailing moisture-laden westerlies swept in from the Pacific, crossed California's vast, flat San Joaquin Valley and hit the westward slope of the Sierras head on. Although atmospheric waves were not that unusual, they were made particularly powerful at Bishop by the topography of the Owens Valley, a deep, north-south rift valley flanked by the 14,000-foot Sierras on the west and the nearly equally high White Mountains on the east. When strong westerly winds flowed over the Sierra peaks at right angles, they caused a horizontal vortex (called a rotor) on the lee side of the peaks, and above that a smooth, powerful, upward-flowing wave. If the jet stream didn't cap the wave, it might go to 65,000 feet or higher. This was known, MacCready explained to Bangs, from the sharp breaks seen in luminous meteor trails passing through the upper atmosphere.

Although Moazagotl clouds had been forming over the Owens Valley since time immemorial, no one understood their significance until the years immediately after World War II, when the owners of a Bishop flying service, Bob Symons and Harland Ross, flew too close to them and suddenly found themselves in such powerful updrafts that it felt as if the hand of God were pulling them up to heaven.

Symons, a former employee of the sailplane pioneer Hawley Bowlus, made his living dropping off hunting parties in the mountains, supplying remote mining camps and rescuing lost or injured hikers. As Colorado pilot and author Robert Whelan explained in his book on the Sierra Wave, *Exploring the Monster,* Symons also had a war surplus P-38 Interceptor, which he used to seed the clouds west of Bishop so as to increase runoff for local hydroelectric plants. Once, as he was returning home from a cloud-seeding mission, he found the Owens Valley totally obscured in blowing dust. With his fuel running low, Symons decided to ease his way into the updraft under a nearby lenticular cloud and suddenly found himself climbing so fast he could shut down both engines in his P-38 and soar the eight-ton fighter plane as if it were a sailplane. He went up to 30,000 feet three different times until finally the visibility at the airport cleared, at which point he restarted the engines and landed the plane.

For sailplane pilots, the possibility that massive atmospheric waves in the Owens Valley could take sailplanes to a greater altitude than any man had ever flown before was such stunning news that for a long time they had difficulty convincing other pilots that such waves existed. Multi-engine pilots had only just acknowledged the presence of the jet stream, and they wouldn't have done so had not B-29 pilots flying at 30,000 feet over Tokyo in World War II reported that 200 mph headwinds were throwing off their bombing runs.

Among pilots it's an ingrained rule not to fly on the lee (downwind) side of a mountain in strong wings for fear of getting caught in powerful downdrafts that can suddenly fling the plane into the mountainside. But if you wanted to get to the Sierra Wave (known as "the elevator" for its 4,000 feet-per-minute upward-flowing winds) you first had to go through the wave rotor, a turbulent area of sudden gusts and powerful shear. One moment the rotor would be slamming you around the cockpit so furiously you'd literally be bouncing off the walls, and a moment later, Whelan wrote in *Exploring the Monster,* everything would be so smooth you'd think you were "sitting motionless inside a hangar." If you didn't look at your rate-of-climb indicator you wouldn't know you were climbing at all. The air felt so smooth it almost seemed electric. "Taut" was the word that Symons used. And everyone who had flown the wave agreed: inside the elevator, the air was taut.

On days when the jet stream didn't put a cap on it, the Sierra Wave could go all the way to 100,000 feet—far higher than anyone could fly without a pressure suit or a pressurized cabin. But when the jet stream held down the Sierra Wave, its energy was redirected downstream. Instead of producing just one big wave, the wind made a whole long line of downwind undulations in the atmosphere, like the undulations in a fast-flowing river downstream of a submerged rock. It was these undulations that caught Mac-Cready's attention.

If he were to take off from Bishop and ride the wave to 45,000 feet, it occurred to him, he could head eastward catching successive upward undulations of the wave across the White Mountains, Death Valley and the Rockies. Because darkness would have descended by the time he hit Denver, he'd have to spend the night soaring back and forth over the same spot using ridge lift. When the sun rose, he'd head east again with the aid of a 100 mph tailwind until he reached the midwestern prairies where he'd have to land.

MacCready prepared carefully for his date with the Sierra Wave, insulating the cockpit of his Polish-built, gull-winged Orlik (eaglet) with fiberglass wool, taking parachute jumping lessons in case his plane came apart in flight, making several simulated trips to 40,000 feet in Lockheed's low-pressure altitude chamber, buying caffeine tablets and forcing himself to practice staying up all night. On December 31, 1948, MacCready took off just before noon and soon encountered a modest elevator that carried him to 29,500 feet, the second-highest glider flight anyone had ever made. At that altitude, soaring over the frozen Sierras was like flying over an alien planet. "You feel all alone in a mighty unfriendly world," MacCready told Scholer Bangs. It reminded him again how "wonderful and fragile" human life really is. His only comfort was the fearsome Moazagotl clouds. "I very quickly developed a feeling that every cloud I contact is a friend," he said, "and that even though I may leave to fly off thirty miles or more on an exploration trip, I always, or nearly always, can count upon finding the cloud waiting for me when I come back."

MacCready stayed aloft more than five hours. As his breath condensed it created such thick hoarfrost that he could hardly see through the canopy. Although his head and shoulders were at 65°F in sunlight, his feet, encased in fleece-lined boots, were at minus 40°F. Two weeks later the big toe on his left foot was still numb from frostbite. MacCready probably could have claimed a world record for this flight but he had heard of an unrecognized flight in Germany before World War II and, characteristically fastidious about not taking undeserved credit, he refused to make a claim. He was so blasé about the flight, Scholer Bangs later complained, it was like "pulling teeth" to get him to recall the slightest "dramatic remembrance."

The day after MacCready's high flight, John Robinson (the pilot who had given MacCready his first glider ride three years earlier) set a new world sailplane record of 33,500 feet before landing 180 miles south of Bishop at Edwards Air Force Base. MacCready had gone up that day as well but, as he would later write, he "chickened out" in order to avoid having to descend through a solid overcast and never got higher than 22,000 feet.

In the end, MacCready says, he never did make any "serious" efforts to break the sailplane distance or time-aloft record. Staying up for extended periods in a sailplane, it dawned on him, wasn't as great a feat as it first appeared. As long as one had ridge lift (wind blowing up sloping terrain) it was possible to stay up indefinitely, slipping back and forth over the same patch of earth. But that wasn't so much a test of skill as a fancy kind of "flag-pole sitting."

When his winter break ended without MacCready's having caught the kind of big booming wave he'd been hoping for, he returned to his graduate studies at Caltech, where, if someone had told him that some day one of his aircraft would be hanging in the National Air and Space Museum next to the *Spirit of St. Louis* and the *Wright Flier,* he would have thought that person deranged.

SEVEN

The Contest at St. Yan

THE NEXT EIGHT YEARS WERE GOOD ones for MacCready. He had won the national soaring title in 1948, 1949 and 1953, and the international soaring championship in 1956. His strong points were focus, strategy and a deep knowledge of cloud physics. In 1947, while daydreaming his way through a Caltech aeronautics class, he had invented the now-famous "MacCready Speed Ring," a simple device that, in conjunction with a variometer (an instrument showing whether the sailplane is in lift or sink), allowed a sailplane pilot quickly to calculate the best speed for flying between thermals.

During cross-country competitions, sailplane pilots depend on thermals to gain the necessary altitude to glide the required distance. When they've gotten the desired altitude from any given thermal (or when the thermal gives out), they stop circling and fly off to the next thermal along their route to repeat the process. Prior to the invention of the speed ring, determining the best speed to fly was a slow, iterative process. The advantage of the speed ring was that it allowed the pilot to determine the best speed, in MacCready's words, "virtually without thought," thus allowing the pilot to concentrate on strategy or evidence of lift, such as evolving clouds, circling hawks and vultures, smoke, dust and surface winds.

MacCready flew in his final competitive flight in a sailplane on July 11, 1956, the last day of the International Glider Competition at St. Yan, a small town in southeastern France. This competition consisted of seven races and distance flights taking place over a two-week period. MacCready's strategy for winning had been "to do moderately well on each day" rather than try to do spectacularly well any day and thus risk not completing a race.

Even so, he finished first in three of the first six events, leaving him so far ahead in points that, had he been so inclined, he could have skipped the final day altogether.

Such triumphs notwithstanding, MacCready knew better than anyone else that his success wasn't primarily a result of his flying ability. There were great natural pilots with the hand-eye coordination and reflexes of world-class athletes who had never won a national soaring championship. Mac-Cready had already won three of them despite his less-than-precise style. Sometimes when circling in thermals he didn't even bother to make coordinated turns. He'd just lean his head against the side of the cockpit and fly by instinct, sound and feel. He almost preferred to fly in clouds, he once said; that way, no one could see "how sloppily the sailplane was being controlled."

For the 1956 internationals, MacCready was flying a borrowed Breguet 901, the highest-performance sailplane he'd ever flown. It had great maneuverability, a low sinking speed and what for the time was a superb 35:1 glide ratio (for every foot the glider descended in still air it traveled 35 feet forward).

"Paul didn't fly for fun," says Henry Jex, a sharp-tongued former Caltech classmate and personal friend. "He flew because he knew he could win." If that required him to take chances, he didn't flinch. On one occasion he flew up a mountain slope with the rocks barely ten feet from his wingtip. On another, he circled in a thundercloud, in spite of hail, icing and occasional thunderbolts, dimly perceived through the mist.

The task for July 3, the third flying day of the contest, was simply to fly 245 miles in a south-southeasterly direction toward Hyeres Airport. As the afternoon wore on, reports came from one or another of the sixty competing pilots who had landed at airfields en route or had put down *aux vaches* (with the cows). Finally with the sun setting, a report came in that three of the four remaining pilots had landed at what they thought was the last airfield on the route. Beyond that was only the Mediterranean and still there was no MacCready.

As darkness overtook the airfield at St. Yan the pilots found themselves wondering if MacCready's plane was crumpled against a rocky peak or shattered into kindling deep in some mountain crevasse. Finally, nine hours after MacCready had taken off—an eternity for a sailplane—a call came in: "Mac-Cready at the Mediterranean!" Spontaneous cheering broke out. MacCready had flown south until the sun set and he was over water, at which point he slipped in unnoticed at a naval air station on the coast, in the middle of night flight operations. The French were so impressed with this thirty-one-year-old soaring wunderkind that they began calling him *le machine*.

MacCready won the 1956 world soaring championship in a Breguet 901.

The task for the final day of the competition, July 11, was to fly the fastest from St. Yan to St. Auban, 190 miles to the southeast. This involved soaring in thermals, slope lift and waves. What made the flight problematic that day was the nearby Hautes Alps, buried in clouds and buffeted by 50-knot winds. As MacCready described that day in an article for *Soaring* magazine, when he reached the mountains southeast of Lyon he found himself under a thick cloud layer above and scattered clouds below. He held his position for ninety minutes, hoping that the weather would improve. When nothing changed, he started down the western slope of a north-south ridge, only to encounter two successive east-west ridges, where the downdraft from one ridge collided with the updraft from the other. In the wind shear between these two ridges MacCready was hitting violent 8 G updrafts one second and equally violent downdrafts the next.

For most people, wind shear is an abstract concept. If they ever think about wind at all, they tend to envision it as a huge, thick blanket of air moving uniformly over the land like a broad, slow-moving river. And they maintain this view despite having seen kites dancing, diving and swooping in the wind or leaves in courtyards swirling, dashing and twirling about as if caught in a covey of micro-tornadoes.

To the early aviation pioneers, the chaotic nature of wind was a new concept. Octave Chanute—a railroad engineer who invented the strut-braced and cross-wired biplane glider upon which the Wright Brothers drew in part to invent the first powered, controllable airplane—was astonished at the wind's variability when he first began gliding in the sand hills of Lake Michigan in the final decades of the nineteenth century:

> The first thing which we discovered practically was that the wind flowing up a hill-side is not a steadily-flowing current like that of a river. It comes as a rolling mass, full of tumultuous whirls and eddies, like those issuing from a chimney; and they strike the apparatus with constantly varying force and direction, sometimes withdrawing support when most needed.

So unexpected, indeed, was the wind's turbulence that it could be fatal. The famed Otto Lilienthal, the most accomplished and renowned glider pilot of the nineteenth century, died in August of 1996 when an unexpected gust of wind pitched up his elegant bird-wing glider, causing it to stall 50 feet in the air. Without enough altitude to recover, he crashed and broke his spine. As he lay dying in the hospital, he famously told his sobbing brother, "Sacrifices must be made."

But turbulence isn't a problem merely because it can fling a low-flying plane to the ground. Over mountains, high winds can create such strong roiling, twisting shear forces that the joints of sailplanes groan and crack, wooden spars snap in two, cables pop, wings break, instruments come loose, bolts pull out and the aircraft disintegrates in midair. To the pilot it feels as if some giant dog is shaking the plane apart. His head hits the canopy. He can't read his instruments, keep his feet on the rudder pedals or his hands on the stick. The bottom of the instrument panel bangs him on the shins (one reason sailplane instrument panels are padded on the bottom).

Alone in the Haute Alps on the final day of a contest he had already won, MacCready became a victim of such winds when he found himself trapped below the peaks in a small blind bowl with, as he would later say, "no apparent exit." One moment a 100-feet-per-second downdraft would throw him down toward the trees. The next, a similar updraft would toss him up 1,000 feet. He was a chip on the surf in the middle of a typhoon. His airspeed at times dropped to zero. It was all he could do to keep the glider right side up.

Furious for getting himself into such a fix, MacCready did the only thing he could—"hang on and work." Eventually slipping out of the bowl, he made it to the line of thermals where he caught a smooth 1,250-feet-per-minute updraft and shortly found himself at 14,000 feet, a safe altitude from which he was able to glide the remaining 40 miles to St. Auban.

The other American pilot in the competition that year, Bill Ivans, tried the same route as MacCready, but didn't make it out, crashing in a high mountain valley and breaking his back. For MacCready the ride home from St. Auban was the most exhausting of his life. His eyes were bloodshot. He was nearly sick with fatigue and worry about Ivans (who survived this crash but was killed in July 1999 when a rotor tore apart his glider in midair).

That was MacCready's last sailplane contest. He knew it wasn't his flying skill that got him home alive. It was pure luck—what he called "fate's coin flip." After that he never flew competitively again. Life was too short to risk for mere glory.

EIGHT

Midlife Crisis

Wꜱ HEN MACCREADY FINISHED HIS Ph.D. in meteorology and aeronautics at Caltech in 1952 (thesis: atmospheric turbulence) his career plans were uncertain. He knew he didn't want to work for major aerospace companies, which, he once complained, hired "engineers by the acre." A small weather modification company would be great, but since there were few such operations around, MacCready started his own. He had no natural business skills. But he also knew that "the way you start a business is that you just go out and do it."

Calling his company Meteorology Research, MacCready seeded clouds with dry ice to make rain. "When it worked it was fun," he said. "It gave me a feeling of omnipotence." It made a lot of lightning and rain, though not always in the right places. "The people who paid for it were the orchard people," recalled Jex. "But the people who got the worst rain were downstream." Some farmers got flooded and MacCready got sued.

Eventually MacCready concluded that rain-making was a "lousy" niche market with no place to grow and lots of potential for litigation. "You find yourself in the position of arguing, 'You can't prove we did it'" (made the rain that flooded you). The best part about it was the chance to do research. MacCready flew Cessna 180s through thunderstorms to collect hailstones. He investigated cloud physics, turbulence, aircraft wakes and, for the military, the diffusion of chemical warfare agents. "I got someone to be executive vice president and general manager so I didn't have to pretend to be an administrator," said MacCready. Even so, the company went through "a lot of ups and downs." It was getting into instruments, an area where there was plenty of competition. "To compete would take more capital than we had." Deciding that discretion was the better part of capitalistic valor, in 1966 MacCready sold his company to Cohu Electronics, which turned it into a division.

Although MacCready was appointed to the Cohu board, he felt increasingly restless. His former company was doing well financially ("it was Cohu's best division," said MacCready) but he knew the situation wouldn't continue indefinitely. Under Cohu, his old company had no new ideas. "It wasn't getting refueled," said MacCready. "It wasn't going to be motivating for me or the key technical people."

The problem wasn't only his former company and its prospects. "[The sixties] should have been a decade of splendid financial success, the material consolidation of all the promise that had gone before," wrote Morton Grosser in *Gossamer Odyssey,* an authoritative account of MacCready's successful assaults on the first two Kremer prizes. "That didn't happen. People of less intellect, less achievement, and yes, less integrity, were getting startlingly rich. . . . It irked Paul; he envied it, he talked about money quite a lot, and his friends noticed some of his father's attitudes beginning to show around the edges."

Deciding it was time to move on, MacCready resigned from the Cohu board and in 1971 started AeroVironment, a new consulting business in the fields of air pollution, hazardous waste management, pollution monitoring devices and windpower.

AeroVironment was growing, but it wasn't so profitable that MacCready could stop worrying about money. In 1969 his brother-in-law, Kirke Leonard, a southern California aerospace engineer, had asked him to co-sign a bank note for $100,000 so Leonard could buy a small Hermosa Beach fiberglass boat company to build 15-foot catamarans to compete with Hobi-Cats. Leonard was a good designer and a gifted craftsman but it became increasingly evident over the next six years that he wasn't a salesman and, for that matter, neither was MacCready. The company failed, and as MacCready later said in a speech, "I was stuck with the obligation of paying $100,000 to the bank which I assure you I didn't have."

By the summer of 1976, MacCready was worried about his future. His "most important helper/mentor/friend," his father, had died the year before. MacCready had no special gift for management and business demands were unrelenting. Thinking he needed a vacation, he packed up his wife, Judy, and their three sons for a trip across the country. It was a good time to get away from work and to revisit former interests that he'd neglected in recent years, for instance, his love affair with birds.

DURING WORLD WAR II, a meteorologist by the name of Alfred Woodcock had written a paper called "Soaring over the Open Sea." On an ocean voyage he noticed that the birds, as MacCready explained it, sometimes "soared in circles, straight lines, or didn't soar at all." Wondering if their flight behavior was in any way correlated to meteorological conditions, Woodcock began measuring the temperature difference between the water and the air and plotting that on a scatter diagram against wind speed. To his surprise, he found that the data neatly clustered in three groups depending on whether the birds were engaged in wave soaring, thermal soaring or flapping flight. Basically he had discovered the existence of big convection cells over the ocean, which were "exactly analogous" on the kilometer scale to the behavior of millimeter-sized Benard convection cells, whose behavior scientists had long studied in the laboratory by heating a shallow fluid on a plate.

"I thought this was a wonderful research project," said MacCready. "Woodcock didn't need a cyclotron or a huge radar. He just had some educated eyeballs, some insight and he used birds as free sensors." In the process, Woodcock managed to pull off a broad, fundamental study at virtually no cost and with no equipment other than a thermometer and a wind speed indicator. It was an "elegant" scientific tour de force that left MacCready "indelibly impressed." For years afterward he wondered if he could do something similar.

On his 1976 summer vacation, MacCready finally figured out what that something might be. As he drove through Arizona on his way across the country to Florida, listening to the Beatles and Monty Python tapes that his three sons endlessly replayed, MacCready diverted himself by sticking his head out the window, watching the sky and checking his wristwatch. MacCready's oldest son, Parker, thought his dad had gone "nuts"—he had become obsessed with hawks and vultures.

On any list of best-loved animals, vultures don't rank very high. They have bald, red heads, which they thrust into the rotting carcasses of cows, sheep and coyotes. They enthusiastically eat the bowel movements of cats and dogs. In hot weather they cool themselves—as much as 36 degrees—by defecating on their hind legs. When threatened, they hiss, engage in projectile vomiting up to ten feet and, if that doesn't work, cravenly roll over and play dead. Charles Darwin had nothing but contempt for the vulture, which he called "a disgusting bird with its scarlet head formed to wallow in putridity."

But vulture lovers, who are actually much more common in the United States than one might suspect, claim that the turkey vulture, the most common species in the country, has been egregiously maligned. Unlike European vultures, which are more closely related to hawks, or the aggressive American black vulture, known to attack people, cows, horses and dogs, the easily domesticated turkey vulture (also known as a buzzard) is a gentle, intelligent, highly social, fun-loving creature which quickly becomes emotionally attached to its owner, follows him around like a dog and loves to play tug-of-war with a favorite toy. People who live in parts of the country inhabited by turkey vultures, now nearly all of the United States, report that wild vultures will voluntarily adopt particular humans. One bird would follow a little boy to the bus stop every day and then wait for him in the afternoon to escort him home. Domesticated vultures have been known to sidle up to strangers to nibble playfully on their sneakers or go hopping along after them in the vain hope someone will rub their heads.

Turkey vultures live up to sixty years and mate for life. Creatures of enduring habit, they sometimes roost on the same branch in the same tree for years on end. Although notorious for their carrion-loving ways (unlike hawks, their beaks aren't strong enough to tear fresh meat), turkey vultures mostly eat leaves, seeds, grass, insects, reptiles, rodents and other small animals. They have such a keen sense of smell that natural gas line operators use them to locate leaks. (Workmen pump a foul-smelling gas, ethyl mercaptan, into the pipeline and then watch to see where the vultures congregate.)

Compared with powerful birds like pigeons or geese, vultures are such low-metabolism, weak fliers that they wait patiently on their roosts until the midmorning sun heats the earth sufficiently that thermals begin to form. Eventually one vulture—what MacCready calls "the wind dummy"—will venture out. If it fails to find a thermal, it returns to the roost. "When it finally catches one," says MacCready, "they all go out."

In light winds, vultures are consummate fliers, holding their six-foot wings in a distinctive dihedral. In contrast to the high-aspect-ratio wings of sailplanes or albatrosses (wings that are long in relation to their width), vulture wings are short and broad. Although most short-winged birds (and aircraft) suffer from high drag, vultures overcome the problem with exquisitely sensitive emarginated primaries—long, separated wingtip feathers, each of which serves as a kind of individual high-aspect, high-efficiency airfoil. Such feathers give the vulture the ability to pivot on a wingtip and thus take advantage of even the lightest gust or smallest bubble of rising air. The vulture is an atmospheric performance artist, contends Bill Kohlmoos, president of the Turkey Vulture Society: "He can feel the air as he plays updrafts and minor variations with his wing-tip fingers, much as a pianist plays classical music on a Steinway."

MacCready's sudden interest in the turkey vulture on his cross-country vacation wasn't purely aesthetic. He had taken up hang-gliding in recent years and had noticed that when a hang glider and a turkey vulture were in the same thermal, the vultures clearly flew better, making tighter turns, circling closer to the ground and climbing faster in lighter winds. If you were going to improve hang glider performance, he reasoned, you could do a lot worse than study turkey vultures.

A few scientists had tried to measure the flight efficiency of birds by training them to fly in wind tunnels. But such tests were difficult and expensive; it was hard to convince birds to fly in wind tunnels and the lift coefficient data was far higher than some observers, including MacCready, thought it should be.

In the tradition of Alfred Woodcock's nearly equipmentless experiment employing the flight techniques of ocean birds, it was MacCready's great insight to realize that he didn't need a wind tunnel to measure a bird's flight efficiency. All he really had to do was find a bird soaring in a thermal, measure how long it took the bird to do a complete 360-degree turn and then use a protractor to estimate its bank angle. From this it would be possible to calculate the bird's speed. Then, by combining this number with the bird's wing loading—its weight divided by its wing area (readily available from ornithological reference books)—MacCready could determine the bird's lift coefficient, a dimensionless number measuring flight efficiency, to an accuracy of 10 percent.

Pretty soon he was comparing the performance of turkey vultures, which flew slowly, had light wing loading and were able to fly in light, early-morning thermals, with the performance of black vultures, which had heavier wing loading, flew faster and didn't take off until much later in the day. To his surprise, he discovered that the lift coefficients of some of these birds when thermaling was a "very reasonable" 0.9. Black vultures and hang gliders had virtually the same wing loading (around 1.33 pounds per square foot), flew at the same speed (24.4 mph) and made the same radius turns in thermals (80 feet). The much more efficient turkey vultures, on the other hand, had half the wing loading and half the turning radius of black vultures, and they flew at three-quarters the speed (17.4 mph).

To MacCready the implications were obvious: The trick to making a hang glider soar like the highly efficient turkey vulture was simply to make it bigger while keeping the weight the same. The bigger the glider, the lower the wing loading, the slower the hang glider would fly and the less power would be required to keep it in the air. In fact, it dawned on him, if the wing loading was low enough, the plane would fly on no more power than that put out by a well-conditioned athlete. It was an insight that would change MacCready's life, redirecting his focus and revitalizing his career, even as it changed the lives of many around him too.

NINE

Man's Innate Desire to Fly

TWO-THIRDS OF ALL SPECIES fly at one time or another in their life cycle. Flight allows a creature opportunity to explore his environment, escape predators and find food. A mouse on the ground, MacCready points out, can cover only one-third of an acre a night foraging for food, at the risk of "falling in mud puddles and being eaten by snakes. The mouse's cousin, the bat, the same size as a mouse, will fly and cover 2,000 square miles in that one night." As for birds, they must be doing something right, says Mac-Cready. They sailed right through the great extinction 65 million years ago.

Perhaps in recognition of such power, in earlier societies birds were regarded as omens, spirits, portents or beings with special wisdom. Mac-Cready regards birds as "the essential spirits of nature." Naturalist John Burroughs once noted that birds seem to have mastered the secret of eternal life: "You grow old, your friends die or move to distant lands. . . . Yet there in your garden or orchard are the birds of your boyhood, the same notes, the same calls, and, to all intents and purposes, the identical birds endowed with perennial youth."

For much of man's history, bird flight was regarded as equivalent to total freedom. Freud thought the wish to fly was an infantile desire for absolute power. Charles Lindbergh claimed that flying allowed him to live "on a higher plane," giving him insights about himself, about life and the universe he lived in. "I may be flying a complicated airplane, rushing through space, but in this cabin I'm surrounded by simplicity and thoughts set free of time," he wrote in *The Spirit of St. Louis*.

How detached the intimate things around me seem from the great world down below. How strange is this combination of proximity and separation. That ground—seconds away—thousands of miles away. This air, stirring mildly around me. That air, rushing by with the speed of a tornado, an inch beyond. These minute details in my cockpit. The grandeur of the world outside. The nearness of death. The longness of life.

Although pilots in everything from Cessna 150s to B-29s have claimed to feel spiritual uplift, psychological insight, or just plain euphoria in the air, it wasn't necessary to fly over oceans at night or high above the clouds to appreciate flying. Low and slow was better still. And for doing that, nothing beat a hang glider.

Hang-gliding was the modern equivalent of those wild leaps made by tower jumpers in ages past. There were no rules or regulations or any need for towers, runways, expensive instruments or noisy engines. The hang glider, which usually weighed only one-third as much as the pilot, could be carried on a van, rolled up and stored in a garage. All that the pilot needed to take off was a moderately sized hill and a light breeze. A few running steps and he was airborne. The wings were so light they become an extension of the pilot's arms. He could turn, soar and, with the benefit of ridge lift, remain aloft for hours. Because he hung in a harness under the wing, the pilot literally had a Godlike view. When hang glider pilots looked down from 5,000 feet, they weren't just taking in the real estate, they were also looking inside themselves.

"When you fly really high the people start looking like ants and the roads start looking like ribbons," says Ken deRussy, a twenty-five-year veteran of the sport, who for many years ran a Santa Barbara hang glider flight school. "That's when you become acutely aware how no one in the world can have an impact on you. No one is going to panhandle or ask for the rent or tell you to get back to work. The police aren't going to tell you that you can't sit there or park there or that you got to have your seat belt on. You have incredible feelings of peace and great serenity and independence of soul."

At the same time, says deRussy, "you also become acutely aware that there are no tall ladders, nets or helicopters that can come and bring you back down. It is a wonderful paradox in that you are completely in your own destiny and that feels good. But you are the only person in your universe that can get you back down safely too."

And your problems weren't over just because you landed. Hang glider pilots who landed in national parks were sometimes arrested, stripped of their gear, taken to jail, charged and fined. Even if you were merely passing over private property, people would phone the police to complain that you were violating their airspace. "Every time I hear a siren when flying I just assume someone has reported me for something" says deRussy. Then when he landed, the police would always demand to see his hang glider "license."

But he didn't have a license. No one did. That was the reason thrill seekers and dirt bikers flocked to the sport so readily in the early days. There were no guidelines, safety rules, required training or even, at times, adult supervision. People were taking off (sometimes in flimsy, homemade contraptions) without bothering to strap in. They flew in high winds, into wires, into hillsides, stalled out and made high-speed downwind landings. They overstressed spars and wires, got flipped upside down, got wrapped in their sails or went into full-luft vertical dives, a condition where the sail just flaps futilely in the wind.

In hang-gliding's early days, the sport was killing fifty people a year. If that rate had continued for a decade, it would have killed the industry, just as the light plane aviation industry was almost killed by a tidal wave of liability suits in the eighties. But between 1970 and 1980 the hang glider accident rate plummeted as pilots moved up the learning curve and manufacturers went from bamboo, plastic and cheap aluminum to high-quality, aircraft-grade components.

But the essential element of the sport wasn't the danger; it was the intense thrill of flight. New pilots sometimes found the experience so deeply moving, deRussy discovered, they gave him personal credit for their ineffable joy, confessing to him as they would to a priest or doctor. And it wasn't hard to understand why. When conditions were just right, hang-gliding was as close to true bird flight as anything yet devised. On sunny afternoons, friendly hawks and vultures joined you in a thermal. When you took off from a ridge top just as the sun was setting, you saw golden cobwebs slowly floating upward, back-lit by the setting sun. You flew silently over rabbits, foxes and mice coming out for their evening meal and understood, for the first time, how hawks made a living. And one day, feeling euphoric and full of gratitude to hang-gliding's early pioneers, you may have remembered Richard Miller.

TEN

Hang-Gliding in Southern California

ALTHOUGH PEOPLE TOLD ME Richard Miller was an "Eastern mystic" and "cosmic sort of guy" who was "into transcendental aerodynamics" and lived on "fruits and nuts," from the tone of his initial e-mail messages I half-expected a rigid autocrat. In fact, when I met him in the vitamin aisle of a Santa Cruz health food store, I discovered he was a tall (6'2"), thin, painfully vulnerable man with a white goatee, looking like a combination of Vladimir Lenin and Sir Alec Guinness. He was wearing a sweater, a dirty jacket, too-short pants and a pair of eyeglasses with a piece of tissue paper taped across one lens. He made his living by intuiting his clients' glandular deficiencies, then recommending appropriate nutritional supplements. He came across as highly literate, intelligent, candid and shy. The year 2000, he told me, had been "both the best and worst year of my life." The best part, he said, concerned Dharma or destiny, performing one's role in "the cosmic play" and "fulfilling the obligations of one's existence." The worst part had to do with declining health and acute poverty. "I've never had money," he said. "I've never felt I was meant to have any."

What he did have was the respect of hang glider people everywhere for having helped introduce the sport to America. In the fall of 2000, when southern California hang-gliding pilots held a ceremony at Dockweiler State Beach to dedicate an official hang-gliding training site, the organizers sent Miller an airplane ticket to permit him to attend. Miller hadn't been on an airliner in thirty-five years. "We went to 35,000 feet [on the flight from San Jose to Los Angeles]," he kept saying in amazement. All day long he sat bundled in a parka and sweater while various people took turns thanking him for having paved the way by flying his first glider, the Bamboo Butterfly, in that same spot some thirty years before. One fan even told Miller he had built a new Bamboo Butterfly in his honor: "It took five hours and three beers."

When I first met Miller he was living out of an ancient oxidized-orange VW van with a broken grill, busted running lights and rusted hubcaps. He kept the inside clean and tidy with a little table and seats, a battery-powered clock, and a roll of toilet paper sitting on top of neat boxes of clothes in the rear. Like the Roger Miller character in *King of the Road,* he knew the best places to park a van, where no one would bother him, and where in the neighborhood to find the cleanest fiberglass toilet.

In the late 1960s he lived on the $4 or $5 a day in mail-order profits from a book he had written on soaring flight, *Without Visible Means of Support.* At other times he had made his living going out each morning on his bicycle to salvage items from Dumpsters that he could sell at swap meets. He was one year older than Paul MacCready, he says, and ever since they first met as boys their lives had followed "parallel tracks," the difference being that, in contrast to the high-achieving MacCready, whose ambitious father lavished sailboats and model airplane engines on him, Miller's father abandoned his family shortly after Richard was born, and his mother put him in a foster home. Although she later retrieved him when she remarried, there was no love in the family. Growing up in Chicago, Miller had "a reoccurring nightmare of being dropped into a black bottomless pit."

He escaped into model planes—"I like to think when the curtain rises on poor little Richie Miller he was born with a kit of a Fokker D7 in his lap." The generation that grew up in the thirties and forties were just so privileged, says Miller. "For ten cents you could go down to the stationery store and buy yourself a model airplane kit. You got some strip wood, sheet of wood, tissue to cover it with, a turned hardwood nose bearing, a machine-cut propeller, and the plans to build it, all for ten cents. God what happy years they were." For Miller, model planes were his "savior," the "most precious thing" in his life and, at times, the cause of his greatest humiliations too.

In the summer of 1940, the sixteen-year-old Miller put his planes in the basket of his bike and rode forty minutes to the field at 69th and Cicero in Chicago, where the model airplane championships were being held that year. "I can remember quite well my big flight, which was with this huge stick model which I had built with all my hopes," says Miller. "On launching, it curved up to the right and crashed into the ground."

Richard Miller, demonstrating "personal motorless flight" in 1966 in the Bamboo Butterfly.

The reason, says Miller, was that he was all alone. He didn't have a father or knowledgeable friend to teach him model-building principles and as a result he didn't even understand mere fundamentals, such as avoiding warped wings or attaching them firmly to the fuselage. The other factor was more pervasive—"I was just a dumb kid. Dumbness pervades my life."

There was one other memory from that day that has stuck in Miller's mind for the last six decades: "Paul MacCready was there. He was junior champion at that meet. And that began for him a life of unprecedented success. You can add them up—World Soaring Champion, all the awards, Engineer of the Century—and parallel to this has been my life of unprecedented failure. I have failed all my life in one way or the other."

Even so, Miller never gave up on flying. At age sixteen he began the independent part of what he calls his "extraordinarily unique life" when he ran away from home, first to work at airfields in the South and then, when the Second World War came along, to maintain aircraft as a Navy machinist's mate. After the war ended he headed for Northwestern University on the G.I. Bill. But he quit after seventeen days, a decision that still puzzles him today. "Why does a dog bark?" he says. "I didn't attend any classes."

All through this, he had one consolation: when everything else failed, he still had flying. Miller subsequently moved to San Francisco, joined another model airplane club and began flying a war surplus TG3 glider at Mission Peak south of the city. With the prevailing winds it was possible to fly all day. Rental charges were a mere two cents a minute, a rate so low that even Miller could afford it. "I took any job I could get," he says. "I was living at the bottom of the social scale. The average amount of money I had in my pocket at any one time was something like $3.83."

Wanting a change of scenery, Miller sold his car, made his way to Mexico and caught a tramp steamer to Marseilles. Eventually ending up in Paris, he joined the government-sponsored Aeroclub de France, which allowed him to fly gliders for free, and supported himself with small roles in several "Captain Gallant" films starring Buster Crabbe. He also did some dubbing in an Orson Welles film, *Mr. Arkadin*. "Talk about real alpha males. He filled the room. He was absolutely in charge." The rest of the time Miller made the rounds of Paris cafés, eking out a living photographing the patrons. "I was living by my wits," he says. "And also I had the G.I. Bill."

In 1951, after some correspondence with the famed Norwegian adventurer Thor Heyerdahl, the twenty-seven-year-old Miller decided it would be a good idea to raft across the Mediterranean, just as Heyerdahl had rafted across the Pacific on the Kon Tiki. Then, figured Miller, he could sell the story to *Life* magazine and make himself a bundle. "With a few associates I searched for a café, which is where everybody meets in Paris to plan whatever they're planning," Miller recalls. "It turned out to be the Kentucky Club, pronounced 'Ken-Tooki.' As soon as we heard it we knew we had the name of the raft."

After finishing the *Ken-Tooki* in a chantier (shipyard) on the banks of the Seine, Miller and three friends floated it downriver to Marseilles, where one night they set off from a little fishing village on the lower hook of the bay. The following day the French coast guard arrested them and tossed them in the brig for creating an illegal *corps flottant* ("floating body"). It was, Miller says, another "one of life's little lessons in how to fail, at which I became increasingly adept."

Having had enough of France, Miller returned to New York in September of 1955 and again took low-wage, "shitass jobs you get when you haven't got much self-confidence or skills," working for the post office at Christmas, as a photographer's assistant and as a bookstore clerk. Through it all, his one anchor was model planes. Miller joined another model building club, the Brooklyn Sky Scraper, and began writing articles for *Model Airplane News* and *Air Progress*. Obtaining an assignment to interview Paul Garber, the aeronautical impresario behind the Smithsonian's Air and Space Museum, he went to Washington, D.C., where during a visit to the Academy of Model Aeronautics he happened to bump into John Worth, a government employee in charge of the Rogallo project at Langley Research Center.

The project was named for Francis Rogallo, a NASA engineer who had invented a substitute for the traditional parachute. The principle was very simple: during flight, air pressure will hold a soft fabric covering against three spars in a delta shape, thus creating a low-performance glider. For a while NASA had flirted with the idea of using the Rogallo wing to bring back space capsules from orbit, but nothing ever came of it. During their chat, Worth drew a diagram of the Rogallo wing in Miller's notebook and, when Miller moved to California, he used some bamboo poles from a rug store to build a man-carrying Rogallo glider, which he called the Bamboo Butterfly. It was diamond-shaped with two 16-foot leading-edge spars that met at an 80-degree angle. It had a 22-foot keel and was covered with a 16-by-16-foot square of clear polyethylene, held in place with duct tape. Total cost for materials was $9.

As a glider it was only slightly more inefficient than a brick, having a glide ratio of 3:1 (for every three feet forward it dropped one foot). To get airborne required a steep hill and a stiff breeze. Even on a good flight Miller rarely got more than a few feet above the ground (one reason an early hang-gliding magazine was named *Groundskimmer*). A hundred feet was considered a long flight. In contrast, Otto Lilienthal had been making quarter-mile flights in rigid-wing gliders seventy years before in Germany, and in Phoenix, contemporaneously with Miller, other Rogallo enthusiasts were getting as high as 80 feet and gliding 200 yards.

At this point neither Miller nor MacCready knew much about the other. They once rode together to San Diego, where MacCready was giving a talk to an aviation group. "It was just two guys talking," says Miller. "I was ignorant of the magnitude of his accomplishments as a soaring pilot then." But by 1965, Miller had become editor of *Soaring,* the journal of the Soaring Society of America. One day when MacCready came by the office, Miller offered to demonstrate the Bamboo Butterfly to him at Playa del Rey, a beach near Los Angeles International Airport with steep hills and a wide sandy beach. As there wasn't much wind on that occasion, the Bamboo Butterfly barely got airborne, leading a skeptical Paul MacCready to run down the hill without the glider, holding out his arms instead. "I went farther and stayed up longer without the Rogallo," he told Miller.

In the meantime, to help spread the word about hang-gliding, Miller had encouraged a fellow sailplane pilot, Emil Kissel, to publish a hang-gliding newsletter—initially called "Low, Slow and Out of Control." Other people began to write to Miller asking for information on the Bamboo Butterfly. When Miller sent photos and details to a correspondent from Texas, the man drew up plans for what he called the "Bat Glider" and began advertising them in magazines at $5 a set. One excited reader who quickly sent in his money was a bright, deceptively mild-mannered seventeen-year-old Pasadena high school student named Taras Kiceniuk.

ELEVEN

The Earth-Flip Hypothesis

WHEN I WENT TO VISIT Taras Kiceniuk he was living in the agricultural town of Santa Paula, California, in a converted barn with rough stone steps, an ancient four-legged bathtub in the grass, and some highly aggressive geese. When they got loose, explained Kiceniuk, they would grab his pant cuffs in their beaks, and beat his shins with their wings. "It really hurts," he said.

Kiceniuk turned out to be very friendly, very low-key and surprisingly thoughtful. If, in the struggle to understand some unfamiliar technical point, I said something obviously wrong, he wouldn't so much seize upon my error as gently suggest that there were other ways to look at the matter that I might find even more rewarding.

Kiceniuk, who had a meteoric career as a hang-gliding pioneer, began to fly sailplanes at age fourteen in Kanpur, India, where his father was a professor of mechanical engineering. In 1968, the family returned to southern California where, during the seventies, his father was superintendent of Mt. Palomar Observatory. Taras in the meantime took sailplane lessons with Alec Brooks, a junior high school classmate with whom he flew model planes before class and built a plywood railroad handcar with which he traveled the San Gabriel Valley tracks at night.

Although Kiceniuk loved flying, he was less enthralled with the adult supervision and what seemed at times an overabundance of rules. When a friend pointed out a magazine ad offering "Bat Glider" plans for $5 he quickly sent in his money. When the plans arrived, he cut down some bamboo poles from a neighbor's front yard, bought a 16-by-16-foot square of 4-mil black polyethylene plastic drop cloth from Sears and hastily taped, tied, stapled and screwed together a glider, which he called the Batso.

The Batso, an indirect copy (by way of Texas) of Richard Miller's Bamboo Butterfly, wasn't much of a flier, but if you found a steep enough hill and got a couple of friends to tow you into the air, you could make some short, fast flights and some gentle S turns. Pretty soon Kiceniuk was gliding off ever higher, steeper and more rocky hills, careening over crevasses and engaging in such highly athletic maneuvers that he once caused a passing car to spin out in a cloud of dust. Kiceniuk was thrilled. After all the rules of flying sailplanes, making a hang glider out of bamboo and plastic and then running down the nearest hill and getting airborne without a license, without permission, was for Kiceniuk "pretty much total freedom."

Quickly realizing the limitations of the early Rogallo glider's meager 3:1 glide ratio, he built a series of rigid-wing, tailless biplane gliders (the Icarus and Icarus II) and followed that up with an elegant, high-performance, rigid-wing monoplane, the Icarus V. At a time when Rogallo wing gliders were struggling along with 3:1 or 4:1 glide ratios he had glide ratios of 10:1. When he had first started out, hang-glider flight times were measured in seconds. Now he was launching at the top of the 300-foot seaside cliffs down at Torrey Pines and riding back and forth for hours, then just as the sun was setting, landing back where he started or, if the wind died completely, gliding down the beach to touch down lightly on the sand.

Kiceniuk's exploits made him into a hang-gliding equivalent of a teenage rock star. Younger aviation-minded teenagers followed his career the way earlier generations followed Mick Jagger or Bob Dylan. *Soaring* magazine put him on the cover. Stories about him and his increasingly sophisticated hang gliders appeared in magazines like *National Geographic, Popular Science, Air Progress, Private Pilot* and a dozen others. When I went to see Kiceniuk, one dusty, yellow Icarus V was still on his hangar wall.

Initially Kiceniuk and I talked at the Santa Paula airport. For anyone who has even the slightest attraction to aviation there's something inordinately pleasant about sitting inside a cool hangar, looking out the big open doors and watching small planes touch down on the runway. (For me it has the same calming effect as sitting by a table at a hillside café in Naples, looking out on the Bay of Capri.) Later we drove over to his house, where he showed me the February 1972 issue of *National Geographic,* with multiple photos of himself

A teenage Taras Kiceniuk in the Icarus.

flying a bamboo and black plastic glider, including one from the May 1971 Otto Lilienthal Meet, an event as significant to hang-gliding pilots as Woodstock is to rock fans. Before I left he also demonstrated a model he had built to illustrate his latest scientific theory, the "earth-flip hypothesis."

Because Kiceniuk's theory involved a lot of vector mathematics, a field in which he seemed to have immersed himself during his Caltech days, it wasn't easy for laymen to understand. For a visual aid Kiceniuk had made a small, smooth Styrofoam model of the earth mounted in a nearly frictionless, air-cushioned cradle, powered by an aquarium pump. When Kiceniuk gave the globe a sharp spin, it whirled freely in the air cradle just as the real earth does in space.

To simulate an exaggerated nonuniform planet, Kiceniuk had buried unevenly distributed weights within his globe. To make the motion easier to follow, he painted an orange spot and a green spot at diametrically opposed positions along the equator. When he spun the globe on a vertical axis with the north pole on top, the ball would continue to spin in a simple, stable fashion. But if he spun the globe starting with the green equatorial spot on top, it underwent a series of dramatic but predictable gyrations until it completely flipped ends, leaving the orange spot steady on top. After a brief steady-state period, the ball would begin gyrating until it flipped again, this time leaving the green spot on top. As long as the ball kept spinning, it would continue to flip periodically.

What did all this flipping of the model have to do with the real earth?

To Kiceniuk's thinking, quite a bit.

As he explained to me, and in a series of papers he posted on his website (icarusengineering.com), scientists have never satisfactorily accounted for three major geological processes: (1) what causes ice ages? (2) what keeps the earth's interior so hot? and (3) where does the energy that moves tectonic plates around come from? Kiceniuk's theory suggested that the surprising answer to all three questions was sunlight. In a process not unlike the workings of a huge steam engine, the earth's (wobbly) rotation took the seasonally varying energy of sunlight and converted it into mechanical energy, causing the earth to wobble even more and thus creating internal friction, which then greatly heated the earth's interior, with profound consequences for both the planet and all life on it.

Although the details of Kiceniuk's "Planetary Heat Engine Theory" involved tensor mathematics and references to angular velocity vectors, system 'Q', maximum moments of inertia and chaotic neutral points, his main ideas were pretty simple:

1. Planets not only spin, they also wobble.
2. When you add energy to a wobbling system it increases the amount of wobble.
3. In winter, ice and snow build up in the northern latitude land masses (and in summer, sunlight melts and evaporates the ice).
4. The increased winter weight causes the land to sink, like the downward stroke of a huge piston engine.
5. This piston stroke adds energy to the earth, which in turn increases the earth's wobble.
6. Due to the Coriolis effect (a deflection of moving bodies caused by the earth's rotation), the wobble causes ocean currents to move faster and change direction.
7. Ocean currents are strongly correlated with snowfall distribution and ice buildup, which together increase the force of the piston stroke and further excite the wobble.
8. The increasing wobble causes frictional stress in the earth's crust and mantle, which heats up the earth's interior and drives the movement of tectonic plates.

In the past, scientists have tried to explain the earth's hot interior by reference to "primordial heat" and "radioactive decay." But the numbers just weren't big enough. Kiceniuk's calculations, on the other hand, showed that a planetary heat engine could generate 300 trillion watts, enough to explain both the shifting of tectonic plates and the heat coming out of the earth's interior.

Kiceniuk's theory depended on the fact that the earth doesn't merely spin on its axis, it also wobbles, albeit more slowly, not unlike a football does when a quarterback throws a less-than-perfect spiral pass. The wobbling, called the "Chandler Wobble," has a period of about 425 days. During this time the earth pendulums around in such a way that the latitude of each point on the surface changes back and forth by 1/10,000th of a degree (about 10 meters).

This pendulum-wobble movement can be exacerbated by changes in surface loading caused by shifting ice deposits, moving water or, as recent

work at the Jet Propulsion Laboratory in Pasadena has shown, pressure fluctuations on the sea floor. It was Kiceniuk's contribution to suggest that during ancient ice ages the size of the wobble was much greater than today and
that the motion was driven by changes in glaciation (ice buildup and decay).

The more that ice buildup excites the wobble, the greater the wobble
becomes. If the earth were to remain relatively solid and rigid, its wobble
would eventually become so great that the planet would flip, like Kiceniuk's
little Styrofoam globe. The good news for the earth is that the wobble appears
to be self-regulating. As the internal friction from wobble heats the interior
of the earth, the earth becomes fluid enough that the surface piston stroke
of the seasonally varying ice load gets progressively decoupled from the wobble. As the wobble fades away, the earth's interior slowly cools until it becomes
relatively solid once more, whereupon the process starts all over again.

"This feedback process provides an internal thermostatic action for
spinning planetary bodies," wrote Kiceniuk in a paper published on his website. "Perhaps it's an aspect of Gaia theory (the living earth postulate). Animals that thermoregulate are called warm blooded, but who ever heard of a
'warm blooded planet'?"

Kiceniuk was excited about his theory, which he planned to present
in a lecture at Caltech, and I was excited for him. If it were true, it seemed
to me, it was a major discovery, like finding a coelacanth off Madagascar or
discovering that an asteroid impact in the Yucatan killed off the dinosaurs.

Kiceniuk's lecture was in a small academic auditorium with stadium
seating on the Caltech campus. Perhaps a hundred people were there, including faculty members, former classmates, Kiceniuk's wife and mother and
Paul MacCready, who didn't recognize me when I shook his hand.

The earth-flip lecture was a big occasion for Kiceniuk. He had his
spinning-globe model set up on a lab table at the front of the room and a
video camera to project it on a large TV screen. To demonstrate the difference between stable and unstable rotations, he threw balls into the air and
flipped tennis tickets. At the blackboard Kiceniuk had the polished academic
manner of someone who had been teaching many years. The talk went on
for perhaps forty-five minutes, after which Kiceniuk solicited questions.

Coming into the lecture I didn't know what to expect, but the thought
had occurred to me that in this modest Caltech lecture hall I might be wit-
nessing a modern-day equivalent of Einstein's first speech explaining relativity at the Carpenters' Union Hall in Zurich. If the room had erupted into

thunderous applause and a standing ovation, I wouldn't have been all that surprised. Instead, the audience was completely silent.

Kiceniuk asked again, this time almost plaintively: "Doesn't anyone have any questions or comments? Any at all?"

Suddenly a Caltech professor made some highly technical and surprisingly angry objections to what he regarded as Kiceniuk's unwarranted assumptions regarding the magnitude and frequency of ice/snow buildup. I was taken aback by the out-of-the-blue ferocity of his opinions. But Kiceniuk seemed totally unfazed. He thanked the professor for his observations and that was that. As the people slowly filed out of the auditorium, MacCready went up to the podium, watched the earth-flip model and then bent over and blew on one side of the still-spinning globe. "That's the solar wind," he said.

Kiceniuk was such a genuinely nice guy that I felt disappointed on his behalf. He later told me the muted response was actually pretty "normal" for Caltech. Most of the time, he said, people took the attitude, "Okay, that's your shtick. That's fine. The donuts were good."

A few weeks later I later spoke with Kiceniuk's good friend Bill Watson, who ran a model-building business in Van Nuys for the film industry and aerospace. They were old friends from Kiceniuk's high school days. After Kiceniuk gave up hang-gliding, Watson had helped him build a ground-effect vehicle in an early attempt to win the Kremer Prize, and together they had helped build the Gossamer Albatross, the first man-powered aircraft to fly the English Channel.

When I went to see Watson I found he was a big, tall guy with prematurely white hair. Kiceniuk told me that Watson did the "most delicate work" anyone could imagine. But when I saw him, he had been installing new front-wheel brake pads on his GM van. As he sat in his workshop driveway wiping grease from his fingers with a paper towel, he told me that he was more than a "little irritated" with Kiceniuk. He'd been the greatest hang glider pilot of his generation and on top of everything else, he had a first-class mind to boot. "He's one of the smartest people I know," "intuitive," "creative," "probably smarter than all of us." But he never took it to the next stage. "He could have advanced far more than MacCready—or any of us. He could have had his own business or whatever. I know two or three people like that. They hate being in the workshop. You have to pay them a huge amount of money to get them through the workshop door and then they want to leave as soon as they can."

On the other hand, Watson knew, if following other people's rules had been important to Kiceniuk, he never would have been a hang-gliding pioneer in the first place, designed the Icarus V or appeared on the cover of flying magazines everywhere. And he certainly wouldn't have shown up, along with hundreds of other people, at the Otto Lilienthal Meet in Orange County one Sunday morning in May of 1971, to create the sport of hang-gliding in America.

TWELVE

The Otto Lilienthal Meet

IN THE LATE NINETEENTH CENTURY an American civil engineer and railroad builder named Octave Chanute had designed a foot-launched, rigid bi-wing glider with a horizontal and vertical stabilizer. Although associates of Chanute (who himself was elderly at the time) made thousands of success-ful gliding flights on his gliders, the Wright Brothers' success with powered aircraft caused his earlier and, in some ways, more advanced gliders to be nearly forgotten. Every decade or so a magazine like *Boy Mechanic* or *Pop-ular Mechanics* would rediscover the Chanute glider and republish plans, and then there would be a minor revival with a small number of people building gliders, after which the subject would fade away for another decade. During World War II, when it was illegal to fly powered planes within 150 miles of the coast, Volmer Jensen, a self-taught engineer from Glendale, Cal-ifornia, built quite sophisticated, Chanute-like, foot-launched, rigid-wing gliders with full three-axis control. Although Jensen made even better glid-ers after the war, in those days America was in love with radios and rockets. The zeitgeist wasn't right for lightweight, foot-launched flight and, aside from a few isolated individual planes and fliers, nothing ever came of it.

By 1970, though, says Kiceniuk, "the collective psyche and the tech-nology" had finally met. It was during that time that Jack Lambie, a science teacher, aviation writer, efficiency aficionado and all-around raconteur, decided to supplement his instruction in aeronautics by having his sixth- and seventh-grade students at the Collins School in Long Beach build a replica of Chanute's bi-wing glider. As with all of Lambie's projects it was a low-key, low-cost affair. Lambie spent $10.50 for 14 feet of Douglas fir doorjamb, $3.20 for Mylar sheeting, and 50 cents for bailing wire. As neither Lambie's students nor Lambie himself were skilled craftsmen, the glider's bailing-wire-braced and turnbuckle-tightened frame was too flexible to make a decent airfoil. And when it made a hard landing, the struts popped out of their bottle-cap holders. Still, with a student holding the end of each wingtip, it was possible to run down a hill on a windy day and sort of get airborne. Lambie called his modified Chanute glider the "Hang Loose," a reference both to the haphazard way it was built and to Lambie's deeply relaxed philosophy of life.

In the spring of 1971, Richard Miller and Jack Lambie got together on a hillside in Mission Viejo. Lambie brought a disassembled Hang Loose and a class of sixth and seventh graders to help him put it together. Always on the lookout for anything that would help him satisfy his inner craving for what he called "famousity," Lambie had also invited an aviation photographer to cover the event and eventually the spring 1971 issue of *Sportplanes* magazine carried a cover photo of Lambie and the Hang Loose with the title, "The aircraft you can build for $24.86." To his amazement, Lambie found himself inundated with thousands of orders from everyone from young boys to airline pilots, many of whom enclosed passionate notes, such as "This is something I've dreamed of all my life." Lambie's younger brother, Mark, a gifted draftsman with a *Mad Magazine* sense of humor, drew up a breezy, three-page mimeographed set of plans, which Jack sold for $3. Suddenly, home-built Hang Looses were appearing everywhere.

Popular as they were, Hang Looses weren't the only inspiration. In recent years, hang-gliding had been bursting out in multiple places, helped by such Australians as Bill Bennett, who started flying on large water-ski kites pulled by speedboats back in 1957, and John Dickenson, who built a speedboat-towed Rogallo in 1963. Richard Miller began flying the Bamboo Butterfly in 1965 on bluffs above the beach just south of Los Angeles International Airport. In 1969, Bennett flew over the Statue of Liberty and landed at its base. Another Australian, Bill Moyes, flew a Rogallo wing off the rim of the Grand Canyon to the valley below and was fined $150 for staging an event without a permit. In 1971, Dave Kilbourne soared for an hour on Mission Peak near San Francisco. The same year, Joe Faust wrote a piece for *Soaring* magazine on the hang-gliding phenomenon. Seeing which way the wind was blowing, Richard Miller realized one day that the number of gliders within a 50-mile radius of Newport Beach was growing so rapidly that a celebration was in order.

Top, Jack Lambie casting his fate to the winds in the Hang Loose.
Above, Richard Miller gliding downhill in the Conduit Condor in 1971.

"When I got home, San Clemente at the time, I consulted the calendar for a likely date," Miller later wrote, "and what should I discover but that—*Shazam!*—Lilienthal's birthday, May 23rd, fell on a Sunday just a few months ahead." Miller immediately wrote to Lambie suggesting that they stage a glider meet in honor of the nineteenth-century German visionary Otto Lilienthal. As the Irvine Company owned most of the undeveloped land in Orange County, Lambie went first to them. Although not opposed to the idea, they also required that Lambie have a million dollars worth of liability insurance, the same as for a motorcycle race. At $400 to $800 a day, that was out of the question.

Figuring he wasn't going to get anywhere following other people's rules, Lambie found a site on a hillside, belonging to a memorial cemetery in Newport Beach, that "nobody seemed to be using," as his brother Mark put it, and he invited people just to show up. If the police showed up as well, the participants would all take the position that it was not an organized event, no one was in charge, they were just a group of flying enthusiasts who had spontaneously gotten together for a weekend outing.

There was method to Lambie's madness. As he later explained to writer Maralys Wills in *Manbirds,* it was a lot harder to defeat a group of people who had no leaders than it was to defeat one led by a powerful authority. Cortez had only four hundred men when he conquered Montezuma. If the meet had no organizers, there would be nobody for the police to threaten with arrest.

On the day of the meet, several hundred people showed up with fourteen gliders. There were eleven brightly colored Hang Looses and three Rogallos: Kiceniuk's Batso, a jib-rigged Rogallo by aeronautical engineer and sailplane enthusiast Bruce Carmichael, and an advanced flying wing by Richard Miller called the Conduit Condor (for its aluminum electrical conduit frame). In this, Miller made the longest self-launched flight of the meet—280 feet. "Hang Looses flew slow and graceful," Taras Kiceniuk recalls. "[But] the Conduit Condor (actually a prototype tailless flying wing) was by far the most advanced plane there. It was ten years ahead of everyone else."

For safety's sake (the rule in those days was never to fly higher than you're willing to fall) they had picked a hill with such a gentle slope that— the Conduit Condor excepted—the gliders generally had to be towed or pushed into the air. The longest-duration flight of the day, made when Taras Kiceniuk was towed aloft on the Batso, was twenty-three seconds.

As a rigid-wing plane, the Hang Loose had much better glide performance than the flexible-sail Batso-type gliders, but it also had some major limitations, the greatest being that it was hard to control a Hang Loose by weight shifts alone (it had no other controls). If a wing hit the ground, the pilot could find himself doing cartwheels down the hill.

As Lambie later wrote in an article about the "mayhem" of the Lilienthal meet, some Hang Loose owners had only just built their gliders and had never flown them before. Some of their launching assistants had even less experience. They'd grab the wingtips and the tail assembly and together the group would try to push the plane into the air. Sometimes the people on the wingtips would let go while the tail man kept pushing, which caused the glider to flare up in a full stall. At other times, the front would hit, causing struts to collapse and the tail to snap off. Or one of the wing men would let go while the other kept pushing, causing spectacular ground loops (horizontal spins, like a car on ice).

After half a dozen crashes, the airframes became so twisted that it was impossible to fly the aircraft straight and level no matter how skilled the pilot or ground crews. The Rogallos were much easier to control but they had terrible glide ratios. As the gliders were visible from a nearby highway, soon thousands of spectators had gathered, not to mention a squad car and police helicopter. Through loudspeakers the police repeatedly ordered the event organizers to report to the squad car, but because there were no organizers, there was no one to arrest, and in the end, the police left the fliers alone.

Keenly alert to the advantages of publicity, Lambie had arranged for a photographer from *National Geographic* to cover the meet. Stories appeared in the *Los Angeles Times, Science, Soaring* and *Popular Mechanics.* Joe Faust, who had helped arrange the meet with Lambie, was contacted by Merv Griffin, CBS and the *London Times.* The news traveled to England, Germany and France, where it stirred up such great excitement that Lambie held a second meet in San Diego a few months later.

In the meantime, at El Toro Marine Air Base, where Mark Lambie had just started work, the regional newsletter of the Federal Aviation Agency got a call noting that Lambie had made the longest-duration untowed flight at the Lilienthal meet. Lambie recalls,

The next day, two guys from the Long Beach Flight Standards district office showed up at the facility and wanted to talk to me. They wanted the names of all the pilots who had participated. They were going to charge us with flying unregistered aircraft, flying inside the Orange County control zone, flying near crowds, flying aircraft repaired with duct tape and on and on and on. Believe me, they were out for blood.

Lambie, who professed not to have recognized anyone there, quickly realized that the investigators really didn't want to arrest anyone. They had been embarrassed by the *Los Angeles Times* story and were just looking to give themselves a little cover in case anybody complained. Amiable and good-natured, Mark Lambie was happy to provide it. "Well, you know," he said, "we were tethered."

"*What???*"

"All the planes were tethered to the ground."

That was exactly what the inspectors wanted to hear. If these gliders were tethered, they were man-carrying kites, not aircraft, and thus not the FAA's responsibility after all. For years afterward, some southern California hang glider pilots dangled tow strings from the front of their gliders in case an FAA inspector showed up.

Despite the poor performance of the gliders, the participants went away from the Lilienthal Meet with the sense that they had been present at the start of something new in America. In the years that followed, the Otto Lilienthal Meet would take on a legendary status among hang-gliding pioneers. But surprisingly, the one observer at the meet who was not overly impressed was Paul MacCready. "What good is it?" he asked as he watched one pilot after another stumble and stagger down the hill. "It's like rolling down-hill on a bicycle with the steering locked and seeing who can go the farthest before crashing."

THIRTEEN

Taras Kiceniuk and Icarus Ground Effect I

ALTHOUGH TARAS KICENIUK HAD MADE the day's longest-duration flight on his Batso, it was clear to him that the rigid-wing biplanes had far better performance than the Rogallos. He subsequently built a swept-back, rigid-wing, tailless biplane with twin rudders, which he called the Icarus. It was a quantum leap forward in performance from the Rogallos. A subsequent improved version, the Icarus II, was the first hang glider to make a complete 360-degree turn in flight, allowing Kiceniuk to spiral upward to 1000 feet in a shear line out near Palmdale.

At the Otto Lilienthal Meet, Kiceniuk had given MacCready a 15-foot-high towed flight in the Batso. Afterwards, Kiceniuk begun hanging out at AeroVironment with MacCready to talk about low-speed flight. "I used to pal around a lot, visit and ask questions," says Kiceniuk. "I realized he was really alert and really listening. We were having a conversation in real time. It wasn't just a case of people playing our own tape loops."

Their relationship proved hugely beneficial to Kiceniuk. At a time when many hang glider designers were proceeding by trial and error, Kiceniuk was able to use AeroVironment's Hewlett Packard computer to run an elegant airfoil design program written by AeroVironment aerodynamicist Peter Lissaman to calculate pressure distributions. The result was Kiceniuk's most elegant design, the highly efficient Icarus V mono-wing, with a 10:1 glide radio, low stalling speed and, as Kiceniuk wrote in his Icarus V manual, "a large usable range of flying speeds and excellent controllability."

For Kiceniuk, who wasn't yet out of his teens, these were thrilling times. People were buying plans from him and building their own versions of the Icarus gliders. Soon it seemed everyone was designing and building hang gliders, including some people who should have stuck with dirt bikes. There were broken bones, concussions and herniated disks. Some of Kiceniuk's friends got killed. One guy fell out of an Icarus V while flying at 10,000 feet over the Colorado Rockies. "Since it was a plane that I designed," says Kiceniuk, "it affected me a lot."

Deciding that hang-gliding was just too dangerous, Kiceniuk gradually phased out of the field and decided to put his considerable energy into human-powered flight instead. While still an eleventh-grade student at Pasadena's John Muir High School years before, he had heard about the longstanding Kremer Prize for the first person to make a one-mile figure-eight flight in a human-powered aircraft. In those days he was still flying the Batso, so he used his high school's IBM 1620 computer to calculate just how much bigger he needed to make the Batso in order to win the Kremer Prize. "It had sixteen-foot leading edges," says Kiceniuk. "I determined that if I made the leading edges fifty feet longer it would get down into the range where it could fly on human power."

Considering a plane that size a little bit daunting, Kiceniuk gave it up. But after he had phased out of hang-gliding, he decided to try winning the prize with a ground effect vehicle—a vehicle that takes advantage of the greater lift of a wing when it traps air between itself and the ground.

The Kremer Prize was named for the British industrialist Henry Kremer. Starting with a small particle board company, he quickly moved on to make the plywood used in the de Havilland Mosquito bomber during World War II. He later built fiberglass radar domes, radar-jamming chaff and electroviscous fluid suspension systems for tanks. A lifelong physical fitness buff, he jogged regularly and in winter swam in the ice in London's Highgate Ponds in the belief that the shock of cold water stimulated the immune system. Hoping to inspire some British athletes to make comparable efforts, one afternoon in 1959 he offered to fund a prize for man-powered flight, whereupon the Royal Aeronautical Society's man-powered flight group drew up what proved to be an inspired set of criteria for winning the Kremer Prize.

To encourage every sort of innovation, the terms of the competition required only that the pilot complete a figure-eight course around two pylons a half-mile apart and clear a 10-foot hurdle at the beginning of the flight and at the end. Aside from these rules (and the original restriction—soon dropped—that only British citizens were eligible), there were no other major limitations. Initially the prize was only £5,000, but as the years passed and the great difficulty of the task became increasingly apparent, Kremer raised the purse in increments until by 1973, the year that Kiceniuk began his ground-effect machine, it was worth £50,000 ($85,000 to $100,000, depending on the exchange rate).

Kiceniuk got the ball rolling by asking Bill Watson to help him. Watson, who was a couple of years older, was living with his parents in Van Nuys at the time. He had previously built an Icarus V hang glider from Kiceniuk's plans, "one of the nicest ones that had ever been built," says Kiceniuk. Watson wasn't much interested in academics. He was more a "natural-born engineer/aerodynamicist/inventor" with extremely delicate hands. Although he built anything that flew or moved—his garage storage area is a working museum of everything from side-by-side bicycles to flying fifties-style Martian spaceships to gas-powered boomerangs—his first love, as with so many MacCready associates, was model planes.

With Watson's help, Kiceniuk decided to build a "ram-wing hover craft" that would ride on a cushion of air between the wings and the ground, thus dramatically reducing the amount of power required. The idea was that for most of the Kremer course, Kiceniuk's plane would fly a mere 3 inches off the ground supported on an air cushion, then "zoom up" to clear the 10-foot barriers that marked the beginning and end of the course.

It took Kiceniuk and Watson two years to build the plane. The first trials were at El Mirage dry lake in the Mojave Desert in 1974. The results were disappointing. The best they could do was get "the wingtips to rise," says Joe Greblo, a Los Angeles hang-gliding pilot and instructor, "but we were no closer to getting off the ground than I was in my car." Finally in 1975, Dave Saks, a 125-pound bicyclist, managed to make a three-second flight, rising to a height of 18 inches and covering 50 feet. It was the first human-powered flight in the United States. But there was no possibility of the plane flying anything remotely close to a mile, let alone zooming up to clear two 10-foot barriers.

FOURTEEN

How Henry Kremer Changed
Paul MacCready's Life

ETWEEN 1959 AND 1976, there were over fifty official entrants in the Kremer competition and not one had come close to succeeding. A German
professor even argued that man-powered flight was impossible, while a British
aerodynamicist at the University of Liverpool described the task as equivalent to the "Wright Brothers attempting to fly the Atlantic in 1903." Like
many other sailplane pilots, MacCready had idle thoughts about winning
the Kremer Prize over the years. But then he saw a film at an MIT conference about the fast, clean and exquisitely crafted British entrants for the
prize and he lost all hope. "They [the British] had very large teams, lots of
resources, lots of brainpower, huge computers and they made planes that
couldn't even come close to winning the prize," MacCready says. "And I was
thinking, 'Hey, is there a simpler, more fundamental approach?' But every
time I tried to think how to do it, it came out like their approach. So I gave
it up."

In the summer of 1976, two simultaneous events gave MacCready the
conviction that the Kremer Prize was winnable and he was the man who
could do it. The first was a news item noting that the value of the British
pound was now almost exactly $2, which in turn meant that the Kremer
Prize, recently raised to £50,000, was worth nearly $100,000, the same
amount as MacCready's bank note. It was a eureka moment. Suddenly, says
MacCready, human-powered flight was "the most interesting thing in the
world."

Second, when MacCready took his family across the country on a
much-needed summer vacation, listening to his sons' Beatles tapes and tim-

ing the orbits of thermaling vultures, he had an insight that changed his life. As he drove along watching turkey vultures and black vultures, he realized that they occupied different niches. The turkey vulture with its low wing loading flew on small thermals early in the morning. The more heavily wing-loaded black vulture flew faster and glided further later in the day. These observations made MacCready begin to wonder: Could a hang glider fly at the same speed as a turkey vulture? What would its turning radius be? How much power per pound did a turkey vulture need to stay aloft?

"I was doing the scaling laws in my mind, which are pretty simple if you are an aerodynamicist," says MacCready. And suddenly it dawned on him that if one wanted to win the Kremer Prize, there was an approach that no one had ever used before.

> If you keep the weight of the plane the same and increase its size in some magic way, the power to fly goes down. If you triple its span and its chord the power is cut to a third. And so you take a hang glider, which I knew took about one and a quarter horsepower to fly, and triple the size up to a hundred-foot span but keep the weight the same, the power would be down about .4 horsepower. And a good cyclist can put that out. And the light bulb was glowing over my mind. And once I realized that it could be [aerodynamically] ugly but if it was large and light it could win the prize.

At this point MacCready was thinking way outside the box. The other contenders for the Kremer Prize had always assumed that the way to win was to construct a plane that was superefficient. This meant smooth, perfectly contoured, cantilevered wings (like those on airliners, which are attached to the fuselage but have no other supports). MacCready's inelegant but highly practical solution was to forget about cantilevered wings and instead revert to the kind of wire bracing reminiscent of aviation's early days. The other designers were building such fast, ultra-efficient aircraft that they couldn't use wire bracing. But MacCready's proposed plane would fly so slowly (8 mph) that any parasitic drag from the wires would be too small to worry about.

Once MacCready decided to go with a very large, superlight, wire-braced plane, the aircraft practically designed itself. "It was just a big model airplane," he says; "6 sticks and 72 piano wires connecting everything to everything." The design couldn't have been simpler—three lightweight, wire-braced aluminum tubes at right angles to each other, a seat underneath for the pilot, a small horizontal stabilizer (known as a canard) on a boom out front, and two wire spreaders. The stabilizer, whose job it was to hold the wings at the correct angle of attack, could either be in front, as on the Wright Brothers' planes, or in the rear, as it was on conventional planes. Since Mac-Cready's design already called for a forward-looking boom for attaching the wires that kept the trailing edge of wings taut, he found it convenient to put the canard out front too. This allowed him to put the propeller in the rear, where it was more effective anyway. The chord (wing width) was 12 feet because aluminum tubing came in 12-foot lengths. The wingspan was 96 feet because the hangar at Mojave (where they did their initial flight testing) couldn't accommodate a bigger plane than that. He decided to call the plane the Gossamer Condor because the condor was "a large impacted" bird and gossamer meant "fragile, light and frail."

To help him, MacCready decided to ask Jack Lambie—"He was smart. He was a self-starter. He built things with his hands. And he was available."

FIFTEEN

Lambie Luck

Jack Lambie, who had just come back from an around-the-world bicycle trip, was at first skeptical when MacCready asked him to help build a man-powered plane. Like most sailplane pilots he knew that British and Japanese engineers had repeatedly tried to build these beautifully constructed ultralight planes to win the man-powered flight prize and all of them had failed. Except for MacCready's reputation, there was no reason to think his design would be any better. It looked like a big jack with kingposts and wires. He didn't even have any blueprints. He drew his plans on cocktail napkins and brown paper bags. On the other hand, Lambie had to admit in later conversations with his brother, Mark, MacCready certainly had an original approach. "You know," Lambie told Mark, "there is a possibility this could work."

For two people so little alike, MacCready and Lambie got along surprisingly well. MacCready was rational, introverted and shy around women, while Lambie, a bold, muscular type, was intuitive, gregarious and an inveterate ladies' man. But they did agree on one thing: neither one particularly cared how something looked as long as it worked. "If it's worth doing," Lambie was fond of saying, "it's worth doing poorly." It wasn't that he didn't care about craftsmanship; he was quite gifted in making models of things he really cared about, such as marble women's torsos and wooden penises. He just knew that craftsmanship came at the cost of other things, some of which were even more important, such as getting the job done at all.

Unlike MacCready, who wasn't especially coordinated, Lambie was a natural-born pilot with an unequaled ability to make tight coordinated turns at low speeds. He flew hang gliders, sailplanes, single-engines, multi-engines, motor gliders. In the early seventies he owned a yellow Piper Cub with big fat tires, which he liked to take down to San Felipe in Baja California. "I tend to get claustrophobic in planes," says Lambie's articulate and gregarious fourth (and last) ex-wife, Karen Hoiland, "so he used to fly it really slow, really low and keep the windows open. He could land that sucker anywhere. He liked to drop it down in the middle of the street. I swear he could land it in a kitchen." Once, he landed his glider in a nudist camp, where he felt so much at home that he stayed for dinner, took off his clothes and gave a speech.

Unlike most pilots, who worried constantly about running out of gas, Lambie was no more concerned about his plane's fuel supply than he was about the gas level in the old Corvair vans he liked to drive. After he sold his Piper Cub, he bought a little Fournier motor glider (a sailplane with a small Volkswagen pull-start engine) that he used to fly from Lake Elsinore to San Francisco. If he ran out of gas, he'd just work thermals and ridge lift until he finally had to land—on a private strip, alfalfa field, barren hillside, or country road. Before long someone would come by and offer to help. And Lambie was such a genial conversationalist that pretty soon they'd be asking him to dinner, finding him some gas and inviting him to stay the night.

"He loved the feeling of adrenaline," observes Charlie Webber, an old friend from the days when Lambie was so destitute that he lived in a hangar at Riverside County's Flabob Airport. "He loved being scared. He had testosterone coming out of his ears and his pecker." Once on a trip to South America the fuel pump for his reserve tank (a borrowed automotive Honda pump) quit over the jungle, six hundred miles from civilization. He didn't panic, says Webber. "When he came to a fork in the road he took it." If he had to put his plane down, he figured, he'd just hike his way out. On this occasion he didn't have to, the problem being the typically casual way he had wired the fuel pump power supply.

Though outwardly dissimilar in almost every way, Lambie and MacCready shared an ingrained appreciation of efficiency. Lambie streamlined everything he owned—bicycles, all his cars and a tractor-trailer truck (he helped develop the now-ubiquitous streamlined fairings used on tractor-trailers). He would take his trailer truck, named the Drag Queen, out to Kellog Hill at the intersection of the 57 and 210 freeways near Pomona, put it in neutral and coast downhill, seeing how long it took to reach a given speed. With full fairings it was possible to cut wind resistance—and thus fuel consumption—up to 18 percent. Even partial fairings cut fuel consumption 4 to 10 percent. But they were a hard sell, says Mark Lambie.

Jack Lambie fed his baby ravens a mixture of raw hamburger and cottage cheese directly from his lips.

What we found is that the truck driver would get out there and all of a sudden he would have the equivalent of 50 more horsepower at road speed. What does he do? He goes ten miles an hour faster. So the fuel burned between Los Angeles and San Francisco was the same as before, except the driver got there an hour and a half earlier. It was a nice pay raise for him.

For personal use, Jack drove Corvair Greenbrier vans. To compensate for their blunt, air-resisting fronts and deeply inadequate air-cooled, six-cylinder engines, he would completely overhaul the vehicles, adding full underpans and wheel fairings, and shaping their fronts into huge bulbous noses. He taped little tufts of yarn to the windshield so he could monitor the airflow. He removed the side-view mirrors to reduce drag and replaced them with vertically mounted slit mirrors. He cut off the rubber molding that held in the windshields and filled the cracks with Bondo. He bought sound-deadening insulation/padding of the sort used in military helicopters and covered the insides with it. He went to enormous pains to make his cars totally aerodynamic, but he never bothered to take the last step and have them painted. He put surplus DC-8 passenger jet windows in one of his Corvair vans, which made it look like something out of a Mad Max movie, but it could hit 90 miles per hour with an 84-horsepower engine.

Along with Chet Kyle, a former mechanical engineering professor at Long Beach State University, Lambie founded the International Human Powered Vehicle Association and then staged a meet for streamlined bikes. Lambie was subsequently caught on video describing a rider at that first event. "He got up to fifty miles an hour, then he crashed and went around and around," said Lambie, twirling his finger in the air to show how the bike went into a vertical spin. "Then he went this way and around that way. I said to Chet, 'This looks like this is going to be a lot of fun.'"

People who knew Jack Lambie felt he was one of those people who could have been practically anything he wanted. He was smart, charming, persuasive and decisive. "He had incredible chutzpah," says Karen Hoiland. "He could tell a story like nobody's business. He could hold a room. He embellished the truth quite a bit. He told people he was thirty-nine well into his fifties."

Hoiland met Lambie when he came to speak at the U.C. Riverside Glider Club. At the time she was an 18-year-old college freshman and he was a 41-year-old father of five with three ex-wives (he claimed to be 39, with three children). "I sat in the front row," Hoiland remembers.

> And on my part it was love at first sight. Absolutely. I was completely besotted with this man. I just looked up and I was in love. He looked like Papa Hemingway. He just oozed confidence. He was a wrestler in college and always felt in control of any situation. That's why we never had any guns around our house. No matter what kind of situation we were in he always felt quite capable of taking care of himself and us. He just exuded it.

For Hoiland, that first meeting with Lambie opened up a whole new world in that suddenly she found herself meeting "all these wonderful and incredibly neat people.

> I was eighteen. I should have just been going to school and doing my thing. And I instantly went from this little tiny small town girl who had never been anywhere to someone who was flying all over Mexico, having all these wonderful trips, riding bikes, having airplanes. It was a great leap, a logarithmic leap.

The downside was she had to recognize that he was totally in charge and she had to do whatever he said.

Except perhaps in flying, Lambie wasn't necessarily more talented than other people. The difference was that he approached everything and everybody totally without fear. The prospect of failure never occurred to him. He gladly threw himself into any situation whether he was qualified or not. He once got a job as a copilot on a Citation twin-engine jet for Getty Oil after falsely claiming to have a commercial, multi-engine, instrument rating. He did fine when it came to flying the plane. What got him fired was his unwillingness to bother with everything else—filing flight plans, using checklists, getting the weather briefing or calculating fuel loads. He didn't care about such things. He considered them mere busywork. He thought that people who followed procedures were lacking in spontaneity.

He placed a lot of faith in what he called "Lambie luck." He truly felt that (1) no really bad thing would ever happen to him and (2) if it did, he could certainly talk his way out of it. When he got a job delivering a new motor glider from Los Angeles to Paraguay, he wrangled an assignment from *National Geographic* to photograph Andean condors along the way, but in typical Lambie fashion he didn't bother with visas or paperwork. He mounted remote-actuated Olympus cameras on the plane's tail and wingtips and carried hundreds of rolls of film. When he landed in Peru (in the middle of yet another coup), the military took one look at his photo system and concluded he was a spy. Lambie only talked his way out of it by convincing his captors that he was on a photo mission to document their glorious country's magnificent birds.

Despite his charm as a great raconteur, Lambie's disorganization and messiness made him hard to live with. He could go for weeks without remembering to take out the garbage. He survived on Miller beer, cashews and marijuana. His den was so filled with books, papers, beer bottles and shavings from whatever model he happened to be working on that it was a challenge to get from one side to the other.

Inordinately hard-headed, Lambie was famous for never changing his engine oil. He claimed that every-3,000-mile oil changes were merely a scheme to make oil companies rich. He would drive all the way to Oregon to register one of his beat-up old cars because registration fees were cheaper there. Oblivious to the danger, he drove around with five-gallon water bottles full of gasoline in the trunk of his cars and put a TV in the front of his van so he could watch movies while driving down the freeway.

A great fan of ravens, he would capture them as chicks and raise them himself, feeding them a mix of cottage cheese and raw hamburger directly from his own lips. He liked to talk politics, as much for the joy of arguing as from any deep conviction. "Jack's politics were a bottle of beer in one hand and a broad in the other," says his old friend Charlie Webber.

If there was one thing he regretted, it was not being more famous or respected. "He loved the accolades," says Karen Hoiland. "He loved giving talks. He loved being the center of attention." To him, being ordinary was worse than being dead. "He would do anything to avoid a life of quiet desperation. And that's what he thought most people lived. He was obsessed with not being ordinary."

For a while during their marriage, Hoiland and Lambie lived on Heart Street in the city of Orange. It was only a three-bedroom tract house, but there were so many people coming and going that Hoiland began calling it the Heart Hotel.

We had roommates all the time. People were always showing up. They'd stay a couple of months or six, anybody who needed a home. Jack would bring whole families home who were destitute. One of Jack's kids was always coming to visit. It was like a dorm or sorority house filled with college kids who never outgrew it. There were always good discussions at dinner. We could talk till ten at night. Jack was so much fun to be with—it was like living with an artist and a writer and a raconteur all rolled into one.

Unlike most people, Lambie lived comfortably on the edge. He didn't believe in long-range planning for retirement because he was permanently retired from around the age of forty anyway. He didn't pay taxes. He never had any insurance on his house, his car or himself. If he needed to see a doctor, he would enroll in a junior college and use the student clinic. It was impossible to embarrass him because he simply didn't care. Once when he hadn't gotten around to buying an airplane ticket, he walked out on the tarmac, climbed the ramp and seated himself in first class. When the stewardess asked for his boarding pass, he brushed her off—*"Don't you know who I am?"*

He supported himself with a series of low-paying jobs: writing books on ultralights and airplane construction, serving as a parole officer, selling driveway repaving jobs and hearing aids ("the little old ladies loved him," says Hoiland) and teaching people how to fly. "He was a very easygoing instructor," recalls Webber. "He wasn't dogmatic or over-controlling. He read sex magazines during the flight. He never got excited. He would let you go right to the edge of really screwing up before taking over."

Lambie worshipped the female anatomy, especially the "aerodynamic" shape of the buttocks. He had "the gift of seduction," says his brother Mark, coupled with a total lack of social inhibitions. As soon as he saw someone he liked, he'd invite himself to stay the night. "It's okay," he would tell her. "I'm Jack Lambie."

Although Lambie took great pride in his flying skills he was prouder still of his 8½-inch penis. He made balsa wood models of it and then spent hours sanding them smooth. He once made a sculpted model airplane with a penis for the pilot.

Lambie kept a table and a typewriter in the garage, where he used to sit naked all day with the garage door open, writing books and magazine articles on aviation. He yearned to be a better writer, but his high point was winning second place in a bad-Hemingway contest ("Across the Parking Lot into Harry's Bar and Grill").

Physically he was a bull. He would fly up to San Francisco and ride his bicycle back to Los Angeles along the San Andreas Fault. He entered 200-mile bike races (known as "double centuries"), which were so grueling that he was left without feeling in his hands for months afterward. When he was 45 he sold everything he owned, cashed in his teacher's retirement plan and took off on a 15-month ride around the world on a tandem bike with his new, young wife, Karen. Calling it their "honeymoon vacation," they wet the wheel in the Pacific at Costa Mesa and then started east. It took them 42 days to cross the country. Karen had long blond hair and an engaging personality. "They would meet people and be instantly taken in by them," says Mark Lambie. "I think he once said in crossing the United States they stayed at other people's houses 34 times."

AFTER 15 MONTHS AND 15,800 MILES, having pedaled across Ireland, Europe, the Alps, the Middle East, Africa, Australia and Bali, the Lambies returned home to find Paul MacCready waiting for them. "We were sitting in his office telling him about our trip," says Karen Hoiland, "and Paul said, 'Well okay, you can tell me about that later. I've been thinking about [building a man-powered plane] and you're just perfect. You are perfect, Jack. I've just been waiting for you to come back. You just got to do this, Jack. You are the man who can do this.'"

MacCready offered to pay Lambie $5,000 if they won the Kremer Prize, whereupon Lambie went to the hardware store and started buying things and putting them together. For the power train, he borrowed a crank-and-pedal assembly from one of his brother's racing bikes. MacCready rented the pavilion where they build floats for the Rose Parade in nearby Brookside Park in Pasadena to use as a temporary hangar.

To keep MacCready's design a secret, wrote Morton Grosser in *Gossamer Odyssey*, Lambie variously told curious onlookers that he was "building a sculpture for the Pasadena Museum of Modern Art" or that it was a Rose Parade float depicting "government meddling in private affairs." Within two weeks—a leisurely pace by Lambie standards—Lambie, MacCready and MacCready's brother-in-law, Kirke Leonard, had put together a prototype. I once saw part of the pedal structure of one of the early versions of the plane in a hangar at Gillespie Field in El Cajon. It looked as if someone had taken a piece of scrap aluminum, clamped it in a vise and worked it over with a hacksaw, which is probably exactly what happened. The wings were covered with clear Mylar polyester, making the plane look like a big, floppy, billowing kite covered with the kind of thin plastic bags that dry cleaners use to protect the clean clothes. A two-inch chemically milled (thinned) aluminum tube formed the wing's leading edge. A few widely spaced ribs were connected to that to give the Mylar polyester covering a rough cambered shape. A wire ran along the trailing edge to keep the Mylar taut.

The night before they had to vacate the pavilion for the beginning of the Rose Parade float-building season, the crew took the prototype outside for a hand-towed test flight in a grassy field across the street. A light drizzle was coming down, which made the wings sag. The plane had no pilot, no seat, no chain drive, no propeller. It was little more than a flying wing.

Despite the rain and darkness and the fact that on the way back to the hangar a gust of wind snapped a wing, MacCready was encouraged. The wings had lift. They tugged at the restraining ropes. Even in the rain, the plane obviously wanted to fly.

SIXTEEN

A Human Test Stand

I N LATER YEARS, FORMER AEROVIRONMENT vice president Ray Morgan
would say that one reason MacCready has accomplished so much is that
"he knows a lot of smart people and he is very good at getting people to tell
him what he wants to know for free. Most people love doing that. They're
flattered that [someone with MacCready's] credentials would want to know
what they know." And it wasn't a one-way street. "He tells you what he
knows too."

The first time that MacCready came by to ask Joe Mastropaolo what
he knew was in late summer of 1976. "He was at the brown bag stage," recalls
Mastropaolo, a physiologist at Long Beach State University.

> He took out a brown bag and made a little sketch. He said he was in
> debt. He went on a vacation. He watched some hawks circling. He
> remembered that it took about a horsepower to keep a hang glider up.
> It had a 30-foot wingspan. He figured if "I triple the span I can cut
> the power to a third of horsepower." That was where he was at.
>
> MacCready said, "What are your ideas?"
>
> I said, "I don't think there is any doubt. You need to train the pilot
> on an ergometer."
>
> MacCready caught on right away. "Ah," he said, "a test stand for
> the engine."

That impressed Mastropaolo. Unlike some other teams that had been
trying unsuccessfully to win the Kremer Prize for nearly seventeen years,

MacCready immediately understood the value of having a precise way to measure pilot output. Some British teams just sent their pilots out on long bike rides. But without an objective way to measure their performance, says Mastropaolo, they couldn't tell if their pilots were improving or not.

In person, Mastropaolo is a genial, grandfatherly man who looks like Joe DiMaggio in his later years. He's got a comfortable living room with crucifixes on the wall, Bibles on a stand and pictures of his three grandchildren scattered about. He doesn't hide his opinions under a bushel basket. The first time I called to ask if I could talk to him about physiology, he launched into an explanation of why bicycles were the most efficient and healthiest mode of transportation ever made but could never replace cars unless whole road systems were completely redone. Bikes weren't compatible with cars. Drivers hated them so much they ran bicycle riders off the road. "I knew a guy who had rearview glasses," Mastropaolo said of one bicyclist. "He saw someone leaning out of a pickup truck, about to hit him with a two-by-four."

When Mastropaolo worked at Douglas Aircraft, he rode a bicycle to work. He could maintain 20 miles per hour, which was faster than rush-hour traffic on the freeway. But he quit after being hit by a car.

> I started to tell people about it and they said, "Don't tell us. We'll tell you. You were hit by a car you didn't see." They were right. Riders pay attention to cars on their side of the road. Someone from the other side of the road made a high-speed left turn. He never saw me. I broke his rear window with my shoulder. It knocked me unconscious. I was lying in the street. When I came to, he was standing over me swearing. Bystanders were ready to grab him. It looked as if he were about to assault me. He blamed me for the accident.

As a longtime fitness physiologist, Mastropaolo had been interested in the Kremer Prize from the moment he first heard about it in 1960, long before he met Paul MacCready. "I thought it could make a tremendous difference in the fitness of our population because it had the two essential ingredients. One was a high degree of adventure and the other was you had to be continually exercising large muscle mass in order to enjoy the adventure. I was very intrigued."

Although building human-powered planes wasn't in Mastropaolo's job description, he thought Douglas might want to humor him, given that in 1968 he had helped the company win a half-a-billion-dollar contract to build an aero-medical evacuation aircraft for the Air Force. "It was a dead heat," recalls Mastropaolo. "The Air Force had been up to Boeing and back down to Douglas. Then up to Boeing and back down to Douglas again. They really couldn't make up their minds. The planes were about as equal as if they both came off the same assembly line. There was no objective way to break the tie."

Finally, says Mastropaolo, his supervisor sent him to meet with the Air Force evaluation team. The Air Force generals were on one side of the table and the Douglas people were on the other. Mastropaolo asked the general in charge, "Why does the Boeing plane have an 800-pound curtain in it?" The general said it was to muffle the engine sounds in the intensive care area so the doctors could hear the patient's breathing and heart rate. Then Mastropaolo made an offer.

> I said, "General, would you like to trade those 800 pounds for 8 ounces?"
>
> There was an absolute silence.
>
> I said, "General, I believe I can make you an electronic stethoscope that would give you all the intensive care data that you would need and it would allow you to abandon the 800 pounds of curtains." I said, "I can make it lighter than 8 ounces."
>
> A major jumps up. "We already tried that. It won't work."
>
> So I said, "I have already solved this problem for a higher noise environment than our aircraft. I would only require a very small grant and then you and your physicians be the judge. If we fail, you have lost perhaps $5,000 or $10,000 and if you win you relieve the aircraft of 800 pounds."
>
> The general said, "You have the grant."
>
> So I built it and we flew it. And they said, "Yeah, we hear the blood pressure sounds and the breathing sounds. Sounds okay to us." And lo and behold, we got the order. The Air Force said they believed they could depend on Douglas for more and better medical backup. They realized our aircraft would be 800 pounds lighter and that broke the tie. I was called up to the vice president's office and he gave me a citation for excellence in aero-medical factors.

On the heels of that success, Mastropaolo felt secure enough later that year to put together a team of twenty people to develop a plan to win the Kremer Prize. "We had people in aerodynamics and airfoils and all of the disciplines having to do with aircraft. We even found someone who was an expert in low-speed airfoils." What he didn't have was a small amount of money for basic materials. Mastropaolo made the case with management that it would be good publicity for the company. "The budget was in the noise level," says Mastropaolo. "But they wouldn't have any of it." It didn't fall within the "scope" of the company's long-range plans.

Shortly afterward, Mastropaolo left what was now McDonnell-Douglas to teach exercise physiology at Long Beach State. He used stationary bicycles (ergometers) to measure human power output in his lab. Sharing the gymnasium building with him was Chet Kyle, a mechanical engineering professor who, as a founder of the Human Powered Vehicle Association, had long been interested in streamlined bikes. Kyle had done bicycle coast-down (efficiency) tests down a long corridor next to the gymnasium. He'd lay down strips of tape, sprint to top speed, and then coast between the strips. Mastropaolo would be in his exercise lab with the students laboring away on instrumented stationary bikes and he'd look up and there would be Kyle on a bike flying past the door.

The day that Kyle brought MacCready by, Mastropaolo told him everything he knew about the benefits of an ergometer "test stand" for the pilot. "I thought, 'He's an interesting friend of Chet Kyle,'" Mastropaolo says of MacCready.

> I enjoyed meeting him. [But] I didn't expect to hear much about him after that because there is nothing imposing about him—not his manner, not his speech, not his vocabulary, not his physiognomy. There was nothing about him that was so imposing to make you think he was really going to tackle this project and go after it the way he did.

Later that fall, Mastropaolo got a call from MacCready, who said he was testing a man-powered plane up at the Mojave Airport. He wanted to fly it himself. And he was wondering if Mastropaolo would design an ergometer conditioning program to help him get in shape.

SEVENTEEN

Tales of the Mojave

W HEN TWENTY-MULE-TEAM WAGONS first began hauling borax out of
Death Valley in the 1860s, Mojave was the place they hauled it to. By
the time MacCready moved the Gossamer Condor project up there in the
fall of 1976, it was a small, hot, dusty little high-desert junction town ninety
miles due north of Los Angeles on State Route 14. On one side of the highway was the busy Southern Pacific railroad line and on the other was a long,
thin strip of gas stations, cheap motels, coffee shops, hamburger stands and
liquor stores advertising "ice and ammo." Tractor-trailer trucks rumbled
slowly down the street, followed by automobiles full of campers headed for
the high Sierra or skiers bound for Mammoth. A mile east of town was the
10,000-foot Mojave Airport, a former military base used to refurbish old
aircraft, maintain privately owned military jets and provide hangar space for
people who wanted to build their own planes.

Originally MacCready had thought he could win the Kremer Prize
with a single-surface airfoil—a cambered wing with a top but no bottom,
of the sort used on the thin-film, oversized, ultralight indoor models he used
to build as a kid. But the early versions of the plane (there would be perhaps a dozen of them by the time they were finished) barely flew, didn't turn
and sometimes broke even before they became airborne. Because MacCready
had insisted that the Gossamer Condor had to be as light as possible—author
Morton Grosser once quipped that from a distance it looked like "a small
bicycle attached to a large television antenna"—even slight stresses caused
poles to buckle and wires to snap. In turbulence, the ultrathin, chemically
milled aluminum tubes that made up the plane's structural components bent

like so many "wet noodles in the sky," recalled James Burke, a former Caltech classmate of MacCready's. "The landing gear was laughable: two tiny,
hollow plastic wheels from a toy fire engine." With MacCready's 108-pound
son, Tyler, as the pilot, it could fly a mesmerizingly slow 6 mph before it
stalled and settled to the ground.

Although it was theoretically possible to make the wings more rigid,
and therefore more aerodynamically efficient, by adding additional poles,
wires, braces and ribs, this added more weight, which in turn required more
power from the pilot, who was already at his limit.

MacCready had good reason to be concerned about finding a top athlete to fly the plane. Every day, just as dawn was breaking, they'd pull the
Gossamer Condor out into the cold morning air and the pilot would pedal
furiously, whereupon the plane, with many a warp, ripple and crackle, would
mush along for at best 500 feet. In the meantime, in 1974, a British pilot
had flown the elegant Jupiter, a man-powered plane, 3,500 feet. And shortly
after New Year's Day, 1977, Nihon University's Stork B flew a stunning 7,000
feet down a runway in Japan. Neither of the two planes had come close to
winning the Kremer Prize because neither had figured out how to turn without crashing. But overcoming that, MacCready suspected, was just a matter of time.

Initially, MacCready thought he could win the Kremer Prize in three
weeks—"One week at the Rose Bowl to build the plane, one week at an airport, and the third week to go to London and cash the check," says Taras
Kiceniuk. Although it quickly became clear that winning the prize would
be more difficult than expected, MacCready's enthusiasm and confidence
were such that people jumped at the chance to work with him.

It was the notion of working on a small project with a tight schedule,
limited funding and a single goal that attracted James Burke, a square-jawed
former Navy seaplane pilot, director of the Ranger space probe at Pasadena's
Jet Propulsion Laboratory and member of the board of AeroVironment, the
environmental research and consulting company MacCready had started
five years before. From his years in aerospace, Burke knew that a lot of projects went bad because the workers got sidetracked into investigating things
that weren't on the critical path. MacCready, in contrast, had the self-discipline
to focus on a single goal: getting the thing around the Kremer course, period.
"We had all kinds of opportunities to do other research," said Burke. "He
resolutely said, 'No, we are only out here to do one thing and when it's done
we're through.'"

In short order, MacCready had assembled a formidable team around the project. Peter Lissaman, a wavy-haired and erudite South African with degrees in mathematics and aerodynamics from Cambridge and Caltech (and a vice president of AeroVironment), designed the propeller, wings and canard. MacCready's quiet-mannered brother-in-law, Kirke Leonard, a catamaran builder, volunteered, as did numerous Los Angeles bicycle and hang glider enthusiasts. The gregarious Jack Lambie, for his part, commuted from the Los Angeles area in his little Fournier motorized glider. With a Volkswagen engine, its radar signature was zero. "When Jack went [up to Mojave], he would fly over the mountains and across the dry lakebed at Edwards Air Force Base at 15 to 20 feet," says Edmund Burke, a commercial pilot who once roomed with Lambie. "They couldn't pick him up on radar." Edwards was one of the most secure areas in the country, but Lambie would fly right over it rather than make a 100-mile detour.

The weather at Mojave presented its own problems for a plane as aptly named as the Gossamer Condor. It had the fragility of a bicycle made from soda straws. A minor wind gust could snap a wing. Even a 2 mph wind would cause so much turbulence (and increased drag) that the pilot couldn't keep the plane in the air. It did no good to wait for the wind to die down because too often it never did. The airport was located in a wind tunnel—the Tehachapi Pass.

Mojave was "a cold beautiful wonderful place," MacCready later concluded. But it was no place to test fly such a light, fragile, underpowered plane. Deciding not to waste any time, in mid-February MacCready moved the project to Shafter Airport, a former army flight-training field in the San Joaquin Valley that was now virtually unused.

EIGHTEEN

The Shafter Connection

SOME OF THE PEOPLE WHO WORKED on the Gossamer Condor at Shafter Airport in the spring and summer of 1977 remember it now as one of the best times of their lives. Shafter was a huge, near-deserted airport covering an entire square mile near Bakersfield. The military had built it to train pilots during World War II, when it was known as Minter Field. Glenn Miller once entertained the troops there. By the time MacCready moved his operation to one of the old military hangars, the field was mostly abandoned. Barn owls nested in the rickety old wooden hangars. There was no tower, restaurant or other amenities. Crop-dusting companies used it as a base for spraying nearby cotton fields.

At Shafter the volunteers quickly developed a routine. They'd get up at four or five in the morning and go flying in the Condor until it got too windy or until they broke the plane—whichever came first. They'd carry the pieces back to the hangar, have breakfast, then work until lunch time. By then, the temperature was 113, too hot to work, so they'd drive to Bakersfield and float down the Kern River in inner tubes, recalls Bill Watson, who along with Taras Kiceniuk had joined the MacCready project once it became evident that Kiceniuk's ground-effect machine would never work. At sunset the crew would come back to the hangar, eat dinner, throw down a sleeping bag on a runway and sleep until 4 A.M., when they would be awakened by the heavy engines of the crop dusters warming up for takeoff. Everyone would get up in the predawn stillness, push open the hangar doors and do the same thing all over again.

Weekends at Shafter were like holidays, with fifty or sixty people including kids, dogs, cats, skateboards, bikes and model planes. "It was a total happening," says aerodynamicist Peter Lissaman. Private pilots would fly up, kick the tires, look at the Gossamer Condor's front-mounted canard and shake their heads.

"You know," they'd say, "that was not the way God intended man to fly. Otherwise he would have put their tail feathers in front and their beaks in the rear."

"Yeah," Lissaman would answer. "But I've ridden horses for thirty years and it's hard to make them turn by pulling their tails."

Lambie's wife, Karen, who to support herself (and Jack) was running a catering truck business in Orange County, loved the feeling up at Shafter so much she would drive up after work every Friday afternoon. "I was the gopher," she says.

> I would do anything for Paul. It was dirty, it was hot and everyone was equal. It was wonderful and exciting. The guys would just sit around and design things. You could just feel the excitement in the air. Their heads were just spinning. "Let's try this." And then they would stay up all night and try things in the morning. Every day was exciting.

At one point Jack Lambie insisted on substituting a conventional rear rudder and horizontal stabilizer for the drag-producing front canard. "And instead of trying to argue him out of it," says James Burke, "Paul said 'Well, make a model, put a tail on it, see what it does.' That attitude permeated the whole operation. We put an enormous tail on the whole airplane, which of course was ridiculous. It was a horrible appendage and nothing good came of it."

Over the course of the project Lambie went from being perhaps the most important worker to one least appreciated. "He had a remarkable capability for hurting people's feelings," says Bryan Allen, the lean, young bicyclist who flew the Gossamer Condor and Gossamer Albatross on their prizewinning flights. "He was a really interesting guy with powerful opinions but he had a history of going through life using people up." He wouldn't come around all week, and then, when the documentary or TV film crews were coming, suddenly there was Jack. "There were lots of other people who worked harder on the project and they got practically nothing compared to

Lambie and he thought that was wonderful," Allen remembers. "He'd tell people about it—'Yeah, yeah, yeah, har, har, har.'" He considered it a splendid joke.

Some crew members resented him, calling him "Jack the Hack" behind his back. "He would say, 'Oh we can fix this,'" says Allen. "He would wade in with his hot glue gun, smearing little streamers of hot glue everywhere. People who were at a much higher technical level would react in semi-horror—'Don't let this guy close to the plane.'" Then, after breaking something and making everyone mad, he'd leave as suddenly as he came.

MacCready's philosophy had always been never to do anything that didn't directly contribute to the ultimate goal—winning the Kremer Prize. In order not to waste time, formal meetings were conducted standing up in a circle. When a decision was called for, it had to be made before the meeting broke up. No ideas were excluded. "If someone wanted to try something," James Burke noted, "he collected trash from the last crash, went to a corner of the hangar and built it."

One group of builders, long infatuated with the idea of superefficiency, insisted on removing the front canard and turning the plane into a pure flying wing. "The good thing about Paul's approach was that everything was so simple," says Burke. "All you had to do was pull a few pins, undo three or four knots and go flying." It was quickly apparent there was no way to control a human-powered plane without a canard, so they put it back on.

Years later people would remember these experiments as proof of MacCready's fundamental good sense. He didn't insist that everything be done his way; he wasn't frightened by people smarter than himself; and he wasn't wedded to any one approach. His goal was to win the prize and whatever brought that goal a little closer was by definition the right way. As a result, the crew was creative, the work fun and the morale high.

"And always," wrote Jim Burke, "there were the slow dreamlike flights of the great, silent aircraft in the calm of deserted airfields at dawn."

NINETEEN

Reinventing the Wright Brothers

BEFORE MOVING TO SHAFTER, MacCready had built six planes with single-surface airfoils at Mojave Airport. There were some successes at Mojave: MacCready's oldest son, Parker, who would later become an oceanographer specializing in current flow over rough topography, flew for forty seconds on December 26, 1976, and Greg Miller, a professional bicyclist with a strong distaste for anything with a gasoline engine, flew over two minutes in January 1977. But the pilots couldn't keep the plane in the air long enough to fly the mile-long figure-eight Kremer course. And even if they could, no one had yet figured out how to turn the plane. For one thing, it had absolutely no vertical surfaces, which also meant it had no directional stability, and if banked by a wind gust it would just slide slowly sideways into the runway. "It is sort of horrifying to see it crash," MacCready once said. "[The plane] sort of gentles into the ground and then slowly breaks."

To try to get the plane to turn, MacCready initially used upper-surface wingtip spoilers, but the drag was so great that the pilot couldn't keep the plane in the air. Ailerons also failed, a development that left everyone's minds spinning. Aircraft designers had been using ailerons—a hinged section of the wing's trailing edge—to turn planes since the dawn of aviation. If the pilot wanted to turn left, he pushed the stick (or turned the wheel) left. This caused the aileron on the left wing to come up, and the one on the right to go down. Together they simultaneously forced the left wing down and the right wing up, and the plane banked left.

The Gossamer Condor not only didn't bank left with the left aileron up, it rather yawed (rotated clockwise around the vertical axis) to the right.

At the same time, the right wing lost lift and slowly settled into the ground. Its reactions were exactly the reverse of a normal plane. It was as if you were driving a car and you turned the steering wheel left, but the car turned right and all the passenger-side tires went flat.

The problem, it soon became clear, was something called the "apparent mass effect." Normally when a plane is banked in a turn, the wings accelerate air out of the way. With an aircraft powered by an internal combustion engine this isn't a problem, since the aircraft wing is so much heavier than the air it has to move that the weight of the air is of little concern, and in any case the engine has power to spare. But the Gossamer Condor's wings were longer than those of a DC-9. In order to bank into a turn, the wing had to move 600 pounds of air out of the way, a difficult task for a plane weighing only 200 pounds, including the pilot, and operating on a mere 12 pounds of thrust. Trying to bank the plane by pushing down on one wing was like trying to flatten a pillow with a broom held at arm's length. You didn't have the leverage. In fact, it was now evident, the plane was a floater. Once it got to 10 or 15 feet, it pretty much preferred to fly straight and level, and that was all there was to it.

In an effort to reduce the force required to turn the plane, MacCready tapered the wingtips, shrinking the tip chord (wing width) from 12 to 5 feet. Because this made the total wing area smaller, in order to maintain the lift he had to increase the plane's speed from 8 to 10 mph. This in turn increased parasitic air drag, which made it necessary to enclose the cockpit.

To reduce drag caused by the airfoil (something MacCready hadn't initially thought would be much of a problem), Peter Lissaman designed a new double-surfaced, compound-curve airfoil, the Lissaman 7769. Its shape was such that it sped up the air as much as possible at the airfoil leading edge and then gently slowed it down to free-stream velocity by the time it reached the trailing edge, thus eliminating drag-producing pressure spikes. Lissaman was very proud of that. "It's the greatest low-speed airfoil in the world," he says. "And it was designed entirely by mathematics."

John Lake, another hang-gliding pioneer who worked on the plane, came up with the idea of using one-sided corrugated cardboard (the kind used to separate layers in candy boxes), which bent easily but in only one direction, so it could be used to give the wings' leading edges a smooth, rounded shape.

To help the wings maintain the airfoil contour, additional ribs were added and the Mylar was fastened to them with double-sided sticky tape. It was Jack Lambie's brilliant idea to use a hair dryer to heat-shrink the Mylar, thus reducing in-flight billowing. Then, to compensate for the change in center of gravity caused by all the modifications, MacCready swept the wings back.

Because every pound of reduction in weight lowered the required horsepower by 0.75 percent, MacCready announced a $1,000 reward to anyone who could cut a pound off the plane's weight. "Anyone who showed up with an idea was welcome," remembers Bill Watson, a professional model builder who, along with Taras Kiceniuk, worked on the Condor in its later stages. "If someone said, 'Wait a minute. We shouldn't be using aluminum. We should be using wood. It's lighter.' And if it didn't break, that was fine. If something lasted two weeks before it broke, it was too heavy. The idea was to have something break every couple of days."

Although some people got frustrated and quit, Paul MacCready was the force that held the project together. He concentrated on winning the prize, didn't procrastinate and never got discouraged. "Paul never thought he was more than two weeks from winning the prize," says Watson. "And he kept this up for an entire year." No matter what happened, he just plugged away. He believed in getting things done. Anything that was finished, no matter how poorly, was still a lot better than something that wasn't. "So no matter how it was done, it was the right way."

TWENTY

A Turn for the Better

Wɪᴛʜɪɴ ᴀ ᴍᴏɴᴛʜ ᴏꜰ ᴛʜᴇ Gossamer Condor's February 1977 redesign, Greg Miller managed to keep the plane aloft 5 minutes and 5 seconds, a world record for human-powered flight and only 90 seconds short of the time needed to fly the Kremer course. All they had to do now was figure out how to turn the plane.

The solution turned out to be so simple that afterwards the team would wonder out loud why they hadn't done it sooner. Far from being a new idea, it was the oldest in powered flight. The concept was wing warping—pulling one corner of the wing down with a diagonally running wire while pulling the opposite corner up. The Wright Brothers used wing warping on their 1903 *Wright Flier.* When Jack Lambie built copies of the Wright Brothers' plane, he incorporated wing warping too. Many of the people on the project were familiar with the concept and later half of them would take credit for having suggested it. ("In research, that's called 'reviewing the literature,'" says Mastropaolo.) But MacCready had an intuitive sense that wing warping was unnecessary on an aircraft designed to make such gentle banked turns and he had earlier dismissed the idea without doing any calculations.

"I can vividly remember we [MacCready, Lissaman and Burke] were sitting around in front of the hangar," recalls James Burke of the moment the idea finally bubbled up from the group's collective unconscious. "It was hot; the flies were buzzing; the agricultural chemicals were smelling. There was no flying going on because it was too turbulent." By this time the Gossamer Condor was flying well enough in straight, level flight that the team was concentrating on the margins, trying to find small ways to reduce drag and thereby make the plane easier to fly. Someone suggested that they try a symmetrical twist arrangement to unload the canard (take drag-producing weight off the forward stabilizer). As the three were talking about the kind of wire arrangement that they would need to achieve the wing warping, one of them observed that if you were going to twist the wing symmetrically, you could twist it asymmetrically too. *Of course,* the group suddenly realized! Why not use asymmetrical wing warping to turn the plane?

Peter Lissaman, the team's applied mathematics expert, did a few calculations and concluded that it ought to work. Over the next several days the crew rigged wires and installed a twisting lever, which the pilot had to operate in conjunction with the canard. When the pilot wanted to turn left, he would first tilt the canard left. This sideways force on the front of the bowsprit would cause the plane to rotate counter-clockwise (left) around the plane's vertical axis. This would tend to slow down the left wingtip and speed up the right.

Prior to this, the problem had always been that in turns the slower-moving wing would lose lift and settle into the ground. But with the new wing-warping lever, the pilot could force the trailing edge of the outer portion of the left wing to twist downward. This would increase the angle of attack on that wing to create more lift to compensate for the slower speed. Then, as the plane yawed left, the right wing would come up and the plane would make a gently banked and coordinated left turn.

On April 5, with MacCready's middle son, Tyler, as the pilot, the Gossamer Condor made its first flight using both canard tilt and wing warp. The crew was euphoric. The Gossamer Condor was actually banking and turning like a real plane. In the subtle interplay of wing warping and a banked canard, they had found the Holy Grail of man-powered flight—the way to make coordinated turns.

Now MacCready had everything he needed to win the Kremer Prize: a redesigned plane with (relatively) tight, nonbillowing skin; the ability to make 180-degree turns (necessary to fly a figure-eight course); and a strong, increasingly experienced bicycle-racer pilot. Thus it came as a shock in late March when MacCready and the rest of the team received the news that their talented young pilot, Greg Miller, was leaving the project on April 4 to enter a European bicycle race.

WHEN MACCREADY FIRST BEGAN the Gossamer Condor project, he had thought the plane would be so easy to fly that finding a pilot would be the

Flying the Gossamer Condor, Bryan Allen once said, was like "pedaling a house."

least of their problems. Initially he didn't even plan on having a trained athlete/pilot. One of his lightweight teenage sons would fly the plane, he thought, or he'd fly it himself, despite his being fifty-one and little gifted in athletic ability.

In September 1976, MacCready had asked Mastropaolo to draw him up an exercise regime and started working out on a stationary bike. "I began charging ahead," MacCready later said.

> I found that the program by the exercise physiologist was so easy that on the second day I did the fifth day's effort, turned green, went to the hospital. I learned you do what the professional tells you. After two weeks of recovering I went back and started doing what he told me and finally got to the point where I was good but nowhere as good as the top bicyclists were.

Joe Greblo, a lean and athletic Los Angeles hang-gliding instructor who subsequently tried out for one of MacCready's later man-powered planes (the Bionic Bat), says that MacCready's methods were nothing if not rigorous. "He brought me to his house, put me in a bedroom with nothing but an ergometer, table lamp and a pitcher of water. He told me, 'Keep the speedometer at 25 mph for 30 minutes.' After 15 minutes I hit the floor. MacCready came in. 'Hot damn. We're halfway there.' I said, 'Paul, it will never fly.'"

One person who did think the Gossamer Condor would fly was Bryan Allen, a taciturn and wiry bike racer and hang glider pilot. For MacCready, Allen was a good deal: an athlete and a pilot with a quick technical mind. Equally important, he was currently unemployed and MacCready only had to offer him $3 an hour to fly the plane.

"Bryan was the perfect bird-man," says Mastropaolo. He had thick powerful mesomorphic thighs and a thin ectomorphic upper body. Later he would run the length of the 10,000-foot runway at Edwards Air Force Base shouting flying instructions to an Air Force F-102 pilot in the Gossamer Albatross and still not be breathing hard. But in his first couple of flights in the Gossamer Condor, he didn't do as well as MacCready's middle son, Tyler. Pedaling the Gossamer Condor, he once said, was "like pedaling a house." It took Allen three months to surpass Miller's record of 5 minutes, 5 seconds.

FOR AN ENGINEER, MACCREADY had a remarkably relaxed attitude toward crashes. He didn't blame people, lose his temper or go to pieces. The way he saw it, crashes weren't so much disasters as additional data points on the learning curve. That's how you found out what didn't work. In mid-July 1977, the Condor team was testing the plane at Shafter when a Stearman crop duster took off. A Stearman was a heavy wire-and-strut-reinforced biplane with a powerful radial engine, used for pilot training in the thirties and World War II. Knowing that a heavy plane like a Stearman could produce powerful long-lasting wing vortices, Bryan Allen tried to avoid the plane's wake, but five minutes into the flight he ran into it all the same, whereupon the left wing snapped off halfway out from the fuselage. Surprisingly, the plane flew steadily and smoothly for another five seconds before landing normally. It flew so well on half a wing, MacCready later joked, "we were tempted to cut the other wing off."

Because the plane almost never flew higher than ten feet, crashes were slow-motion affairs. Even if the wing was totally crumpled, generally only a single major piece was broken. When the crew repaired the part and spread the wing, everything pretty much went back into place. Repairs were crude and quick. Someone would saw off a broom handle to make a splint and tape it to a spar with duct tape, and then minutes later they'd be ready to fly again.

The Mylar wing covering was a revelation in itself. Although it was only a half-mil thick (.0005 inches) it was amazingly rugged. It repelled dropped tools with impunity. Its weak point was its susceptibility to tears, which if not immediately caught would propagate through the entire wing. To cope with that, the team used hundreds of rolls of industrial/scientific-quality 3M 850 Scotch tape. More of their budget went for that than practically anything else.

The pilot problem was now solved, yet the plane still wasn't flying the way it was supposed to. The Mylar crackled and fluttered in flight. And virtually any wind at all caused so much turbulence that the plane wouldn't fly.

The solution was obvious: since there was no way to make the plane any bigger (they had already pushed chemically milled aluminum tubes as far as they could), the only way to win the prize was to make it more efficient. Although some of the workers had known this for a long time, they weren't sure MacCready felt the same way. It sometimes seemed to them as if he didn't give craftsmanship the attention it deserved. The first time Ray Morgan—a former Lockheed Skunkworks engineer who had left aerospace to help MacCready with his subsequent Solar Challenger project—saw Mac-Cready's craftsmanship in action, he was appalled. They had built a plane of beautiful carbon-fiber composite tubes, but in covering over a joint at the top of the fuselage, MacCready had taken a piece of paper-thin plywood, punched it full of holes and tied it in place with string. "It was the crudest thing you could imagine," says Morgan.

MacCready's indifference to craftsmanship was a great virtue early in the project, when the important thing was just to prove the concept, but at this point some team members thought it was what was keeping the Gossamer Condor from making it around the Kremer course. One of these was Vern Oldershaw, a retired pilot, sailplane builder and, says Kiceniuk, "a very, very talented builder and clever, dedicated and meticulous worker who was there every day. He took what was a good but very shaky physical contraption and kept fine-tuning it and fine-tuning it and developing it. Without Vern the plane would have broken too many times, been too wrinkly, been too heavy, too crude to do its job."

Oldershaw, with his great attention to detail, had long felt that the fuselage needed more streamlining. But every time he brought the subject up, MacCready told him the old one was fine. Since it was clear that Mac-Cready didn't much care how things were done as long as they worked, Oldershaw privately took it upon himself to redesign the fuselage. He figured there'd be time to tell MacCready soon enough.

In August that time arrived. Allen was flying through a patch of convection turbulence when a pulley broke, causing Allen to lose pitch control and smash into the runway. Not only did Allen suffer bruises and abrasions, the plane was totally wrecked.

MacCready was "discouraged in a way that I hadn't ever seen before," Oldershaw's wife, Maude, told Morton Grosser, author of *Gossamer Odyssey.* Seeing his discouragement, Oldershaw figured the time was right to take MacCready aside and show him the new fuselage, which, being nearly six pounds lighter than the old one, flew on 4.5 percent less horsepower.

MacCready, never one to stay disheartened very long, was impressed. "Vern had come in with kind of a U-shaped stringer that was convenient, light and easy to apply," he said. But it wasn't just the better fuselage that made success inevitable. Everything was coming together. The crew was getting much better at the never-ending problem of tightening the Mylar without melting holes in it or causing new wrinkles somewhere else. And Allen's flying skills, good from the beginning, were improving every day.

Once the new fuselage was in place, Allen found the plane so much easier to fly that MacCready immediately scheduled another attempt to win the Kremer Prize. Whereas in the past, flying the plane had been an incredible workout, now it was almost fun. "Because of the huge surface there were so many little zephyrs and they would lift and give you little sensations," Joe Mastropaolo would later say. "You could feel every draft and ripple from so many different directions, front to back, side to side, even diagonally."

It was evident from the first flight that this version of the Gossamer Condor was capable of winning the prize. Allen failed on one attempt only because a downdraft caused the plane to touch the runway, and on another because he couldn't spot the 10-foot-high T-bar that marked the end of the flight.

On August 23, 1976, MacCready called in the reporters, cameramen and official observers, whereupon Allen, making his 223rd flight in the Gossamer Condor, began to pedal. Despite turbulence from a 2 mph wind, the plane was in the air within 5 seconds. As Allen pedaled, two crewmen rode bicycles at his wingtips, calling out encouragement and warnings not to get too low. Sprinting all out at 11 mph on the final leg, he cleared the 10-foot barrier that marked the end of the course by an easy 2 feet.

MacCready had known there would be publicity for the feat. He had arranged much of it himself, calling local TV stations and reporters to document the occasion, not to mention author Morton Grosser and film maker Ben Shedd, whose half-hour documentary *Flight of the Gossamer Condor* would later win an Academy Award. Still, MacCready would later say, he never expected to be fielding calls from the *Wall Street Journal,* the BBC and even specialized aerospace journals.

There was something else he didn't expect either. From takeoff to touchdown the flight lasted only 7 minutes, 27 seconds, but it changed MacCready's life, transforming him overnight from an obscure businessman in a niche field to an internationally known luminary and "genius" inventor.

Surprisingly, two people who made critical contributions to the plane didn't even know an attempt was being made that day. Peter Lissaman learned of it only when he came to work at AeroVironment and found the place abuzz. And Lambie, who was home in bed making love at the time, didn't find out about the successful flight until a friend called to give him the news.

TWENTY-ONE

The Case for Apparent Altruism

WHEN REPORTERS RETIRE AND write their memoirs about their forty years in the newspaper business, one of the characters they always seem to include from their cub reporter days is the cigar-smoking, hard-bitten veteran newsman who sits in the corner of the newsroom, phone against his ear, taking a report from the scene while he furiously pounds out the story in one take. Then, slamming down the phone, he yanks the copy out of his typewriter, fires it off to the composing room, and returns to the racing sheet.

The cub reporter naturally is blown away by the old hand's speed and proficiency, given his near-total lack of interest in language, literature or anything else related to the written word. Then one day the young reporter wanders by the old hand's desk and in his open drawer sees a stack of prototype stories for every common incident—a fire, auto accident, plane crash, murder, obituary and so on. When a call came in from an on-scene reporter, the only decision the seasoned reporter had to make was how to pigeon-hole it. If it was a fire, he'd just pull out the fire prototype and fill in the blanks as he typed—the time, address, number of alarms, quote from fire captain, suspected cause, and dollar estimate of the damage. It was no wonder he could write a story in six minutes; he had already written the exact same story hundreds of times before.

Maurice Sendak, the curmudgeonly but deeply talented author-illustrator of the classic children's book *Where the Wild Things Are,* made a similar complaint about the press when I interviewed him years ago. Most reporters, he said in warning, were always trying to pigeon-hole him as some kind of child-centered elf living in the "woods under the mushrooms." In fact, Sendak was a bitchy, aging artist with a catty streak who lived alone with his German shepherd and, as far as I could tell, didn't even like kids.

When I began looking up articles about MacCready, I found that reporters had occasionally indulged in a similar kind of benign caricature about him, presenting him as a shy, unassuming, whimsical soul with an astronomical IQ, who walked around in a childlike state of wonder like the wild-haired genius inventor in *Back to the Future.* In this vein, *Soaring Museum* magazine called him "the Tinker General of the United States," and *Esquire,* in naming him first among the top twenty-one people whose work was transforming society ("then there is one who is so full of invention, influence, and delight that he had to come first"), photographed him in a black bowler as if he were a beloved but eccentric Englishman, standing out in the noonday sun on a dry lakebed, hurling a model plane aloft. The accompanying text described him as "a kid at heart, part Tom Swift, part Bucky Fuller."

To some extent MacCready encouraged this treatment himself. "He once told me the best policy is 'apparent altruism,'" says Bob Boucher, a solar-power pioneer who helped MacCready build his man-carrying solar-powered plane. "Altruistic. He has positioned himself as an altruistic guy. He's not going to tell you that. That's what he said to me."

Still, his altruism had its limits, especially around journalists. When I once called him to ask if I could spend the day with him while he was teaching hands-on aerodynamics to a group of high-achieving middle school students, he suddenly lashed out, complaining that he felt besieged, "cornered" and pursued by "paparazzi." It annoyed him that I would go out and interview "his" friends. "I guess you have to feed your family," he said, "but what do I get out of this?" Then suddenly he surprised me by asking what appeared to be a genuine question: "What should I do?"

Disappointed and more than a little angry myself, I told him that while I hoped he would make himself available for interviews, in the final analysis it was a decision he'd have to make himself. The choice he made, as it turned out, was not to invite me to any of the sessions with his superstar kids, but he did invite a *Pasadena Star News* reporter, who wrote a perceptive story about the class, and CBS News, which missed the point.

MacCready, it seemed, relished publicity even as he resented the time he had to spend with reporters in order to get it. Once in a phone interview he mentioned that during the time we had been talking, four other people had called wanting to speak with him. In another interview he noted that he spent so much time dealing with administration and the need to answer "twenty e-mails a day" that he never got to do any work, meaning his own projects, until the afternoon, on weekends, or at the airport while waiting for his flight to be announced.

For someone who was in the public eye so much, MacCready's personality was a curious one. As an introvert he tended not to talk very much, unless you found his favorite subject. "Then," Boucher remarks, "you couldn't shut him up." Boucher says he once saw MacCready giving a speech in the San Fernando Valley when, without warning, he just suddenly stopped. "Nobody knew if it was over or what." But that indifference to (or unawareness of) social convention was also what made MacCready good at what he did. "He's not a politician and he is not a bullshit guy," says Boucher.

> Everyone who works for Paul likes him. He knows how to get things done. He knows how to get his hands on the money. None of the people at AeroVironment have anything bad to say about him. Of all the people I've ever worked with he is probably one of the easiest guys to work with because he gives you all the room to do what you need to do. He just wants you to get something done. He's not a nuts and bolts guy. He's like Reagan. He has an idea and he's going to be the spokesman—"You guys figure out the details."

Peter Lissaman, who was forced out of AeroVironment after working for the company for two decades, once told me that MacCready reminded him of Buckminster Fuller, a person Lissaman knew quite well, except that when it came to getting the job done, MacCready had the real stuff whereas Fuller "operated entirely on charisma.

> When you read his speeches it was just a bunch of jumbled bullshit. I'll tell you this about Paul. He is not a bullshitter. He never makes grandiose remarks. [When it comes to his own work] he's very modest.
>
> When I first joined him, everybody told me how lucky I was to work with that guy. I'd be a millionaire. I damn near went bloody well broke. He's a truly unusual person. You have to take his words seriously. He has many features of great integrity.
>
> Everyone thinks when they first get to meet him that they are going to meet some Leonardo da Vinci type character. [In reality,] the guy has no aesthetic sense at all, he is not interested in beautiful women, he says things to people that hurt their feelings. Once when he got the Lindbergh

award, I said to him, "I wouldn't mind winning that." He said, "I don't think you have the stature." He fires people. He thinks its okay. He says, "Nobody wants to have a job he isn't capable of handling." I told him that most people in the world can't do their jobs and they still want them.

Winston Churchill once referred to Clement Atlee as a "desiccated calculating machine." Some might think that description fits Paul, except he is a calculating machine with idiosyncrasies. He has very, very interesting ideas. He looks at things differently. It's a cliché but Paul does think outside the box. He has a lot of courage, a lot of determination, and he takes risks. On the [Sunraycer], the Solar Challenger, and the Gossamer Albatross he was there every goddamned second making decisions and making good decisions. He made the decision to go [fly the English Channel]. It turned out that was the one day for the entire summer when conditions were okay. I don't know where he gets his fucking luck. He has astonishing luck. Of course he doesn't believe in luck. He believes in rational decisions.

One good example of MacCready's rational decision-making process was described by Paul E. Teague in *Design News* when MacCready, out for a solitary hike on a late fall day in 1993, found himself cold and lost on a ledge in the San Gabriel Mountains:

The tiny, rocky outcrop was an unlikely easy chair, but it did provide the lonely and scared climber a place to rest and wait for rescue. He had been stranded there on the down-sloping ledge for hours, inches away from a 70 ft vertical drop to eternity. Night was falling, the temperature was dropping, and there was no sign that anyone had heard his cries for help. Legs and arms aching, heart pounding with fright and fatigue, his mind raced with the usual thoughts of someone in danger: How did he get into this spot? How would he get out? If he didn't, would his family be okay without him? What would be the best design strategy for low-speed flight?

Design strategy? Low-speed flight?

Yes, in one of the most perilous situations of his life—stranded overnight while climbing in California's San Gabriel Mountains on Thanksgiving Day 1993—Paul MacCready was still thinking of pioneering design ideas. By the time of his early-morning helicopter rescue, he had actually come up with a draft concept.

TWENTY-TWO

The Channel Crossing

WHEN MACCREADY'S BRITISH COMPETITORS saw how crude the Gossamer Condor was, it practically made them sick. "They couldn't believe they'd gotten beat by a flying laundry bag," says Ray Morgan. They had assumed that the only thing that could win the Kremer Prize was an elegant, superefficient, handcrafted, cutting-edge expression of the aerodynamicist's highest art. Instead they'd been trounced by some inefficient, backward-flying, Saran Wrap–covered, mobile sculpture that wasn't even "a proper plane."

And that, of course, was MacCready's great insight. Back in 1976, when he first conceived of the Gossamer Condor, he had realized that if you make something big enough and light enough it will fly on so little power that aerodynamic efficiency (almost) doesn't matter. But other than that, there was nothing particularly sophisticated about the Gossamer Condor's design. Any aeronautical engineer could have figured it out in a few minutes. ("All inventions are obvious once you have the solution," MacCready told Kenneth Brown in *Inventors at Work*.) Nor was there anything special about the materials used in the plane. If anyone had wanted to, they could have built it in 1915, MacCready once observed, the only difference being that one would have had to use wood and silk in place of aluminum and Mylar.

Because it had taken the Gossamer Condor one year and 223 flights to win the Kremer Prize (and no one else had come close to winning it at all), it was easy to underestimate the plane's true capabilities. When the Royal Aeronautical Society announced a second Kremer Prize—this one for the first human-powered flight across the English Channel—they assumed that because it had taken eighteen years for anyone to fly just one mile on human power, it might very well take another two decades for anyone to fly twenty miles. For one thing, a twenty-mile flight might take as long as two hours, whereas the longest anyone had stayed in the air to date (and even this was pushing the limits of exhaustion) was a mere seven and a half minutes. Consequently, in recognition of what they regarded as the exponentially greater difficulty of a cross-Channel flight, they increased the prize money to £100,000, which made it the largest aviation prize in history—over $200,000, depending on the exchange rate.

In fact, cyclist-pilot Bryan Allen would later say, they didn't realize how close the MacCready team already was to winning the cross-Channel prize: "All they had to do was look at the human power curve. It's not twenty times as hard to fly twenty miles as it is to fly one. The difference between one mile and twenty miles is a little bit of technology." All the MacCready team needed to do was build a cleaner, lighter version of the Gossamer Condor with lighter, modern, high-tech materials. That in itself would cut power requirements by 20 percent, whereupon pilot endurance would go up "by a factor of ten."

The Gossamer Condor, because of its overflexible aluminum spars and billowing Mylar wings, required 0.4 horsepower or more to stay aloft if there was even the slightest wind. Even first-class athletes had trouble putting out much more than that for over ten minutes. On the other hand, the power-versus-endurance curve flattened out very quickly. The same pilot who could put out only 0.4 horsepower for ten minutes, could put out 0.3 horsepower for two hours and 0.2 horsepower indefinitely. By MacCready's way of thinking, the Channel-crossing prize was already in the bag. All they had to do was redesign the Gossamer Condor to make it lighter and more aerodynamically efficient, and the way to do that was replace the aluminum tubes with carbon-fiber composites, increase the aspect ratio (the ratio of wing length to width) and add more ribs.

Compared to wood, which has a tensile strength of 18,000 pounds per square inch, or even steel, with a tensile strength of 50,000 pounds per square inch, carbon fiber was an incredible boon, having a tensile strength of 600,000 pounds per square inch. By making the spars of the cross-Channel plane, which MacCready was now calling the Gossamer Albatross, out of carbon fiber, he was able to cut the number of support wires and the associated drag.

At the same time, because carbon fiber was so light, he was able to put in a lot more chord sections (the cross-sectional pieces in the wing that give the airfoil its shape and maintain its efficiency).

For help, MacCready called upon his brother-in-law, Kirke Leonard, who knew carbon-fiber fabrication techniques inside out from his boat-building days. To make a spar (main wing support member), he wrapped a hollow aluminum pole with carbon fiber material, baked it to cure it and then dissolved the aluminum in chloric acid. The result was an ultralight, superstrong structure of surprising rigidity. Whereas under stress the thin, chemically milled aluminum spars of the Gossamer Condor bent like noodles in the sky, the Gossamer Albatross was a finely turned airfoil with a wingspan of 96 feet but a weight of only 56 pounds (14 pounds lighter than the Condor). Although the press tended to ignore the contribution of carbon fiber to the plane's success, geodesic dome designer Buckminster Fuller understood instinctively why the Gossamer Albatross was such a wonderful success story—despite its 96-foot wingspan, it was so strong and light "you could hold it in one hand."

Before the Gossamer Albatross crew left for England in late spring of 1979, Bryan Allen made the final test flight early one morning at Harper Dry Lake in the Mojave east of Barstow. Jack Lambie arrived overhead by plane just as Allen started his flight. When he spotted the Albatross skimming across the lakebed far below, he recalled, he had "the intense sensation of being in an ocean of air and watching a giant fish swimming below us. With the slowly spinning propeller and the glittering, floating, flexing wings, it seemed like a monstrous aquatic creature gliding over a lake bottom."

TWENTY-THREE

Vikings versus the Emerald Isle

THE MYTH ABOUT THE English Channel is that for most of history (and prehistory) it protected Britain, kept it isolated, deterred invaders and gave that country its distinctive national character. In fact, until the end of the last ice age ten thousand years ago, the English Channel wasn't so much an obstacle as a highway—a wide, shallow plain that nomadic hunters walked across, as they had for eons, following the game and their age-old instinct to explore. Later, as the planet warmed, the ice retreated and the water levels rose, creating the white cliffs of Dover on the English side and what, during World War II, became on the French side the deadly heights of Omaha Beach. But the fact that the twenty-mile-wide plain between Britain and Europe was now under 130 feet of water didn't stop either prehistoric hunters or invaders. They just traveled in small boats when they had them and big baskets when they didn't.

The invasions went on for centuries—Angles, Saxons, Jutes, Romans. Given the ease of water travel by comparison with the extreme difficulty of moving armies and supplies across roadless terrain, the English Channel wasn't a barrier; it was a wide-open thoroughfare that practically invited intruders to drop in any time.

In A.D. 410, after nearly four hundred years of peaceful, prosperous and, for the day, enlightened rule, the Romans abandoned Britain. Their troops were needed to defend Rome from the Huns and, if truth be told, the sun-loving Romans had never much liked what historian R. J. White called Britain's "mists and half-light where the ghosts of the dead floated about, crying with the weird voices of sea birds."

Between A.D. 950 and 1300 the world's climate grew warmer during "the little optimum." In Scandinavian countries the pack ice retreated so far that for the first time in many centuries, Viking ships had access to the entire North Atlantic. As their population exploded, the Vikings came pouring out of Denmark and Norway in their dragon ships in search of gold, silver and slaves.

For residents of Britain, it was a medieval "War of the Worlds." With what Winston Churchill called "the gleam of steel and the scent of murder," Viking ships would appear out of the mist and fog, touching down like so many alien spacecraft. Sometimes the ships, which each carried around eighty men, arrived in small flotillas of two or three craft, sometimes in huge fleets of three or four hundred. With their shallow three-foot drafts they could follow England's broad, slow-moving rivers far inland. The Vikings' swords and battle-axes were the best in Europe. British farmers and sheep herders were no match for warriors who considered it an honor to die in battle. The appearance of a single Viking could send ten Britons fleeing for their lives. British farmers would meekly stand by, one British bishop bitterly complained, while a dozen Vikings in succession "insulted" their wives.

When William the Conqueror (a French-speaking descendant of a Viking, from Normandy), crossed the Channel in 1066 and conquered Britain, he subsequently turned what had always been a nation of farmers and sheep herders into a seafaring, empire-building country. The English Channel, which had always been the broad, undefended highway over which everyone always attacked England, now became a graveyard for England's enemies as English sailors exploited the Channel's winds, fogs, tides and shoals to strike at the enemy fleets at will. The result was such a dramatic improvement in England's ability to defend itself that no one ever successfully invaded the country again.

A thousand years later, the English were still using their mastery of Channel weather to defeat their enemies. In June of 1944, English, Canadian and American forces under Supreme Allied Commander Dwight D. Eisenhower were poised to invade Normandy when yet another storm hit the Channel, pouring green water across the bows of the invasion fleet and filling the troop compartments with the acrid smell of vomit. Across the Channel, the German defenders of the Atlantic Wall hunkered down in their bunkers and kept their patrol boats in port, so confident were they that the Allies wouldn't invade in such weather. But, as historian Stephen Ambrose has written, Eisenhower's weather forecasters had spotted an upcoming hole

Flying the Gossamer Albatross across the English Channel, Bryan Allen was so exhausted he had cramps in his legs and the taste of blood in his throat.

in the endless storms—thirty-six hours of clearing skies, mild winds and moderate swells. With horizontal rain still pelting the windows at Allied Headquarters at Portsmouth, Eisenhower sucked in his gut and said, "Okay, let's go," thereby launching the biggest amphibious invasion in the history of man.

As the Albatross team sat on the beach at Folkestone in southern England on the morning of June 12, 1979, waiting for the area's infamously bad weather to improve, the crew knew exactly what Eisenhower's weather forecasters had to contend with thirty-five years previously: the English Channel was a tumultuous sea of strong currents and dramatic tides, sudden gales and smoking waves. Every day it was the same thing—15-to-20-knot winds under gray skies, accompanied by everything from fog and scattered showers to pouring rain and thunderstorms. It was the "rainiest May in two or three hundred years," said Bryan Allen. The weather was so variable that Allen saw flowers blooming one minute and snow falling on them the next.

For MacCready, the toughest part of winning the cross-Channel prize wasn't building a plane adequate to do the job. It was the logistics necessary to support that plane: getting it to England in the first place, finding a suitable hangar, quartering the crew, coordinating the attempt with the French and British aviation authorities, chartering a power cruiser for a command center and finding four inflatable Zodiacs with outboard motors.

One Zodiac was to warn Bryan Allen if he got too low. Another was a craft for rescuing Allen, who couldn't swim. The others would keep the many media boats and onlookers away. If Allen signaled that he couldn't pedal anymore, Bill Watson would snag a hook on the front of the Albatross with a fishing pole and then, using the Zodiac, they'd tow the plane to whatever shore was closer. It was such a tricky maneuver that they'd never even tried it before. In the meantime, MacCready broke his ankle jogging and was wearing a cast on his foot. There were a lot of people, a lot of international press, including some who had been waiting for months for MacCready to make the flight. Communications were a horror. Just to call someone, MacCready had to ride a mile and a half on a bicycle. "It was like running the Normandy Invasion from a phone booth," he said.

Before going to England, MacCready had been so confident about flying the Channel that at one point he thought that after crossing in one direction they might just turn around and fly back the other way, thereby avoiding any need to dismantle the plane for shipping. In fact, he quickly realized upon his arrival in England, the Channel turbulence, not to mention the weather, was so bad that just making it across one time was going to be incredibly hard. He knew from historical weather records that there were only two or three days each summer suitable for making the flight. But even if they were lucky enough to have light winds and sunny skies, there was still the traffic problem. The English Channel was the busiest waterway in the world; 500 to 1,000 ships sailed up, down and across it every day. Because the Gossamer Albatross didn't fly higher than 10 or 15 feet, it would have to fly around any ships in its path. The biggest worry was supertankers, which left turbulent air in their wakes for miles. It did no good to ask them to change course. They were tanker captains. They deviated for no one.

Mastropaolo had done what he could to prepare Allen for the ordeal ahead. While waiting for the weather to clear, he made Allen train indoors until the sweat pouring off his body left a puddle on the floor. Still, Mastropaolo was worried. The only way Allen could get across the Channel in two hours was for everything to be perfect, with no tankers, no headwinds, no equipment failures or navigation mistakes. Rationally it didn't seem possible—if for no other reason, thought Mastropaolo, because Allen was certain to overheat in the Albatross's nearly airtight Mylar cockpit. The cockpit air would get so supersaturated with condensing moisture from Allen's breath that he would lose the effect of evaporative cooling. If he ran out of drinking water, he was finished.

But MacCready and Allen didn't see any need to carry more than two liters of water. Allen would be flying only a few feet above the waves. If he even so much as touched one, the flight wouldn't count. In such a situation every ounce was critical. Besides, two liters would last two hours. By then Allen would be either in France or in the Channel. In neither case would he need more water.

Although Mastropaolo was a physiologist, he also considered it his duty to prepare Allen psychologically. A few days before the flight, he took Allen and the backup pilot, Kurt Gibony, out for dinner. After they had eaten, Mastropaolo posed a question: What were they going to do during the flight if they got too tired to continue? One of them, recalled Mastropaolo, answered "ditch" and the other said "call for a tow."

"Negative," said Mastropaolo. "If you ditch or call for a tow that means you lose the prize. That means we came all this way for nothing.

If you think you are going to get across the Channel without thinking that this is the hardest thing you have ever done in your life, then
we have made this trip for nothing. You don't come down unless you
are a quivering mass of protoplasm. As long as you have one ounce of
energy left, you stay up there. Because if you're not willing to do that,
step aside and let the old man do it, because I won't bring it down
otherwise.

Mastropaolo meant it too. Although he was 52 and Allen was only 26,
they'd been having endurance contests on the bicycle ergometer. Mastropaolo
would set a record and Allen would beat it. On the morning of June 11, 1979,
Mastropaolo set yet another record, putting out 0.32 horsepower for two
hours, enough to fly across the Channel and then some. Although Allen
vowed to beat this, he never got the chance. Shortly after noon that day,
MacCready told everyone to return to quarters and get packed because there
was a possibility the weather would break on the following day. Mastropaolo
was delighted that his challenge to Allen was left hanging in the air. "I would
like to say I planned it that way," said Mastropaolo, "but it was absolutely
fortuitous."

For his part, Allen had more on his mind than beating Mastropaolo.
Earlier that year, he'd written MacCready a long letter complaining about
MacCready's disorganized management style which left him spread so thin,
says Allen, he wasn't in command of the organization details. "Then he'd show
up and make a snap decision." In addition, his crash-first-and-fix-it-later philosophy ignored the pilot's (which is to say, Allen's) safety, while his financial
stinginess was alienating the very people he needed most. Allen recalls,

I was telling him, "Hey, pay people what they are worth," and pay
attention to the details of being in a relationship. And he was coming
at it from a businesslike attitude. His attitude was to get people to
agree to work for whatever you can get them to work for. He was very
up front in saying, "Look we have a big philosophical difference in
terms of how people should be paid and I don't think we will ever
solve that but some of that stuff in how the project is being managed,
yeah you're right."

Basically, says Allen, he had told MacCready, "You're screwing up," and Mac-
Cready, to his credit, was "open to that."

Still, MacCready found it hard to understand all the resentment. It was not as if the Gossamer Albatross were some incredibly difficult plane to fly. After the first Kremer Prize had been won, everyone on the project had flown the Gossamer Albatross's predecessor, the Gossamer Condor, including Maude Oldershaw (Vern's wife), a sixty-year-old grandmother. Ground school was five minutes. Once the plane was in the air, its response time was so slow that even inexperienced pilots could stay ahead of the plane with the aid of ground observers calling out corrections.

Ray Morgan would later say that neither Allen nor MacCready fully appreciated what the other was doing for him. Without MacCready, Allen would never have had the chance to leave his name in aviation history books. MacCready, on the other hand, so minimized the need for an exceptionally fit and coordinated pilot that at one time he thought he'd simply fly the plane himself. In fact, as the flight itself made clear, the chances of success without Allen were slim to none.

As THERE WAS NO PLACE to hangar the plane at the takeoff site, it was tucked away disassembled in a railroad shed down by the beach. In the early morning hours of Tuesday, June 12, the crew gathered to reassemble it. "We got up at midnight and started to put the plane together at 3 A.M. using floodlights and Coleman lanterns," says Kiceniuk. "[For a runway] we used a big concrete pad used to stabilize the beach against erosion. By the time it got light we were ready to take off."

At this point the main concern was the weather. MacCready was getting reports from three different weather sources (the British, the French and a private service) and "nobody agreed."

To get across in two hours, Allen needed a 2 mph tailwind. "What we were getting from the mid-Channel buoy was a seven-mile-an-hour headwind," Watson would later recall.

And starting at 1:15 in the morning we got a weather report every fifteen minutes of a seven-mile-an-hour headwind. So at 1:30 it was a seven-mile-an-hour-headwind, 1:45, 2:00 A.M., 2:15, 3:00, 3:15. Finally the plane is [ready to go]. It is about 4:15 A.M. Finally at 4:30, it's a nine-mile-an-hour headwind and MacCready was just smiling, beaming, happy, dancing around—"We have great news from the weather station! Great news from the weather station! The wind is beginning to fluctuate!" So the news that the wind was increasing was the best news he could possibly get. Fluctuations were beginning. It was going to die down. When it got down to a two-mile-an-hour headwind we took off.

When I later repeated this account to MacCready, he smiled and said it sounded "glorious" but "I don't remember that at all." As he recalled that morning, Allen initially had a small tailwind for takeoff, but on the takeoff roll one of the Albatross's small plastic wheels veered into a crack and broke, delaying departure for forty minutes. By the time the wheel was replaced, the tailwind was gone and the headwinds had started to build at the mid-Channel buoy.

At the time of his liftoff at 5:51 A.M., Allen was carrying with him two liters of water, a makeshift radio altimeter from a Polaroid autofocus camera, and enough radio batteries to last two hours. MacCready thought that Allen's chances of making it on the first try were about 20 percent. For that reason, they used the heavier, dirtier backup plane and saved the cleaner, lighter version for a better day.

Initially the plan was to fly right above the waves, where it was thought that the cooler surface water temperature would minimize turbulence. Allen pedaled steadily at 70 rpm. At one hour and forty-five minutes into the flight he encountered a 4 mph headwind, which reduced his ground speed to 7 mph. Additionally, the moisture from his breath had condensed on the inside of the cockpit, fogging the Mylar so badly he could barely see out.

Outside the cockpit, the eastward-tending swells were pushing around a lot of air, causing so much turbulence in the process that Allen had to pedal harder than expected just to stay aloft. At times he was only a few inches above the waves, a perilous place given that even momentary contact with the water would disqualify the entire attempt. Concluding that he would never get to France at this rate, Allen signaled the Zodiacs to move in for a tow. As he climbed to fifteen feet to make it easier to attach the fishing pole, he suddenly discovered that the pedaling was a good deal easier.

Despite being near the limits of his endurance, he decided to push it as far as he could go, turning what he had expected to be a brisk but otherwise normal workout into an excruciating ordeal. After two hours, his radio batteries were dead, his water bottles empty, he tasted blood in his throat (a sign of impending exhaustion) and he had a cramp in one leg. He found it difficult to keep his mind focused. It was the hardest thing he had ever done.

Still he churned on until eventually the beach came into view, protected by a rocky breakwater. Realizing that he didn't have the strength to go around it, Allen began checking out the possibilities of landing there. "I was thinking, 'Hey, crash on the rocks,'" he later said. "'That counts. We win the prize. We're done.'"

As Allen's course began to drift toward the rocks, flight director Sam Duran immediately realized what was going through his mind. "I think I know what you're doing," he told Allen over the radio from his Zodiac. "Don't go for the rocks. You can make this. Come on. Turn a little more to the left."

Allen tried to comply, but as he went around the breakwater, turbulence made the left wing flex so violently that the aircraft creaked and groaned. He knew what the sound meant: the spars were starting to snap. He had to use full control deflection to maintain attitude. Then suddenly, he was past the jetty and over dry land. When he looked out he saw cheering people running alongside the plane. When he stopped pedaling, the Gossamer Albatross hung in the air for what seemed like endless seconds and then lightly touched down in the sand above the water line.

Allen tried to push his way out of the canopy, but breaking the sealing tape required three pounds of pressure, which was more than he could muster. When someone finally opened the door, Allen nearly fell out. He was almost incoherent with fatigue. He'd been in the air for 169 minutes, one minute short of what Mastropaolo had calculated would be his point of total exhaustion. "If it had been high tide he wouldn't have made it," MacCready later said.

When Mastropaolo went back to the Royal Air Force hangar to collect his gear, some RAF people lounging in the day room cheerfully told him, "We didn't think you'd make it."

"We knew that," Mastropaolo said.

TWENTY-FOUR

Why the British Didn't Win

BRYAN ALLEN WOULD LATER SAY that the Royal Aeronautical Society's Man-Powered Aircraft Group Committee wasn't exactly thrilled at the Americans' winning a second Kremer Prize so soon. For one thing, says Allen, the committee's activities had been funded for the last eighteen years by the interest from the prize money. Now a large part of that was gone. Also, the fact that the Albatross team was made up of easygoing southern Californians seemed to rankle the class-conscious British. Just for turning down the offer of a drink, says Allen, he was met with a sudden "blast of hostility," a shock from which he concluded that it really was true what they said about England—it was "a stratified society" based on "rank and privilege."

There was another problem as well and it went beyond the fact that MacCready had named the plane the Gossamer Condor, not realizing that in England "gossamer" was slang for condom. It even went beyond the fact that the Americans had the embarrassing taste to let a grandmother fly the Gossamer Condor, whereas the British had always maintained that only a super-athlete could possibly fly a human-powered plane. The real problem, Allen said, was that the British felt that the American team wasn't paying proper deference to the nearly two decades of British effort to win the Kremer Prize. No one was saying, "We won because we stood on the shoulders of (British) giants." The fact of the matter was, says Allen, "I don't think a lot of us had much respect for what the British had done."

The British insistence that a man-powered plane should look like a plane doomed their efforts from the start. They seemed unable to make the conceptual leap that the goal wasn't to build an elegant human-powered plane with which they could then win the prize, but to win the prize with whatever worked, no matter what it looked like.

At one point, Allen recalls, many members of the British man-powered aircraft teams came to a reception where the Gossamer Albatross was hanging overhead. Although the Americans had already won the first Kremer Prize for man-powered flight, there still were other, smaller prizes reserved for the first British team to fly the Kremer course. "All they had to do," says Allen, "was start taking pictures, ask questions, order some tubes, and go win the prize. But instead they were reminiscing about stuff that had gone on fifteen years ago. The Human Powered Aircraft Association was well named. They were interested in aircraft and they weren't interested in human-powered flight."

TWENTY-FIVE

Soft Energy and Lissaman's Broken Heart

IN THE 1970S, PETER LISSAMAN had what seemed at the time to be an incredible stroke of professional good luck. After the United States sided with Israel in the 1973 Yom Kippur War, the Arabs retaliated and the price of a barrel of oil shot up seven times. Suddenly energy conservation was in vogue. The government began funding research into alternative sources of power such as wind, solar, wave, methane, ethanol and other alternative fuels. Insulation became sexy, as did efficient refrigerators and high-mileage cars.

For an applied mathematician and aerodynamicist like Lissaman, it was the best of all possible times. As the son of a South African British motor car importer, Lissaman had grown up, loving "everything that moved or flew." He initially studied mechanical engineering at South Africa's Natal College, where he became interested in the effect on combustion of cylinder head design. Realizing that he needed a greater knowledge of theoretical mathematics, he got a master's degree in math at Cambridge and then a Ph.D. at Caltech, where he discovered aeronautics and the deep satisfactions of airfoil design. In 1971, MacCready asked Lissaman, who had been running a research lab at Northrop in continuum mechanics, to join him at AeroVironment, the consulting company he had founded to deal with energy and environmental issues. "We thought we were going to become millionaires by being smart with wind energy, solar energy, water energy," says Lissaman.

Lissaman didn't just bring a knowledge of theoretical math to the job. Unlike the quieter, lower-profile MacCready, Lissaman was a raconteur, bon vivant, horseman and lifelong student of Leonardo da Vinci. He had helped with the hull design for *Stars & Stripes,* the 1987 Americas Cup winner. He designed a monobeam transportation system, a submarine periscope that produced minimal wake, and a marine turbine to harness the power of the Gulf Stream. He wrote a paper on the formation flight of birds showing that when geese flew in formation they could go 70 percent further than birds flying alone, albeit at a slower pace. He patented toy designs, investigated Frisbee aerodynamics, high-tech wind-powered ships and windmill-powered land cruisers (they work, he says, they're just not very practical). In the seventies, seeing what appeared to be a huge potential transportation market, Lissaman patented the first airshield device for tractor-trailer trucks (called the Aeroboost). "I was convinced, absolutely convinced, that this was a breakout product," Lissaman would later tell a business reporter. "But we thought it would sell itself. We've always assumed around here that if you made a technologically superior mousetrap—not a cheaper one, not a flashier one— the world would rush to lay money on you. Well, it isn't true."

Throughout the seventies and into the eighties, says Lissaman, he poured himself into chairing wind power conferences, writing papers on wind turbine aerodynamics and creating software to help design wind farms. "This filled me with joy because I thought I could use my skills as an aerodynamicist to do good and do well—make a lot of money and help society at the same time." Lissaman recommended that people put wind turbines in valleys all over the country, but what happened instead was that "everybody lost his ass. You'd put a wind turbine in a little village in Alaska and the guy would say, 'Oh Christ. It's a lot of hassle and it doesn't work and what do you do if the breezes don't blow? We'd just rather fly in a forty-gallon oil drum and have a diesel motor generator.' "

Nobody wanted to face the facts, but there were no good high-energy-density replacements for fossil fuels. Wind, wave and solar didn't have the energy density. Electric cars had too short a range. Lead acid batteries were heavy and polluting. "My god, I spent so much time trying to make a buck out of alternative energy, it really sort of breaks my heart," says Lissaman. "I spent a lifetime looking at windmills, wind turbines, ocean energy, solar energy, wind-powered ships and solar-powered cars and what has it all led to? I went all over the world talking to people about putting in energy and it all sort of drifted away."

TWENTY-SIX

How the Oil Crisis
Changed the Country

To JIMMY CARTER THE 1970s energy crisis was the supreme test of his presidential leadership. The American public had always been used to cheap, abundant oil and by the time Carter took office in January of 1977, the country, it appeared, was rapidly running out of it. In response, Carter attacked the energy shortage on all fronts, using conservation, rationing, price controls and government-funded research into alternative fuels. To set an example, he had heated the reviewing stand at his inaugural parade with a solar system, though, in a preview of things to come, it worked so poorly that Vice President Walter Mondale was seen walking away after the ceremonies, rubbing his hands and saying, "So much for solar energy."

Quite correctly suspecting that most Americans didn't really believe that sacrifice was good for the soul, Carter tried to rally the nation with inspirational speeches, including one where he wore a cashmere sweater while sitting in front of a White House fireplace (which contained a rolled paper log so as not to pop and crackle into the microphone). Telling the American public that the energy crisis was the "moral equivalent of war," Carter did his part by turning the White House thermostats down to 68 degrees and installing solar water heaters. White House secretaries began wearing gloves to type while First Lady Rosalynn Carter put away her dresses in favor of pants and long underwear.

In fact, as William Tucker wrote in an insightful 1981 article for *Harper's*, the oil price shocks and shortages of the seventies were a "self-inflicted wound," when one considered that the Organization of Petroleum Exporting Countries had been around since 1960 and in all that time had never been anything more than "a moribund debating society." It couldn't drive up oil prices by setting production quotas because various member states invariably cheated by pumping more oil than their quotas permitted. Then in 1971, Nixon gave OPEC an incredible gift. He imposed price controls on essential commodities, including oil. As shortages predictably arose, the limits of price controls as an economic tool became glaringly evident and the controls were phased out—on everything but domestic oil. This exception, wrote Tucker, kept the price of gasoline artificially low, discouraged domestic exploration and made domestic demand unnecessarily high. The oil companies responded by importing more cheap foreign oil.

At first Americans were happy because gas was both cheap and abundant. But then America supported Israel in the Yom Kippur War and, in retaliation, OPEC (temporarily) halted oil sales to the United States. As prices shot up, it suddenly dawned on OPEC that it had, in Tucker's words, "a stranglehold on the Western oil market." OPEC subsequently raised prices to seven times the 1970 levels, setting in motion what was later called "the greatest transfer of wealth in history."

For American motorists, accustomed to cheap (and, when adjusted for inflation, even decreasing) gas prices, the shortages came as a huge shock. As pump prices doubled and even quadrupled, lines at gas stations grew up to a quarter-mile long. For fear of not being able to buy gas, people topped off their tanks at every opportunity. When people tried to break into gas lines, fistfights broke out. Motorists suffered heart attacks. Some women traded sex for gas. Vigilantes began shooting out service station windows at night.

President Ford offered a quite reasonable solution to these problems in his 1975 State of the Union Address when he proposed abolishing Nixon's oil price controls and taxing imported oil instead, but Congress was far more interested in punishing the oil companies' "windfall profits" than it was in letting the market control the price naturally. At the urging of such liberal politicians as Toby Moffett of Connecticut, Edward Kennedy of Massachusetts and Howard Metzenbaum of Ohio, not only were price controls on domestic oil extended, but the Energy Research and Development Administration instructed the oil companies to lower the price.

Without a mechanism to restrain demand, noted Tucker, the United States imported ever-increasing amounts of foreign oil, thus enabling the OPEC cartel essentially to name its own price, Still there were no more shortages (as long as one was willing to pay the price) until the Iran hostage crisis of 1979 interrupted supplies again.

On that occasion the U.S. government exacerbated the situation by allocating fuel supplies on the basis of past demand. People in the city quit taking trips, while rural districts were awash in gas. Yet it was illegal to transport oil from places that had oversupplies to places that had shortages. Instead of rewarding people for taking the initiative to solve a supply problem (and make a few bucks in the process), tank truck drivers were prosecuted as economic profiteers who greedily took advantage of a national emergency to line their pockets at the expense of everyone else.

In places like Los Angeles, where inexpensive gasoline was regarded as a kind of implicit amendment to the Bill of Rights, people were irate and irrational. I remember hearing an elderly Beverly Hills resident on the radio demanding that the government use the Marines to seize the Arabs' oil fields. "It's our oil," he said. "We found it. We should send in the Marines and take it back." In the San Fernando Valley, a young woman told a radio reporter she would rather skip work than use public transit. "I've never ridden a bus in my life and I'm not about to start now."

When Jimmy Carter succeeded Gerald Ford, he tried to reduce our dependence on foreign oil, providing tax credits for solar heating and power generation, establishing the Solar Institute with a $128 million annual budget and approving subsidies for wind and water power. Suddenly new alternative power consulting and generating companies were blossoming all over the place. But as the economy remained moribund, Carter finally realized that oil price controls weren't so much the solution as the cause of the problem. Although he announced plans to phase them out by the fall of 1981, he never got the chance. Turned off by Carter's mismanagement of the gas shortages, inflation, the economy and the hostage crisis in Iran, voters overwhelmingly voted for Ronald Reagan in the election of November 1980. Within a week of his taking office on January 28, 1981, Reagan announced an end to oil price controls.

Although commentators and consumer groups denounced the decision as a windfall to the oil companies and an unwarranted attack on poor people who, they maintained, could barely afford to heat their homes or fill their tanks already, such critiques were premature. With price controls off, oil exploration dramatically increased. New supplies began pouring into the pipelines. Overnight, what had for most of the seventies been an oil shortage problem suddenly became an oil oversupply consumer bonanza. Gasoline price wars broke out. Heating oil costs plummeted. Alternative energy suddenly wasn't so attractive anymore, which was one reason why Reagan also slashed funding for the Solar Institute and phased out solar tax credits entirely over five years. In short order, solar water-heating went from a billion-dollar-a-year business to virtually nothing at all. In a final insult, Reagan removed Carter's solar water heaters from the White House for being leaky and ineffective.

Although most people sighed in relief at the dropping oil prices, to some in the alternative energy field it was a disaster. Without subsidies there was no way that alternative power sources could compete on their own with cheap oil. For Paul MacCready, Reagan's contemptuous removal of the solar water heaters from the White House was an "unfair slap" at solar power. "It sent a wrong symbol to the country." Reagan, said MacCready, thought conservation and efficiency were "communist plots." Concluding that many Americans had the notion that solar power was too weak to be good for anything other than calculators or wristwatches, MacCready decided to prove them wrong with a stunning counterexample—"I'd make a solar-powered plane."

TWENTY-SEVEN

Bob Boucher and the Eternal Plane

BEGINNING HIS SOLAR PLANE PROJECT, MacCready did what he always did when he had a promising new idea—he went to see the experts. One of the most prominent was Bob Boucher, a cheerfully profane Marina del Rey electrical engineer and manufacturer of model airplane electric motors, who in the early seventies, along with his brother, Roland, had developed a solar-powered, remote-controlled plane called the Sunrise II. With its 32-foot wingspan and very light wing loading it was theoretically capable of reaching 50,000 feet. In a 100-foot version, it could have reached 100,000 feet or more. At that altitude and at the latitude of Seattle, the solar cells would have provided sufficient power, at least in midsummer, to allow the plane to fly enough to keep up with the sun. It would have remained in uninterrupted sunshine, never running out of power and circling the globe nonstop. It would have been the first eternal plane.

Unfortunately for the Boucher brothers, the military didn't want an unmanned aircraft that could fly continually around the world in midsummer at the latitude of Seattle. It wanted a plane that could fly over Vladivostok, St. Petersburg or Moscow year around, which was out of the question for a solar-powered plane. "There's no goddamned sun up there," complained Boucher. "It's black three months a year."

Although Boucher thought of himself as an introvert, to visitors such as myself he rather came across as forceful, outspoken, and so fast-talking that he didn't always bother to articulate the beginnings of words. He worked out of a dreary office in a small manufacturing plant in Marina del Ray in southern California, taking phone calls and shouting instructions out his office door to his office manager.

By Boucher's account, he got into the solar plane business almost inadvertently. After graduating from college in 1955 with a master's degree in electrical engineering, he went directly to work on aircraft power systems, digital computers and radar for Hughes Aircraft. Within a decade and a half he was head of the company's advanced design department in the missile division with a hundred people under him, including numerous ex-captains and three former admirals. That was the way the military-industrial game was played, Boucher explains. "When you go to talk to the Pentagon, it's nice to have someone from Annapolis with you."

One day when his wife told him that he didn't play with the kids enough, he went out and bought his daughter a tow-line model glider. If you set it up just right before pulling it into the air it would circle down slowly after release. After losing a couple of gliders in thermals, Boucher designed an improved model on his own. Pretty soon, it seemed, every kid in the neighborhood wanted one and, in 1969, thinking he was on to something, Boucher and his brother, a Hughes satellite engineer, began building radio-controlled model sailplanes in their garage. They named their plane the Malibu and later that year they took it to Hawaii, where the trade winds blow all day and all night, and set a closed-course radio-controlled glider record of 188 miles.

Calling their company Astro Flight, they made sailplanes for a couple of years until one day they heard that some other people were planning to build an electric plane that would fly indoors towing a banner. "My brother and I said, 'They don't know what they're doing but we can do it,'" recalls Boucher. "That's when we started looking into electric flight."

The physics were pretty simple. The specific energy in a rubber band was 3,000 foot-pounds per pound, good enough for toys, but nothing in comparison to gasoline, which had 4 million foot-pounds per pound. "That's why you love it so," says Boucher. Still, batteries were not without some potential.

In those days, Nicad batteries had 25,000 foot-pounds per pound. So let's say we had a 50 percent efficient propulsion system. That brings our maximum altitude down to 12,000 feet. Now the whole airplane isn't just battery. One third is battery, one third is structure, and one third is the radio. So now you are down to 4,000 feet. So you should be able to climb to 4,000 feet with a Nicad battery airplane.

Deciding that this kind of performance would allow him to build the sort of small stealth battlefield reconnaissance plane that the military needed, Boucher and his brother spent a year constructing a prototype. By 1972, they had a small remote-controlled electric plane that took off under its own power, did simple loops and rolls and, in a demonstration for the Advanced Projects Research Agency, flew 19 miles in 30 minutes at an average speed of 55 mph, a new electric plane record.

That led to a government contract to build a small remote-controlled flying wing capable of carrying a Northrop Aircraft six-pound battlefield surveillance system. In the summer of 1973 Boucher flew the plane on a bank of silver-zinc batteries for 80 minutes at 75 mph. It was vibration-free and inaudible above 300 feet, and unlike hot-running gasoline engines, it gave off no thermal signature. To prove how quiet it was, Boucher flew the plane by remote control at 500 feet over Will Rogers State Park in Pacific Palisades while hundreds of unsuspecting tourists wandered in and out of Rogers' house below.

Unfortunately, the demonstration flight failed to impress the Defense Department, which at the time was far more interested in remotely piloted vehicles with four-stroke gasoline engines and laser payloads. Even so, John Foster, assistant to the director of Defense Research and Engineering and a model airplane enthusiast himself, held out one small carrot, telling Boucher that if he could get one of his small battery-powered models to fly for twelve hours, the Defense Department might be interested.

Boucher had come to a fork in the road. He knew that no matter how good his batteries were, his plane was never going to fly more than four hours. In desperate need of a breakthrough, he began looking at solar cells, which on a power-per-pound basis were actually better than Nicads. The problem was, the military wanted a plane that would operate at night. If your plane depended on solar energy, how could you fly after the sun went down?

It was at this point that Roland Boucher had an inspiration. If they built a lightweight solar-powered plane with a 100-foot wingspan, the plane could fly to 90,000 feet or more during the day on solar power, slowly glide down all night and still be at 20,000 feet when the sun came up again the next morning. Then it could climb back up to altitude and do the same thing all over again. In theory the plane would never have to come down at all, allowing it to do everything from reconnaissance, communications, high-altitude atmospheric sampling and weather reporting, to following migratory birds. Because it flew on solar power, fuel was free; in fact, the higher the plane climbed, the brighter the sun, the cooler the air, the more efficient the solar cells. It would be an eternal plane. Boucher and his brother called the project Sunrise.

Although the Advanced Projects Research Agency didn't buy the notion of Boucher's going out and building a 100-foot-wingspan plane, they were willing to fund a feasibility study on a one-third-size version to be flown on a government test range. ARPA just didn't want to give the contract to a small firm like Astro Flight. "We were basically just two guys in a garage," says Boucher. "ARPA said to me, 'What business you want to be in?' I said, 'The aerospace business.' He said, 'You don't have a plant.' I said, 'Give me two million. I'll buy a goddamned plant in Palmdale.'"

To Boucher's chagrin, the government awarded the contract to Lockheed instead and made Boucher the subcontractor. Boucher was so protective of his plane that when Lockheed wanted to take publicity pictures he wouldn't let them do it. "I said, 'I don't want you guys even close to my airplane. It's my airplane. Not Lockheed's airplane. I designed it. I invented it. I built it and I'm flying it. Give me the money and get the fucking hell out of here.' That's what I wanted. I never got it. I got a lot of bullshit."

The Sunrise was to be powered by 570 watts of solar cells, supplying electricity to a 0.6-horsepower motor that would turn a 30-inch fixed-pitch wooden prop. With its 32-foot wingspan and 23-pound weight, the Sunrise was supposed to fly to 75,000 feet. Unfortunately, the solar cells, when delivered, turned out to be overweight (6.5 pounds instead of 4.5), underpowered (450 watts instead of 570) and, as they were rigid 2.25-inch disks, impossible to attach to the plane's curved upper wing in an aerodynamically efficient manner. This lack of smooth airflow doubled the drag and, when coupled with the overweight, underpowered solar cells, effectively limited the plane's altitude to 5,000 feet. Still, when Sunrise took off from Camp Irwin, California, at 10 A.M. on November 4, 1974, it was an aviation milestone—the first time a plane had ever flown on solar power.

Because of its light weight and large size, the plane had both great performance and serious limitations. Stall speed was a minuscule 9 mph, gliding sink rate was only one foot per second and wing loading was a minuscule 4 ounces per square foot, a fact which made the Sunrise very tricky to fly in high winds. In the Mojave out near Barstow, where Boucher tested the plane, the wind comes up very fast in winter. This, together with a lack of local weather forecasts, eventually caused the plane to be wrecked in a sand storm. "The wind was blowing fifty miles an hour," said Boucher. "The pieces were flying along the ground. We were chasing it in the goddamned truck."

Despite such problems, ARPA was pleased enough with its progress to give the go-head for an improved version, Sunrise II, which used new lightweight Hughes solar cells that produced twice as many watts per pound as the solar cells on Sunrise I. In June, at 30 degrees north latitude, the Sunrise II's service ceiling was calculated to be 75,000 feet.

The Sunrise II made its first flight at Nellis Air Force Base on September 12, 1975. After several weeks of testing, it went up for what turned out to be its final flight. On that occasion, Boucher was using a dry lakebed near a bombing range littered with antipersonnel mines. "They looked like a maple seed—a half-inch-round ball with a three-inch steel leaf," said Boucher. "Just a little charge but it goes off and cuts your heel off. So the Air Force firemen are in a jeep and we're following in their tracks. They know where the mines are laid."

Notwithstanding the circumstances, Sunrise II initially performed well, but then with the plane 30 miles to the south on the far side of a mountain range, at 12,000 feet, the motor generator that powered the ground radio control system suddenly cut out. "Nellis was tracking it on S-band radar," said Boucher "They were telling us, 'take a heading of so and so.' I was just flying instruments. I couldn't see it most of the time. Then the generator craps out and the guy says, 'Your plane is in a spin.'"

Boucher sent for a new generator, re-established contact with the plane and brought it home. "We sighted it overhead at 10,000 feet," said Boucher.

> I saw it cross in front of the moon. We took it up to 20,000 and then we lost the radio or we got jammed or we had a failure in the control system and the airplane went hard over into a spiral dive. Lockheed was tracking it with a 35 mm camera with an 8-inch telescope on an anti-aircraft gun mount. It went into terminal velocity. A wingtip came off then the tail came off. It took 10 or 15 minutes to hit the ground. One wingtip missing. It was spinning around. The tail came down three hours later in Mexico or somewhere. So that was the end of that project.

THE FOLLOWING SUMMER, 1976, MacCready took the cross-country vacation in which he passed the time by watching hawks and vultures soar. The year after that, his team won the first Kremer Prize for manned flight, and two years later, 1979, the team won a second Kremer Prize for crossing the English Channel. When MacCready returned from all the honors, banquets and receptions in England, NASA told him that it was interested in equipping the Gossamer Albatross II with batteries and an electric motor in order to measure its lift/drag ratio. Bob Boucher's firm, Astro Flight, was given the job of building the electric motor and propeller reduction drive (he used the same motor he had used in the Sunrise II), and when MacCready came by to pick them up, Boucher gave him a tour of the building, which included a view of the wings from Sunrise II that had survived the terminal dive at Nellis Air Force Base.

MacCready asked if its solar cells could generate enough power to carry a man aloft. After a few calculations, says Boucher, he told MacCready that there wasn't enough electricity to carry someone like Bryan Allen, who weighed 140 pounds. On the other hand, if the pilot weighed only 80 to 100 pounds it might very well work.

"Great," said MacCready. "My son Marshall will fly it." Marshall, who was thirteen, weighed 80 pounds at the time.

"Wait a minute," said Boucher. "How old is that kid? Does he know how to fly a plane?"

"No, but he can ride a skateboard. If you can ride a skateboard you can do anything."

Actually, says Parker, the oldest of MacCready's three sons, "we were a hang glider family." MacCready encouraged his sons to go hang-gliding even before they had their driver's licenses. "He drove us to places," says Parker. "It was tremendous. We were never hurt. But we could have been. People we know were. It's unusual for the father of teenage children to do that. I guess I can't say anything rational about his risk-taking strategies. He was a little more willing than a lot of people to go out on a limb."

When Parker was seventeen, Joe Greblo, now the owner of a hang-gliding instructional company at Dockweiler State Beach, took him hang-gliding at Telluride. Greblo, a friend and Parker were all in the air when they found themselves suddenly caught in lightning, thunder and heavy wind. "We were lucky to get back on the ground," remembers Greblo.

The wind was so strong it was blowing us backwards. We were looking between our legs to see where we were going to hit. Once we were
back on the ground, we suddenly realized Parker was missing. "Oh
my god," we thought, *"What are we going to tell Paul?"* We packed up
our gliders and got back to the parking area and there was Parker waiting for us. He never got caught in the storm.

The other reason MacCready was so seemingly casual about his boys
flying his planes was that as far as he was concerned, all his planes were
extremely easy to fly anyway. And it certainly was true enough of the Gossamer Condor and the Gossamer Albatross. They were huge airplanes with
oversized wings and such slow response times that people on the ground
could shout corrections before the pilot got himself into trouble. And even
if they didn't listen, the worst that generally happened was that the plane
got into a poor flying attitude, the drag went up, the plane quit flying and
slowly settled to the ground. "The Condor in particular was so big and gentle you really couldn't do anything wrong," said Bryan Allen.

On the other hand, the Gossamer Penguin, built as the second backup
plane for the Channel flight, was only three-quarters the size of the Albatross and, in Allen's words, a lot more "nervous." It had shorter wings (71
feet versus 96), half the wing area, higher speed and, to make it more efficient, much less wingwash (a decreasing angle of attack near the wingtips
for preventing tip stalls). It also suffered from a problem inherent to free-
flying canards at any but the slowest speeds: rapid yaw movements could
"lock out and give you control reversal," says Morgan.

In early May, 1980, Marshal MacCready made a practice flight at
Shafter Airport in the Gossamer Penguin using battery power.

"Marshall had dyslexia," says Boucher, who at the time was pedaling
a bike under the plane and trying to read the bottom-mounted instruments.

Don't ask me what he did. The bottom of the plane is 15 feet in the air
or less. It's got 100-foot wings. It does a snap roll. This wing hits the
ground and breaks off. The plane's in a 90-degree roll. Marshall falls off
the bicycle seat. The cockpit wall is only 2-mil Mylar. He falls through
the Mylar and lands on the ground. The airplane keeps rolling over and
lands on top of him. We drag him out. He's yelling and screaming. He
thinks he's dead. He wasn't even hurt. He was just scratched up.

Ray Morgan, the project manager, had to call MacCready to tell him the news. "Ray was all nervous," recalled Boucher. "He calls up MacCready. 'Well,' he says, 'Marshall is alive and the plane's all busted.'"

Although Morgan half-expected to be blamed for the crash, he rather found MacCready so calm it was eerie: "All he said was 'uh-uh' and 'uh-hu.' There you got to see Paul's full range of emotions."

For Morgan the crash was quite a learning experience. He'd relied on some traditional airplane designers who urged him to trade stability and stall margin for a reduction in the power needed to fly. "We didn't expect to see such a catastrophic indicator that we had gone too far," says Morgan. "We stepped back, put the washout back in and gave up some performance but brought back some stability. Then we compensated for [the lesser performance] by adding more solar cells."

On May 18, 1980—twenty minutes before the eruption of Mount St. Helens—crew members towed the Gossamer Penguin to a height of 2 feet. Then Marshall flew it on solar power up to about 5 feet and guided it down the runway for 500 feet. It was the first time man (or boy) had flown on pure solar power.

ALTHOUGH THE GOSSAMER PENGUIN WAS the first plane ever to carry a human aloft on solar power alone, it wasn't remotely suitable for what Mac-Cready now had in mind—flying from Paris to London. It was a squirrelly test bed, and a fragile one at that. For safety's sake, a real solar-powered plane would have to be as strong as any light plane and capable of flying above 10,000 feet. As MacCready couldn't build such a plane without financial help, he decided to ask Dupont—which made Mylar, Kevlar, Nomex, Lucite and Teflon, all products that MacCready was using or could use in the plane—if they would be interested in sponsoring the project.

As it turned out, Dupont's chairman, Arthur Greenwald, was a good guy, bird scientist and, as MacCready would later say, "a very soft touch." Dupont did agree to sponsor the Paris-to-London flight, but there was one condition: they wanted a female pilot. "They thought it was the thing to do," says Morgan. "It was progressive. It was an Amelia Earhart–type thing. And frankly they thought they'd get more publicity."

This also meant that the pilot, as a Dupont spokeswoman, would have to be squeaky clean, a requirement that unfortunately eliminated anyone who even had a marijuana bust. But then Maude Oldershaw told MacCready about a woman named Janice Brown, a wholesome Bakersfield kindergarten teacher whose architect husband had given her flying lessons as a birthday present.

Brown, a petite, cautious woman, was already a big MacCready fan with a picture of the Gossamer Albatross on her office wall. "Paul called me on the phone," she said. "I was so excited to be talking to a genius. The first thing he said was, 'How much do you weigh?' I said, '103 pounds.' He said, 'Can you get down to 100?'"

The Dupont people, on the other hand, were less concerned about her weight than about her ability to make a good impression. When she talked to them, Brown said, the one thing they wanted to know was whether she could "talk in front of people."

"I'm a kindergarten teacher," Brown answered. "I talk in front of people every day."

TWENTY-EIGHT

From Pontoise to
"a Right Proper Piss-up"

J ANICE BROWN'S INITIAL FLIGHTS in the Gossamer Penguin were literally straightforward. She would fly down the runway a few feet off the ground and land. Then they'd turn the plane around and flip over the solar panel (mounted on two masts above the plane) so it always faced the sun, and she would fly back the other way. Unlike the Gossamer Condor, which flew best in the still of dawn, with the Gossamer Penguin, Brown had to wait until the sun was high enough in the sky to start generating power in the solar cells. Unfortunately, good solar radiation also meant strong thermals. Once when Brown found herself caught in one, she discovered she was "just along for the ride," she says. "It went all over the place. Ray [Morgan] was really upset. When I landed he said, 'Get that plane in the hangar. We're through for the day.'"

On August 7, 1980, with Janice Brown at the controls, the Gossamer Penguin was towed into the air with a bicycle and orange clothesline at NASA's Dryden test facility at Edwards Air Force Base. Brown released the tow line and flew 1.95 miles at altitudes ranging from a few inches to 15 feet in front of hundreds of television and newspaper reporters. "That it flew two miles is an amazing thing," Brown later said. "It was lucky to go that long without being destroyed."

Having established to Dupont's satisfaction that the project was doable, MacCready put aside the Gossamer Penguin and began to design a real plane, which he called the Solar Challenger, that could fly the 165-mile distance from Paris to London. Unlike the Gossamer aircraft, which rarely flew higher than 10 or 15 feet, the Solar Challenger would fly at 11,000 feet, which meant it had to be both light and strong (ultimately it was stressed for more Gs than a Boeing 747). Peter Lissaman lent his airfoil expertise to design a wing that was flat on top, to accommodate the rigid solar cells, and curved underneath. "Paul said it would probably fly better upside down," Janice Brown recalls.

The Solar Challenger was the smallest plane MacCready had built yet. The Gossamer Condor and Albatross had wingspans of 96 feet and the Gossamer Penguin had a wingspan of 72 feet, but the Solar Challenger's was only 47 feet. Although extremely lightweight (220 pounds empty) it more or less looked like a normal airplane with a very large horizontal stabilizer, to accommodate the extra solar cells. One thing it didn't have was a wire-braced kingpost. That would have thrown too much shadow on the solar cells.

Unlike the Gossamer Condor, which either broke or turned rubbery in even mild winds, the Solar Challenger structure was robust, the main problem being an electric motor that ran so hot under the cowling that it sometimes caught fire. "I got good at doing off-field landings," says Brown. "If the motor caught on fire all of a sudden it became nice and silent and smoke would come out."

But the main problem with Solar Challenger was its lack of power. The electric motor (an Astro Flight 2500) was the size of a can of spray deodorant, turning at 7200 rpm. This was gear-reduced with a timing belt and bicycle sprocket and chain to 350 rpm for the 11-foot prop. The samarium-cobalt motor magnets were so strong that in weak sunlight the propeller often had to be hand-swung to get the motor to start turning. Although the wings and horizontal stabilizer carried 16,128 solar cells (4 percent of all solar cells made in the United States that year), they never delivered more than 2,600 watts to the motor, and this was only in the best of conditions—thin, dry air at high altitude. More often, depending on dust, haze, season of year and time of day, the Solar Challenger had less takeoff power than many hair dryers (1,400 to 1,800 watts). Under such conditions, takeoff roll could be anything from 20 feet to 2,000 feet. "If there was a real deep shadow" (meaning bright sunlight), says Brown, "I knew it was going to be a good flight."

On the other hand, when a temperature inversion trapped pollution in a smog layer, a common occurrence at the San Joaquin Valley's Shafter Airport, where much of the initial testing was done, the plane could hardly get off the ground. Because the power output from the solar arrays varied so much with attitude and direction, the pilot had to adjust the plane's

Top, Janice Allen flew the Gossamer Penguin for 14 minutes at Edwards Air Force Base in 1980—"it was lucky to go that long without being destroyed."
Above, The Solar Challenger crossing the English Channel in 1981.

variable pitch propeller continually to ensure maximum power, a demanding addition to an already considerable workload.

On the day that Janice Brown set an altitude record of 14,000 feet in the plane, the air at ground level was so hazy, warm and full of moisture that, in Ray Morgan's words, "we could barely get out of our own way. We were climbing 25 feet a minute, which is hardly climbing at all. But by the time we got to 10,000 we could out-climb any non-turbocharged light airplane. I calculated the peak climb rate for the Solar Challenger would be 250 to 300 feet per minute at 30,000 feet. It could probably sustain level flight at 50,000 if we could get the pilot up there."

For Brown, the demands of flying the Solar Challenger were quite stressful. "Ray [Morgan] had her in Tucson, Arizona," says Boucher.

It was a CIA [airfield]. They were changing colors and paints [disguising aircraft ownership]. We were trying to get Janice to stall the airplane. She won't stall the plane. She came down. Ray's yelling at her. She's sitting on the tower steps crying. I go over. "What's the matter with you?" She says, "They're all yelling at me. They all hate me." I said, "Janice, learn how to fly this airplane or get . . . off the project." She started crying some more.

Although Morgan (and Boucher) could at times be very hard on Brown, the problem wasn't her fault, Morgan says. She was a quite competent pilot in a Beechcraft or a Cherokee. She had commercial, instrument and gliding ratings and later became a flight instructor. "But we totally underestimated the complexity of flying a solar plane." Even experienced pilots were shocked when they saw how flimsy the Solar Challenger was. The pilot sat on a couple of tubes and a shelf with nothing between him- or herself and the ground but a little bit of Mylar, Styrofoam and balsa wood. It was downright "unnerving," Morgan would later say. "There is a natural tendency not to want to bank the airplane because when you look out the window you are looking down at the ground."

The other problem resulted from the solar power system. To get the most out of the solar arrays, the pilot had to fly directly away from the sun in a nose-high attitude that allowed the solar radiation to hit the solar cells at the highest angle and thus generate the most power. But at a high angle of attack the plane was so close to stalling that all turns had to be absolutely coordinated. It made Brown nervous. "The ground was hard," she said. "You can catch your wings on things." It left Morgan frustrated at times. "I know she isn't coordinated," he'd tell Boucher. "She's doing a flat turn."

To help Brown deal with the difficulty of flying an underpowered plane, Morgan hired a twenty-seven-year-old pilot named Steve Ptacek with five thousand hours of flight time in light planes, sailplanes, hang gliders and, for the Forest Service, borate bombers. Having previously been a glider tow pilot, Ptacek knew what it was like to fly at stall speed with no power to spare. When it looked during the test phase as if Brown wasn't going to be able to establish the plane's stall speed and maximum speed (V_{min} and V_{max}) Morgan asked Ptacek to test the plane instead. Because of his initially much greater weight (144 pounds versus Brown's approximately 100), he had to be towed into the air by two people sitting in the back of a station wagon holding on to the tow rope. But he was very confident in the air. Once he got to 500 feet, he let go of the rope, put the nose down, picked up speed and then pulled up until he stalled the plane. Then he went straight down, pulled back and leveled off 10 feet above the ground at 80, 90, 100 miles an hour.

"He says, 'This airplane flies fine. Don't worry about it,'" recalls Boucher.

The closer they got to making the flight from Paris to London, the more worried Morgan became about using Brown as the pilot. Just controlling the solar array was a full-time job in itself. The Solar Challenger had two motors working in tandem on the same propeller shaft powered by five solar panels (four on the wings and one on the horizontal stabilizer). To power up the plane, the pilot had to turn on the switches in sequence very slowly, even out the load on the prop shaft, optimize the climb angle and keep the power constant. Even so, the plane only had about 1,800 watts of power at takeoff, which meant it was nearly always a struggle to get airborne. And there were times, said Ptacek, "when you couldn't fly at all."

Generating maximum power was a tricky business. If the pilot tried to draw too much out of the solar arrays, the voltage dropped off and the power went down. If he didn't draw enough from the arrays, the current dropped off and the power went down. "If you banked the airplane, if the sun went behind a cloud, everything you did changed the optimum point for the propeller pitch," said Morgan. "As a consequence the pilot had to fly the airplane without thinking about it, doing all the things a pilot always does, clearing the airspace, talking on the radio, taking engineering data, while still constantly optimizing that peak power point."

In the end, the fact that Ptacek was, in Morgan's words, "completely at home in the plane" made Morgan decide to go with him over Brown. It wasn't only that Ptacek had 5,000 hours in the air to Brown's 500; Ptacek's life had been dedicated to flight, says Morgan, while Brown "was a school teacher who happened to fly." Although neither MacCready nor Dupont liked the idea of replacing Brown for the cross-Channel flight, Morgan held firm—"If the pilot had to ditch, we wanted the most experienced person possible." Despite Ptacek's greater weight (he eventually dropped to 117), he was so fully at ease in the plane that he could take off and climb out at times when Brown couldn't get off the runway. His takeoffs were models of precision flying, said Morgan—"one inch off the ground, two inches off the ground, three inches off the ground, four inches off the ground. When you watched him fly, you couldn't even see the control surfaces move."

MORGAN IS ONE OF THOSE PEOPLE the engineering profession could probably use more of—articulate, outgoing, good with people and uncommonly tolerant of cats, one of whom, when I went to his home in Simi Valley, had almost completely scratched though the corner of his front door. ("We'll wait till he dies and get a new door," Morgan said when he noticed me looking at it.)

Morgan was born, he told me in his soft southern accent, in Mt. Airy, North Carolina, the same town that Andy Griffith came from. He studied aerospace engineering at North Carolina State University. His senior year he had to take 21 units, all the while working 35 hours a week at McDonald's. "I barely graduated," he said.

> I got by with a little over a C average. I was an oddball because I did really well at English literature. Most engineers did not. I really had to work at math. Double E [electrical engineering] and physics were my weak spot. I struggled. I was not going to be the Ph.D. type. I knew that going in. Also I liked music. I'd played in bands since elementary school. I made the money I went to school on playing in all sorts of different bands. I was a drummer. You could get a gig. You didn't even have to practice, just show up and fake it. I played everything from Dixieland jazz to rock-and-roll to rhythm-and-blues to cool jazz. Whatever it was, that's what I did. I discovered you could get away with a lot provided you followed the lead trumpet and stopped

when everybody else stopped. Sometimes I'd be playing songs I never heard before in my life. If I thought it was about to end, I'd go, "ba-dup doom," like I'm ending. If they kept on playing, I'd go like it was a high jink or something.

Aerospace was in trouble when Morgan graduated from college in 1969 and his only job offer was from Boeing, to work on the supersonic transport. He moved his wife and baby to Seattle, only to be laid off two weeks later with the rest of his orientation class when the SST was canceled. "They laid off the guy who was teaching the class," said Morgan. "They laid off the guy who hired me. Lockheed heard about the layoff and sent up a guy who said, 'I don't know what you'll be doing. I don't know what you'll make. But if you're looking for a job, I'll give you one.' I said, 'That's exactly the job I'm looking for.'"

Morgan loaded his family into his new 1969 Toyota, on which he hadn't even made his first payment, and drove down to Burbank, living on a credit card. He worked on Lockheed's L1011 passenger airliner for about six months and then went into production design on the Viking S3A, a Navy antisubmarine plane to replace the aging but reliable Lockheed P3. "My main office was right off the field," said Morgan. "I spent two years at the production flight line taking flight squawks, tracing it back through the entire system whether it was tooling, manufacturing, suppliers or design. It was the highlight of my career at Lockheed because when I went to work down here I knew all that went into making things work."

Although Morgan did well at Lockheed, being ranked number one, he said, out of six hundred engineers in his classification year, designing a small piece of a big airplane in an enormous company wasn't professionally fulfilling for him. Projects stretched out for a decade. He wanted to see a project through from conception to production, not just build a plane, hand it over to the Navy and then see some panicky pilot accidentally kill one of his own crewmen with it—which is what happened one day when he walked out of his office at the Burbank Airport, headed toward the flight line and heard a big explosion. Over the top of the blast fence he saw a guy come flying up into the air spread-eagled and fall back down again, while his empty ejection seat tumbled down some distance away. Meanwhile two other guys came flying up in their ejection seats, their chutes opened and they floated back to the ground.

As Morgan later learned, a Navy pilot had come in heavy (with a full fuel load), turned off the antiskid locks on his brakes and began fishtailing down the runway. Thinking he was going to ground-loop into a 727 load-ing passengers at the Burbank terminal, he decided to punch out. Instead the plane ground-looped away from the terminal and parked itself at the end of the runway near the blast fence. "We were there at the end of the blast fence," Morgan recounted.

> We saw this airplane sitting there with the engines running. There was nothing wrong with it except two blown tires. There were big black holes where the ejection seats came out. The guy who came out spread-eagled was the crew chief, who, to celebrate his nineteenth birthday and as a reward for being Seaman of the Month, was allowed to ride up in the back seat. His chute never opened. He was thrown out and landed on the runway face down.

When investigators later looked at the brakes, they found nothing wrong. "The tailhook was down," said Morgan.

> They had arresting cables at the end of the runway. He still had 1,500 to 2,000 feet [of runway]. The pilot and copilot had picked up their chutes and were walking around stunned and a 727 lands right through pieces of ejection seat, pieces of ejection canopies on the east-west run-way. They didn't close the runway while they figured out what to do.

It was an experience that Morgan never forgot or cared to repeat. After spending two decades at Lockheed working, as a friend once jibed, "on the left wheel well cover for the left landing gear," Morgan wanted to transfer before he was too old to a small company where he could see a project through from beginning to end. For him, the idea of building a plane that could fly from Paris to London on nothing but "the amount of power in a plane's shadow . . . had tremendous aesthetic appeal." He had always loved the idea of energy efficiency anyway, riding a bicycle to school before it was the thing to do, writing a seventh-grade paper on energy for the Interna-tional Geophysical year, studying the exponential increase in garbage for a college sociology course. For a long time he fantasized about building a windmill-powered house and living in the base. (When he first moved to Los Angeles he surveyed Malibu ridges for a possible home site.) When he heard that MacCready was looking for an experienced aircraft engineer to run a solar-powered plane project, he thought, "If I only do this, I'll have done way more than I ever thought I'd have a chance to do."

At the time, Morgan was working in Lockheed's Skunkworks on the company's version of the B-2 bomber. "I called MacCready. He said, 'Send me a resumé.' I didn't hear from him for three months.' A friend of MacCready's from his sailplane days told me, 'You really ought to call MacCready. He's desperate. He's going to be funded.'"

PRIOR TO THEIR ARRIVING AT CORMEILLES-EN-VEXIN airport at Pontoise, which was the last metro stop out of Paris to the northwest and had been a German fighter base during World War II, Paul MacCready had told Ray Morgan that France was "pretty flat," as indeed it was—for someone in a Messerschmitt. But for someone intending to fly an underpowered, low-altitude flier like the Solar Challenger from Paris to London, it was a different matter altogether. As the crew quickly discovered, the airport was at the bottom of a wide, shallow bowl, with 500-foot hills making up the rim. As the climb rate of the Solar Challenger was only 20 to 50 feet per minute in the hazy sunlight close to the ground, even a 500-foot hill was an insurmountable barrier.

They had hoped to make an attempt to fly to London as soon as they arrived. But day after day it was the same thing—overcast skies and such strong winds out of the north that Ptacek once got to 10,000 feet without getting more than a mile north of the airport (to fly from Paris to London he had to fly a northwesterly course). On another occasion he was gradually gaining altitude but, as the ground was rising as fast as he was, he had to set down.

And always there was the mixed blessing of the media.

Without the possibility for massive publicity, Dupont never would have put $600,000 into the project in the first place. Dupont was so proprietary about publicity, in fact, it tried to stop people from photographing the plane unless the Dupont logo was showing. To keep the press interested during the long weeks that the Solar Challenger team waited for good flying weather, Dupont set up an open bar. "It was a cast of thousands all the time," says Boucher. "CNN, C-Span, Russian reporters, Japanese reporters. The head of Dupont's public relations would get a telegram every morning—'Dupont's name was mentioned 622 times on television yesterday and 300 times in the press worldwide.' And any unfavorable press would be listed."

But such coverage came at a price. On one attempt Ptacek had to put up with photographers who, in their single-minded determination to get the best possible shot, crisscrossed his flight path so much that he couldn't clear a power line and had to set down in a farmer's field. He did a beautiful job, recalls Morgan. "He landed between the rows of some freshly planted corn, then went down the row until he came to a little cross road, where he tilted the wing down. He didn't damage the corn at all."

It was the accompanying media circus that did that. By the time Morgan and Boucher arrived in their Land Rover with the plane's 40-foot travel trailer, hundreds of reporters and spectators were milling about, tramping the farmer's corn to the ground. The farmer was livid. He ran out toward the plane screaming in French.

The Dupont public relations representative was a French-speaking Hungarian who more than earned his salary that day. Quickly assessing the situation, he rushed over to the farmer and, seizing his hand, began congratulating him for being the owner of the field where aviation history was being made that day. "Gentlemen of the press," he said, calling over the media, "this man is a hero. If his cornfield wasn't just in the right place at just the right time the pilot might have been killed. He saved our airplane. He saved our pilot's life." Hardly pausing for breath, he began interviewing the farmer for the benefit of the TV cameras: "What's your name sir? Do you have any kids? Get your wife and kids over here."

By the time Dupont's PR man got done handing out Dupont T-shirts, neckties and ball caps, all the while telling the farmer how brilliant he'd been to have the foresight to own the cornfield where Ptacek came down, the farmer didn't even want to be paid for the damage. "The guy didn't want anything," said Boucher. "He was on TV, the famous star, with all his souvenirs." Instead he gave a speech in broken English, saying how proud he was that the plane had landed on his corn.

Subsequently concluding that it was just too dangerous ever to leave the vicinity of the airport at such low altitude, the Solar Challenger team decided on a new strategy. Ptacek would take off and look for a thermal to help him get above the dust and haze. If he didn't see any near the runway, he'd land straight ahead, turn around, taxi back and start over. Once Ptacek got to clear, bright air at altitude, the solar cells would produce more than adequate power. It was getting up there in the first place that caused all the problems—that and a month of strong north winds, which never stopped blowing.

Thinking perhaps that if Ptacek flew from London to Paris it might be a lot easier, MacCready moved the whole team to England. But they'd forgotten since the Gossamer Albatross days just how bad English seaside weather could be. "The English base was right on the Channel," says Boucher. "The fog was so thick it didn't burn off till 10 or 11 A.M., which was too late to make the flight."

After sixteen days, MacCready got a forecast that the north winds were dropping to the point where it might be possible to fly the original Paris-to-London route after all. Jumping on the Hovercraft, they returned to France and drove all night to return to Pontoise, where, on the following morning, the sun rose on a warm, still day.

On July 7, 1981, Ptacek made repeated attempts in 45 minutes to get the plane in the air. Due to early morning haze, which held the sun's intensity to 85 percent of normal, he was unable to climb out the first seven tries. As the day grew hotter, the cockpit was like a greenhouse and Ptacek, sweating profusely in his rubber skin diver's suit, was close to heat prostration, he recalled in a 1981 article for *Soaring* magazine. Keenly alert to every possible meteorological advantage, MacCready had previously calculated that the first thermals should start breaking off at 11:30 A.M. At 11:28, on Ptacek's eighth attempt, he noticed the grass on the side of the runway "bending and thrashing around" under a beginning thermal. Furthermore, it was moving in such a way that it would intersect a spot on the runway the same time the Solar Challenger did.

At first the thermal was so weak that Ptacek made his initial turn at 60 feet without gaining any altitude. But on successive low-speed 15-degree banked turns, he gradually located the thermal's center, whereupon the Solar Challenger slowly began to rise. By the time Ptacek got to 500 feet the thermal was taking him up at 150 feet per minute. When the thermal topped out at 2,600 feet, he leveled his wings and headed northwest.

The sun was bright, the air was clear and the power strong. The only problem was a media helicopter that kept hovering right in front of him. Because Ptacek could fly a maximum of only 40 mph, there was no way he could outrun the helicopter, whose downdraft could easily force the 200-pound Solar Challenger out of the sky. But when he changed course, the helicopter would reposition itself in front of him. In an effort to escape, Ptacek began flying in the narrow canyons between towering cumulous clouds. Although he didn't lose the helicopter, which was doggedly intent on getting a shot of him crossing the French coast, he did find that the reflected sunlight from the vertical sides of the clouds, when added to the direct solar radiation, dramatically boosted the solar arrays' power output.

To protect the Solar Challenger from the wake vortices of heavy aircraft, Paris controllers had cleared the airspace around Ptacek to a radius of five miles, which still didn't prevent a Lockheed Electra (a heavy four-engined turboprop) from descending across his flight path a mile ahead. Rather than risk encountering the plane's lingering vortex, Ptacek cautiously circled and climbed for twelve minutes before proceeding on course. For the first two minutes everything went fine. Then suddenly Ptacek was thrown so violently against the side of the cockpit that if he hadn't been wearing a shoulder harness and lap restraint he would have been catapulted right out of the plane. The craft was twisted 90 degrees sideways and hurtling downward in a 60-degree dive. Thinking it was breaking up, Ptacek reached back to deploy the ballistic parachute, when he realized the plane was not only intact but actually working fine. He put the plane back in level flight and called Paris Control to ask what was going on. They in turn contacted the Electra pilot, who sheepishly admitted he was 2,000 feet off his assigned altitude.

By the time Ptacek reached the English Channel, the sky was clear and the sun was bright. He flew directly up the Channel at an altitude of 11,000 to 12,000 feet. The twin cobalt motors that Boucher had built for the plane were so strong they went clunk, clunk, clunk. It felt as if he were "sitting on a washing machine with an eccentric load," Ptacek would later say. When he saw the white cliffs of Dover, he knew he was going to make it. It didn't even bother him that he could hear a bearing beginning to fail in one of the motors. "I was thinking they were close to the end of their limited lifespan so I powered back," says Ptacek. "I was pretty much close to the point I could glide to the airport anyway." Five and a half hours after he took off, Ptacek finally landed at the Royal Air Force Base at Manston, a seaside base north of London.

The flight got an incredible amount of attention—British, French, Russian and German TV. A Royal Air Force lieutenant came up to Boucher with an invitation: "The colonel is inviting you lads to a right proper pissup." Boucher had to find an interpreter to discover that they'd been invited to a drinking party.

Although Ptacek made the historic flight, it was Janice Brown who subsequently traveled around the country talking about it. Dupont had asked Ptacek to speak, he says, but after years of trying to get a full-time flying job, he had just been hired by a cargo airline and was afraid they'd fire him if he kept asking for time off. Brown gave so many speeches, she later said, it seemed as if she appeared before every Rotary Club in the area at least three times. The speeches went on for years afterward and the women in the audiences always seemed to ask the same three questions: "How much did you weigh?" (95 pounds). "How did you go to the bathroom?" (she used her empty water containers). "How many nighttime flights did you have?" (none, you don't fly at night in a solar-powered plane).

Once when Brown was giving a talk, MacCready showed up in the audience.

"Afterward he came up to me," says Brown. "He said, 'You know, Janice, the project has been over five years and you're still talking about it.'"

TWENTY-NINE

"A Big Damn Bird
Came Out of the Sky"

AFTER MACCREADY BECAME FAMOUS, he used to tell audiences that he built the Gossamer Condor to win the Kremer Prize because he had a $100,000 bank debt he had to retire. Then he built the Albatross to win a second Kremer Prize, he said, because after deducting expenses from the first prize, he still owed the bank money. He built the Solar Challenger, he said, because he was miffed with Reagan for having pulled the solar water heaters out of the White House and because it dawned on him during the gas shortages of the late seventies that there were plenty of people in this country ready to send his three sons off to war just so they could continue to drive their inefficient gas-guzzling cars.

But in justifying a flapping-wing pterodactyl, said MacCready, he had motivations of an entirely different order. The readiness of people to believe in creationism had always bothered him. If they could just see a flying replica of a 65-million-year-old pterodactyl flapping its way across the National Mall in Washington, D.C., with "kids running after it and dogs barking," he believed, people would realize that such things did exist in the past— they weren't figments of an evolutionist's imagination, and that the world wasn't created, as Bishop Ussher once famously calculated, in 4004 B.C.

MacCready, who was well known for picking up little bits of information here and there and then uniquely putting them all together in one original whole, began thinking about pterodactyls after flying down to Texas to examine the fossil remains of *Quetzalcoatlus northropi*, an enormous pterodactyl found in 1972 by University of Texas graduate student Douglas Lawson in the Javelina formation at Big Bend National Park. His professor,

Wann Langston, subsequently identified the fossil as a three-foot piece of pterodactyl wing dating from the late Cretaceous (65 million years ago).

Pterodactyl wings were very different from bird wings. They had three claws in the middle and a grossly enlarged fourth digit (the "pinkie finger"), which formed the main wing spar. The bone that Lawson had found was part of that larger spar. With nothing to go on but Lawson's three-foot section of pinkie spar, it would have been impossible to say what the creature looked like or how big it was, but smaller, more complete remains of similar pterodactyls were also found thirty miles away. Extrapolating from these remains, Lawson calculated that *Quetzalcoatlus northropi* had a wingspan of 36 to 69 feet, making it the largest flying creature ever found.

In paleontology, the discoverer of a new species has the right to name it. Lawson called it *Quetzalcoatlus* after the Aztec feathered serpent god and *northropi* after Jack Northrop, inventor of the flying wing.

Although MacCready opened a file on *Quetzacoatlus northropi,* he didn't do anything with it for more than ten years. Then he heard that the Smithsonian was planning to make an IMAX film, *On the Wing,* showing bugs, birds and bats in flight. MacCready thought it was a great idea, especially if the film were to be extended to include pterodactyls too. "Everybody loves ugly extinct dinosaurs," he later said. "Wouldn't it be great to have a pterodactyl flying overhead?" Although these flying dinosaurs had long been extinct, MacCready liked to point out, in their day they'd been one of the most successful flying creatures ever. They had survived from 150 million to 65 million years ago, and ranged in size from sparrow-sized creatures to tailless pterodactyls the size and weight of ultralight aircraft. They would probably still be around today had not an asteroid hit the Yucatan 65 million years ago and wiped them out, along with every other dinosaur.

MacCready wrote a letter to Walter Boyne, director of the National Air and Space Museum, suggesting that the film also include pterodactyls. In April 1984 the Smithsonian, and later Johnson Wax, provided MacCready with funding (it would eventually reach $750,000) to build a flying replica of *Quetzalcoatlus northropi.* As no one, at that point, knew what the pterodactyl actually looked like, how much it weighed, how large it was or how it flew, MacCready got a $50,000 grant to convene an informal workshop at Caltech in July of 1984 for three dozen paleontologists, biologists, ornithologists and aerodynamicists who would try to reach a rough consensus on the subject. The grant would cover the experts' expenses, but most of them, according to MacCready, were so excited about the project that they would have paid their own way.

The members of the Caltech workshop had very little to go on: a few crushed bones ("delicate tubes"), very thin-walled, and no soft tissues. "People were taking wild guesses," said MacCready. Originally, the workshop members thought the pterodactyl might weigh 200 pounds and have a 50-foot wingspan. But MacCready calculated that a creature so big wouldn't be able to fly. The final (shaky) consensus was that the *Quetzalcoatlus* had a 36-foot wingspan and weighed perhaps 140 pounds. It was as if one had combined various features of a frigate bird, albatross, pelican and stork, MacCready would later say, "and then increased the size about sixfold."

None of these numbers for the *Quetzalcoatlus* were hard and fast. "They only found a piece of one bone of one wing and from that they specified what it looked like down to the feathers and fur and the size of the eyeballs," Morgan would later say. "If there ever really was a 36-foot pterodactyl, I think they way underestimated the mass of it." One reason for his doubts was that in building the flying pterodactyl, the AeroVironment team had made a Styrofoam model of the torso using the paleontologists' rough consensus specifications. Assuming that the *Quetzalcoatlus* had the same specific density as a duck, Morgan concluded that the torso alone would have weighed 350 pounds. "I mentioned this to MacCready. He sort of dismissed it, saying, 'Oh, it only weighs 150 pounds.'"

In those days scientists didn't know for sure how *Quetzalcoatlus northropi* got airborne. Its hip sockets were more like those of reptiles than birds, which suggested that it couldn't run fast enough on two legs to reach takeoff speed. On the other hand, other scientists pointed out that if it had light enough wing loading, all it had to do was spread its wings in a light breeze and it would be airborne. Still other scientists believed that *Quetzalcoatlus northropi* was too big and awkward to live on the ground, that it lived, rather, on high cliffs or slept in tall trees hanging upside down from branches like a monstrous bat. In that case getting airborne would require nothing more than dropping away and spreading its wings.

Sixteen years after the workshop, University of Texas paleontologist Wann Langston, working with a Memphis engineer and self-taught pterodactyl expert named Jim Cunningham, concluded that there was no way a QN could hang upside down in a tree like a bat. The QN had an 8.5-foot head, a 10-foot neck, an 18-inch-long body and 7.5-foot legs. That's 27 feet right there. To launch itself into flight, it would have to drop away, spread its wings and pull out of a dive, a maneuver that would probably require a 300-foot tree, said Cunningham. As for the notion that QN lived on cliffs

Top, Keeping the *Quetzalcoatlus northropi* flying straight and level was like "trying to shoot an arrow with the feathered end forward."
Above, MacCready's pterodactyl "performed flawlessly" for the IMAX cameras in Death Valley but later crashed in front of 100,000 people at Andrews Air Force Base.

and launched itself into the breeze, there were no cliffs within several hundred miles of where the QN specimens were found; the land was flat. QN lived on the ground.

So how did it get into the air?

It didn't have the physiology to launch itself by running the way geese and ducks do. To get into the air just by flapping would have required six horsepower, far more than it could produce. Cunningham and Langston eventually concluded that it crouched on the ground on all four legs like a frog and simply jumped into the air, opening its wings in the process. By the time it reached the top of its leap, it would already be beyond stall speed. Flapping would start even before the main spar was fully unfolded. Although the QN was a weak flier and could flap anaerobically for perhaps only thirty seconds, by then it would be high enough to catch a thermal, find some ridge lift or locate wind blowing across the freshwater lakes where it made its home. To feed, it most likely zoomed down toward the water at 55 mph, dropped its lower jaw and skimmed the water surface in search of small fish. It stayed aloft perhaps four hours a day (days were shorter then due to the earth's faster rotation). When the local lakes dried up or were fished out, it would migrate as far as 300 to 500 miles in search of better ones.

MacCready's goal in building *Quetzalcoatlus northropi* was to make a full-size, flying, wing-flapping replica that at a distance of 50 to 100 meters could be mistaken for the real thing. It wasn't an easy job. Because he was building an exact replica, he didn't have the option of arbitrarily adding flaps and ailerons, changing the creature's shape or, to make it easier to control, giving it a clear plastic tail. Such fidelity to nature gave MacCready a lot of trouble when it came to pitch control. Initially, the first pterosaurs did have long tails, which they used as stabilizers. But as the eons passed, the creatures got larger and the tails got smaller until, in the case of the QN, paleobiologists concluded, the creature had no tail at all and was essentially a large flying wing, albeit a not very stable one.

Since there wasn't much information in the scientific literature on the pitch stability of birds, the *Quetzalcoatlus northropi* team spent a lot of time at the *Queen Mary* watching birds flying the lee vortex. They concluded that QN's large, slab-sided head acted like a forward-steering canard. The QN turned by pointing its head where it wanted to go. Pitch stability was achieved by sweeping the wings fore and aft. To make banked turns, the QN team twisted the tips of the wings. Three small claws on each wing could be popped up for yaw damping.

"The wings themselves were tuned like a naturally resonating system," says Morgan. "The spring was a rubber bungee made up of hundreds of strands of rubber tied to a very thick fishing line that went out to a pulley in the neck by the head, came back in and wrapped around a spindle that was tied into the gear train that drove the flapping mechanism, which was a jack screw that went up and down." The QN replica was designed for 1 G straight gliding flight. "When it flapped, the motors would push the wing off that natural point at a resonant frequency, like twanging a weight on a pendulum and by doing that the motors didn't have to supply the torque to handle the big bending load of 1G flight. It also meant the motors didn't have to have a reversing mode."

Because the paleontologists had told MacCready there was no tail membrane for secondary pitch control, to make the model more stable, his team had to use reflex in the pterodactyl wings (an upward curve at the trailing edge). Unfortunately, according to Jim Cunningham, this degraded the wings' effectiveness and prevented the model from ever gaining altitude in flapping flight. If MacCready had known then what Cunningham and Wann Langston subsequently discovered—that QN had a big membrane between its legs, which it could use either for turning (by dropping a knee to serve as a rudder) or for supplemental pitch stability—they wouldn't have needed to use the head of the bird as a steering canard. The fact that the AeroVironment team was able to make such a grievously handicapped replica fly as well as it did, says Cunningham, was one of the most "remarkable things I've ever seen in my entire life."

It was also an accomplishment that didn't come easily. Despite all the servos, sensors, onboard computer and resonant-frequency flapping wings, says pterodactyl pilot Ray Morgan, the *Quetzalcoatlus* replica was "unstable in all three axes." When the replica flapped its wings, it created unequal and destabilizing torques. Although the autopilot was supposed to compensate by turning the head, if the required corrections became too large, according to flight control systems engineer Henry Jex, the system would "saturate," a failure mode which on one spectacular occasion sent the pterodactyl spinning into a 16,000-volt power line. "The wings flapping back and forth brought the lines together, threw sparks everywhere and blacked out an eight-square-mile area," recalls Jex. "A farmer told the cops, 'A big damn bird came out of the sky.'"

MacCready never doubted that his team could make the model fly. "Nature did it 60 million years ago," he liked to say. "We should be able to do it too." But live *Quetzalcoatlus northropi* had big brains (thus the big head) and continuous active control, not unlike a rider on a bicycle making continual small corrections. There was no way the fairly simple electronics of the *Quetzalcoatlus* model could match in sophistication the reflexes of a living creature, and as a result, disaster was never more than an instant away. To make it fly straight and level was like trying "to shoot an arrow with the feather end forward," says project manager Alec Brooks. The bird was forever trying to flip over and fly backwards. It did no good to try analyzing it mathematically either. The bird was too flexible and the math too complicated. It was faster just to build a subscale model and proceed by trial and error.

Even then, the pterodactyl crashed so many times that once, when they strung videos of all the crashes together, the tape was half an hour long. "If you make a car and the electronics don't work, you can coast to the edge of the road and figure out what went wrong," says Brooks. But when the pterodactyl crashed "you had $10,000 or $20,000 worth of work to do."

IN MANY WAYS BROOKS WAS TYPICAL of the young engineers who worked for AeroVironment. He was a model airplane fan who learned to fly sailplanes before he was even out of high school. He once built a lightweight plywood handcar that he ran at night on the railroad line east of Pasadena. He also built a recumbent racing bike, a Batso hang glider (from Kiceniuk's plans) and, much later, a very successful one-man, pedal-powered hydrofoil (the Flying Fish) that could beat eight-man racing shells. Graduating from Caltech with a Ph.D. in civil engineering, he asked MacCready to give him a job at AeroVironment. "MacCready was doing bicycles. He was doing human-powered airplanes. It seemed like a good place to go," says Brooks. "I bugged him for quite a while to get an interview. When I went to talk to him finally he said, 'Well, you know, we don't make human-powered airplanes here. We are a real business.'"

The first thing Brooks worked on there was a huge 300-foot-diameter water turbine for generating power by harnessing the Gulf Stream. "It was called the Coriolis," says Brooks. "it was like a big windmill underwater. It was a big marine engineering challenge, quite audacious. It was big as an oil platform." He also worked on a plane capable of flying around the world nonstop, a flight eventually made with a plane designed by Dick Rutan at Mojave Airport, the Voyager. Then finally MacCready tapped him to build the pterodactyl.

Given the tight schedule and relatively small amount of money involved, it soon became clear that they could never build a full-size 36-foot, 145-pound model in time to meet the IMAX shoot in Death Valley in early 1986. Instead, says Morgan, the team "descoped" the project in favor of building an 18-foot, 44-pound model, a development which MacCready put the best light on, calling the half-size model "a temperamental oversized adolescent."

But even on the half-size model the pterodactyl team never did overcome the flapping problem. Although the live *Quetzalcoatlus northropi* engaged in large-amplitude flapping at a rate of one cycle every two seconds, large flapping motions in the replica tended to stall one wing, causing a loss of lift and an increase in drag, which overwhelmed the head and caused a loss of directional stability. In response, the team cut down on the amplitude and increased the flapping rate to 1.3 cycles per second, which made the pterodactyl oscillate in pitch so much that the sweep servos couldn't compensate. The result, says Morgan, was that the pterodactyl was never able to maintain level flight, let alone climb. The most the flapping did was decrease the rate of descent, albeit very realistically.

The end of 1985 was clutch time for the pterodactyl team. They had to be in Death Valley on January 15 for the IMAX cameras, but it wasn't until January 7, 1986, that they had their first successful flight with the finished model. "We went out to Death Valley with a whole load of spare parts," said Morgan. "We thought we would be crashing over and over."

In fact, when the IMAX cameras were running, the model performed astonishingly well, making twenty-two separate flights over volcanic craters, behind peaks and through crevasses in the rocks—all without crashing. Furthermore, in flight it looked remarkably like a live creature.

The paleontologists had told Morgan that the pterodactyl wing looked like a translucent fish fin with little ribs in it, but matching it with artificial material was very tricky. Morgan explained,

It was a very complex design problem because we needed something that was very stretchy. The only thing we could find that could do that was pure latex rubber. We bought pure latex film, three mils thick. Then to put fur on it we sprayed it with contact adhesive, put the fur on upside down and then trimmed off the backing with barber's clippers. Every individual hair was glued down. But the rubber could flex and move like a real skin.

To make the wings the shade of brown the paleontologists had specified, the AeroVironment team used translucent dyes, making it heavy in some areas to hide the carbon fiber C-channel. Toward the wing's trailing edge they faded the color out to nothing. "When you looked at it with the sun behind it, it glowed," says Morgan. "I likened it to looking at the sun through a fish's fin. I was very proud of that."

But the best part, according to Morgan, was seeing the way the autopilot made the head move back and forth seeking the relative wind. It made the creature seem as if it were looking for something. In flight, the fingers were going up and down (acting as miniature spoilers). The wings were twisting. Morgan was astounded at how realistic it looked.

The final shot for the IMAX cameras required the *Quetzalcoatlus northropi* to fly low over the camera operator from the rear and drop down into Death Valley's Ubehebe Crater and fly around the crater walls. "I had to fly it [with the remote control from a station] right next to the camera," recalls Morgan.

> We built a shield for the camera crew. It was very touchy. The winds were up to 25 knots. We'd waited all day for the contrails to go away and for the airplanes and birds that weren't living in that era to disappear. It was very turbulent around the rim of the crater. We had to run the launch cable out along the rim of the crater and it was going through bushes and everything else for the winch. We had several aborted launches where the cable got tangled in bushes and broke. I was very uneasy. Finally we launched on the rim. The pterodactyl flew out and did a circle around and flew five to ten feet over my head and into the picture.

Morgan called this the "suicide" mission because he expected the pterodactyl to crash in the process of filming the sequence. The crater was a quarter-mile across and shaped like an inverted cone. There was no way to set up a landing path. Morgan couldn't even always see the bird. "What happened was, as I spiraled down to this narrowing bowl, I got into a 90-degree bank. The bird stalled and spun, landed in the gravel and didn't get hurt a bit."

INITIALLY, TO PUBLICIZE THE OPENING of the IMAX film, MacCready had wanted the pterodactyl displayed at the Air and Space Museum for a week.

"Then Friday morning," he said, "it would fly across the Mall to the Natural History Museum. And it would sit outside the Natural History Museum for a week and then fly back. It would impress on the populace the connection between technology and nature. It would be dramatic without being preachy. It would be so appealing it would be on every TV station."

Unfortunately "Lloyds of London had a fit," said Jex, the electronics engineer who designed the control package for the bird, when it heard that MacCready wanted to fly the pterodactyl around the Mall and the Washington Monument. "They were afraid the pterodactyl's bill would pierce some senator's daughter." Instead, it was decided to fly the pterodactyl on the runway at Andrews Air Force Base on Armed Forces Day. Even then not everyone was optimistic. Wann Langston, a paleontologist advisor to MacCready on the project, predicted that it would probably crash.

The day got off inauspiciously when, as the crew was preparing the pterodactyl for the flight, someone noticed a crack in the plastic plate on which the head servo was mounted. Normally they would have changed it, but they had only twenty minutes on the runway before the Blue Angels put on an air show. Still Morgan wasn't particularly worried. They'd designed the flight control system to work up to 50 mph, and in this exhibition they would probably never exceed 35 mph. What they hadn't counted on was radio interference on the flight line.

Two different sets of radio controls were used to launch and fly the pterodactyl. These had been provided by Alan Cocconi, a remote-control airplane buff and electronics whiz. But Cocconi had designed them simply to control a model for an IMAX shoot, where, if anything went wrong, you'd simply take the shot over. No one had ever expected that they'd need a bulletproof system that could be used at an Air Force base in front of a huge crowd with all the interference from radars, radios, transponders and emergency vehicles.

The pterodactyl team always launched the bird with the autopilot off. Otherwise it would be fighting the signals to the launch trolley (a detachable wheeled carriage to help get the bird in the air). Once the launch trolley got to altitude, Morgan, who was the pilot, would put the bird and its associated trolley into a bank and turn on the autopilot. If the bird returned to level flight, Morgan knew the autopilot was working. He would pull the trigger to send the signal to release the trolley. As the trolley came down by parachute, Morgan then would use the other controller to command the bird to sweep its wings back and forth, flap its wings and move its head and claws. The frequency that controlled the bird in flight was well protected from interference. But the frequency that controlled the launch trolley, says Morgan, "was the same old model airplane stuff."

Further complicating the problem was a last-minute wind shift requiring the pterodactyl model to be launched downwind, which meant the radio controller was further from the bird, the signal weaker and the chance of interference greater. As the bird was being towed aloft, Henry Jex later said, a fireman keyed his mike to announce, "He's up." This in turn apparently caused the launch trolley to release at 400 feet—200 feet shy of the normal launch altitude.

For a second, Ray Morgan would later say, the people around him thought he'd accidentally hit the release switch. He felt like astronaut Gus Grissom did when, shortly after splashdown in one of the early Mercury flights, something prematurely fired the explosive bolts on his capsule hatch, causing it to fill with water and sink. Although Grissom escaped uninjured, for the rest of his (unfortunately short) life he had to deal with the suspicion that he panicked and blew off the escape hatch himself.

In fact, says Morgan, when the launch trolley prematurely detached, he wasn't so much panicky as extremely calm and alert. He'd done the drill so many times before that he felt like a race car driver in a crash where everything slows down, or a pro quarterback who is so much in the groove that all the other players seem to be going in slow motion.

As the bird flapped and tumbled, Morgan simultaneously pushed the control panel stick forward to sweep back the wings and turned on the autopilot. The bird became stable and was just pulling out of a 70 to 75 mph vertical dive when the cracked plastic plate snapped and made the head fall off. When it tumbled again, Morgan popped the chute. There was just enough altitude that it fully deployed before the bird hit.

The worst part wasn't the crash. It was the three or four hours of humiliation that followed after that. "When you're doing it for the movies you can always do another take," says Morgan. "But we had over 100,000 people there. I had friends I had known from high school who had driven up to Washington from North Carolina to see this flight. My brother and his family had driven up from Raleigh."

Because the contract called for the pterodactyl to remain on display until the end of the day, Morgan spent "the rest of the afternoon with this headless bird sitting on the pedestal" while everybody came by—from the Smithsonian people to Johnson Wax, who were the sponsors, to the many thousands of visitors to the air show, some of whom were quite free with their jokes and ridicule. "If you believe there is no such thing as bad publicity the flight was a success," says Morgan, because the crash made the front page of every newspaper in the country and the nightly news as well. But it was painful nevertheless. His family and friends didn't know what to say. They were trying not to be critical and to be supportive but at the same time they were disappointed and "feeling bad on my behalf."

To the newspapers, of course, the crash was all a splendid joke. The *Los Angeles Times* called it a "Pterrible Ptragedy." The *New York Times* said the pterodactyl obviously had "the wrong stuff." *Miami Herald* humor columnist Dave Barry, in a later recap of the year's news, reported that in May "at Andrews Air Force Base, hundreds of media representatives watched as a 44-pound, radio-controlled, motorized, 18-foot-long model of a prehistoric pterodactyl, which cost $700,000 to build, is towed to a height of 600 feet and released, at which point it flies directly into the ground." Then a month later, wrote Barry, the Defense Department announced plans "to buy 600 radio-controlled pterodactyls."

Although MacCready was quite "annoyed" by the pterodactyl crash, he made light of it in public, saying "now we know why they're extinct." He also knew that in the long run what people would remember about the pterodactyl was not that it once crashed in front of 100,000 people at Andrews but that in the IMAX film *On the Wing* it "performed flawlessly" for millions of people over and over for decades to come.

MacCready, who not only hated not to deliver on a promise but preferred to deliver more than the contract called for, subsequently tried to find support for building what he'd contracted to do in the first place—a full-size 36-foot model. Then, assuming all went well, there would one day be a big outdoor prehistory museum with flocks of pterodactyls soaring the skies and "land dinosaurs as big as bulldozers."

But the days of big expensive flying replica pterosaurs had passed. Bill Watson, who once had built an unpowered model pterodactyl for the movies himself, later said that in his opinion building a quarter-million-dollar electronic bird brain for a mechanical pterodactyl was doing the project the hard way: "I would have just put makeup on a pelican and have a pelican fly-by."

THIRTY

Biking Through the Gene Pool

EVER SINCE THE FIRST BIPEDAL African ape stood up, looked around and decided that there were certain distinct advantages to walking on two feet, man has always looked for the most efficient way of getting around. Walking was fine up to the dawn of civilization, but with the rise of cities people began to congregate on rivers, lakes, inlets and bays to take advantage of the ease and efficiency of water transport for bulky items like wine, wheat, lumber and hides.

In places where there were no available water routes, workers hand-dug canals that were four feet deep, forty feet wide and hundreds of miles long. After the Civil War, canals yielded to railroads, which were a lot cheaper and faster, didn't freeze over and never ran dry. But even trains couldn't do much about getting around inside big cities like New York. People were forced to live close to their work, crammed into tenements and cellars.

To supply their needs, New York freight and transport companies employed some 175,000 horses in the later part of the nineteenth century, each producing 10 to 24 pounds of manure a day and urine so strong that the horses had to be stabled away from the carriages lest the fumes blister the paint. When workhorses died (they only had a 2½-year lifespan), their 1,200-pound carcasses were often abandoned on the spot. Packs of dogs, goats and pigs roamed the streets, scavenging on offal.

The air teemed with bacteria. Tuberculosis was rife. Without traffic lights, teamsters literally had to fight their way through intersections. Residents of brownstones emptied their chamber pots from the upper floors directly into the streets. In 1892, Rudyard Kipling compared the streets of

New York City to the beaches of Zanzibar at low tide, so littered were they with gullies, holes, stones, lumber, barrels and lime. A nineteenth-century American futurist predicted that by 1930 the accumulated manure from all the horses required to provide for the city's ever-growing population would fill the streets up to third-story windows.

Then in the mid-1880s, just when the congestion problem of a horse-based transportation system seemed for many cities insoluble, a remedy appeared: the diamond-frame safety bike with chain drive, pneumatic tires and same-size wheels. The bicycle allowed urban workers to leave their crowded tenements in favor of more spacious dwellings further out from the city center. Bicycles allowed farm workers, who in previous times had only courted women who lived within walking distance, to reinvigorate the gene pool with mates from as far as twenty-five miles away. The bicycle was democratic. Its "sheer humanity" gave ordinary people a sense of freedom, raised their horizons, and spurred social and technological change. It was not just a coincidence that Orville and Wilbur Wright were first bicycle mechanics before they invented the airplane. The bicycle was the "perfect transducer to match man's metabolic energy to the impedance of locomotion," contended Ivan Illich. "Equipped with this tool, man outstrips the efficiency of not only all machines but all other animals as well."

It was a simple matter of physiology. In running, too much energy is wasted in inefficient thrashing about as the legs are thrust forward, suddenly stopped and rapidly pulled back. Whereas a typical man expends perhaps 100 calories to walk one mile at an average speed of 2.5 to 3 miles an hour, a man on a bicycle uses only 35 calories to travel a mile, and he does it three times as fast. In terms of energy expended per pound per mile, a bike is 3 times as efficient as a horse, 7 times as efficient as a dog, 25 times as efficient as a passenger train and 50 times as efficient as a car with a single passenger. Whereas in a bike, 95 percent of the energy applied to the pedals is translated into forward motion, in a car only 15 percent of the energy in a gallon of gas actually serves to propel the car. The rest is wasted as lost heat in the exhaust, radiator, brakes or tires (one reason Paul MacCready called cars "blast furnaces on wheels").

In congested urban areas, bikes are often faster than cars (one reason why bike messengers flourish in San Francisco and New York). On the open road, on the other hand, wind resistance holds a bicyclist's speed to 25 mph or slower, unless he has a streamlined bike, in which case he can hit 40, or a highly streamlined bike, which can go at 60 mph or more. If a rider could

find a place with no wind resistance—the surface of the moon, for instance—
he could hit 200 mph.

As with everything else, getting around on purely human power can
be taken to extremes. A few years ago, as I drove back to Los Angeles from
Los Vegas at 80 mph in air-conditioned comfort, sipping a cold can of orange
soda and listening to Vivaldi, I passed a line of cyclists wearing high-visibility
Day-Glo orange vests, riding on the shoulder with their overstuffed pan-
niers, pedaling slowly through a vast and empty sun-baked landscape, buffeted by passing cars, gasping from the heat, physical exhaustion and tailpipe
emissions.

It didn't make sense. A hundred years ago people set off on foot on
strenuous months-long safaris to the heart of Africa not because they enjoyed
discomfort, danger and disease, but because it was the only way to get there.
It used to be that if you wanted to reach a mountaintop, you had to claw
your way up hand over hand at great effort and risk. Nowadays, one's elderly grandmother could fly quickly and safely to the same peak in a helicopter and be sitting in a rocker on a wool rug sipping tea when you painfully
hauled yourself up the final precipice. In such a situation, doing something
the hardest possible way doesn't seem heroic. It feels deliberately perverse,
a step backward, a neo-Luddite fantasy of returning to some golden pre-
industrial age.

But at the same time, using powerful machines to whisk us anywhere
with little personal effort or involvement doesn't seem quite right either. For
a species which has come so far and done so much walking, over-reliance
on internal combustion engines is a bit like cheating. It puts people with no
strength, courage, determination or skill on the same level as adventurers
for whom in past ages we had the greatest admiration and respect. In the
same way that absolute political power corrupts absolutely, so does the power
of technology. Billy the Kid would have been nothing but a skinny young-
ster from Brooklyn if it hadn't been for his six-shooter, the great equalizer
that allowed physically unimposing teens to face down stronger, older men.
But die-hard internal combustion engine buffs sometimes encounter things
that inexplicably touch their souls, which is what happened to a burly, bearded
Danish-Australian adventurer named Hans Tholstrup when he read about
Paul MacCready's plane, the Solar Challenger, flying in the clear, bright air
at 11,000 feet between Paris and London on nothing but solar power.

Alan Cocconi had "no equal" in analog electronics.

Perhaps it was just high spirits, Viking audacity, or excess testosterone, but as a young man Hans Tholstrup couldn't get enough of gasoline-fueled power. He had circumnavigated Australia in a 16-foot open fiberglass boat, crossed the Atlantic solo in a small power boat skirting pack ice on the way, flown around the globe in a small plane without navigational aids, crossed the Australian outback in a truck, a Greyhound bus and a motorcycle, and jumped a double-decker London bus over 25 Harley-Davidsons (to upstage Evel Knievel, who had announced plans to jump his motorcycle over 24 London buses). Although successful, the jump flattened all the bus tires and nearly broke the frame in two.

If MacCready could get a man in a solar-powered plane to 11,000 feet, Tholstrup reasoned, he could build a car capable of crossing the Australian continent on solar power. Calling his car the "Quiet Achiever," in 1982 Tholstrup crossed 2,566 miles of Australian outback from Perth to Sydney in 20 days at an average speed of 14 mph. Deciding to institutionalize the feat, he created a race called the World Solar Challenge, which would start in Darwin, a steamy tropical town on Australia's north coast, and proceed 1,867 miles south through the sparsely inhabited outback to end up in the Mediterranean climate of Adelaide on the south coast. Having prepared a brochure and a 44-page rule book for entering the race, he mailed the package out to major corporations and universities.

At General Motors, the packet ended up on the desk of Howard Wilson, vice president of GM's newly acquired subsidiary, Hughes Aircraft. For Wilson, a solar race made sense. As a satellite manufacturer, Hughes had a lot of experience with solar panels and space-grade silver-zinc batteries, while its parent company, GM, had some of the best test facilities in the world. The only drawback was that neither company had a small, fast-moving, highly competent "skunkworks" with experience in building solar-powered vehicles. For this, a Hughes engineer and Caltech alumnus recommended that the company contact Paul MacCready, whose solar-powered plane had recently flown from Paris to London on the power equivalent of a hairdryer or two.

GM gave MacCready $75,000 to conduct a three-week feasibility study, whereupon MacCready began preparing an engineering proposal for a lightweight aerodynamic car, combining bicycle and solar cell technology, capable of winning the World Solar Challenge. As the rules posted by Tholstrup said nothing about the shape of the vehicle—only that it had to fit into an imaginary box 6 by 2 by 2 meters and have no more than 8 square meters of solar cells—MacCready's design team explored a dozen or more variations, including (MacCready would later write) almost every kind of sun-capturing configuration that finally showed up at Darwin. In one of the team's more inspired decisions it opted not to go for the obvious solution—a flat panel like the ones used in rooftop installations, which could be tilted directly toward the sun for maximum power—but rather for solar panels that fit the contour of the car, in this case a pumpkin-seed shape. Although such a design would sacrifice as much as 15 percent of available solar power, it would gain more in aerodynamic efficiency.

On March 26, 1987, MacCready, Wilson and Alec Brooks, the AeroVironment engineer who had headed the pterodactyl project and was now project manager for what they were calling the Sunraycer, made their formal proposal to General Motors, which saw an opportunity to refurbish its stodgy image and decided on the spot to go for it.

It was an unusual arrangement for such a big corporation. GM agreed to put up some $3 million for the project (AeroVironment would get a bonus if it won the race but little more than expenses if it lost), while also providing expertise in solar cells, batteries, electric motors, steering, suspension, bearings, braking, reliability testing, driving, training and logistics. At the same time, because GM surrendered virtually all decision-making regarding the car's design to AeroVironment, MacCready, the complete antibureaucrat, had access to all of GM's expertise without having to deal with its notorious bureaucracy.

Without such an agreement, the partnership wouldn't have worked at all. "Because if you were GM you'd spend a year and a half in meetings and then end up deciding that style and color were the most important thing," said Bill Watson, a key builder on the AeroVironment team. "MacCready would just say, 'Okay, make it happen. How long is it going to take? What is the minimum time you can possibly imagine this taking? Five days? Okay, I'll be back in four to see the finished product.' In the meantime, he is off drawing notes in his notebook, solving other problems, worrying about something else."

This wasn't to say that GM didn't hold AeroVironment's feet to the fire. As if to emphasize to AeroVironment that it was now playing in the big leagues, Hughes public relations made a decision to hold a press conference showing off the completed Sunraycer later that summer. "They gave us a nonmoveable deadline in four and a half months where he had to have a complete car," says Alec Brooks. "That gave us another two and a half months for testing."

To figure out the aerodynamics of a vehicle that could withstand the 40 mph crosswinds expected during the race, not to mention the air blast from one of those 130-foot-long, 120-ton, 62-wheel, 3-trailer road trains that one encountered at 130 mph closing speeds on the Australian bitumen, Mac-Cready choose AeroVironment's Bart Hibbs, the talented son of Al Hibbs, the voice of the Jet Propulsion Laboratory, who once won a small fortune playing roulette in Los Vegas, bought a yacht and sailed around the world.

"Bart was the smartest person around with aerodynamics and stream-lining and computers and airfoils," recalls Watson. "He's like MacCready. He has lots of wild ideas for solar energy, windmills, giant towers out in the desert where you put in water vapor, it sucks the air through, makes a ther-mal and draws out five times more energy than anything else.

> Bart said we should design for a 40 mph crosswind, so we had to make extensive modifications to the body shape in the wind tunnel. Orig-inally we had wheel fairings which would direct the flow back under-neath the body, where it would go across the top of the body. And that means extra wind underneath, which means low pressure which would suck the back down—we had this huge area behind the wheels—and the front would take off at 20 miles an hour. It would rotate and try to fly. We redesigned and redesigned and got rid of the wheel fair-ings. We went to higher drag, less efficiency so it could handle 30 miles an hour. Bart said, "That still isn't good enough. We need 40 miles an hour." And we had to put two little turn signals up front which as the air went across the top created a vortex behind it—a little tornado that stuck to the downwind side of the top of the body to lift the body up. Now it would take a 40 mph crosswind.

The car's body, it was decided, would be a Kevlar-Nomex-Kevlar sand-wich mounted on such a light (15-pound) welded aluminum frame that the driver had to use a kind of short portable diving board to enter the car with-out damaging it. The driver's Plexiglas canopy was lined with gold film, which reflected 98 percent of ultraviolet radiation, a necessary consideration in Australia, which, as Bill Tuckey noted in *Sunraycer's Solar Saga,* has the "highest ultraviolet levels in the world."

Because the car was so light, weighing a mere 397 pounds without the driver, the rear tires were vulnerable to skidding in crosswinds. To reduce the possibility of lift generation, the team added two strakes (vertical fins) over the driver's head and six stabilizing fins under the car body at the rear to stabilize any yawing movements from crosswinds. There was no exterior rearview mirror, which would have generated drag. Instead, a fiber optic remote viewer was mounted in the strake, as were the turn signals (required by the competition rules). To recover energy lost in braking, the Sunraycer had a regenerative braking system that turned the motor into a generator when brakes were applied, thus feeding power back into the batteries. To save the batteries, the horn worked off a compressed air canister.

For power, the Sunraycer relied on 1,500 crystalline silicon cells operating at 16 percent efficiency and 8,000 gallium-arsenide solar cells operating at 21 percent efficiency. Together they produced a maximum of 1,550 watts at noon (approximately 2 horsepower, the same as a small lawn mower engine). The battery pack consisted of 68 1.5-volt silver-zinc cells weighing 60 pounds. They were good for only 20 discharges, but they also weighed only one-fourth as much as a comparable lead battery.

To make the car as aerodynamically efficient as possible, the solar cells were molded onto the flattened teardrop outer skin in twenty separate arrays. This way, the power output from cells that the sun's rays were hitting at oblique angles wouldn't drag down the performance of cells receiving the sun's rays directly. Then Alan Cocconi, the electronics expert who designed the remote-control electronics for the pterodactyl, set out to build a peak-power tracker to get the maximum out of the solar cells.

Years later, when Bill Watson looked back on the race, he was really impressed with the insights of Hibbs and MacCready. "They instinctively understood the important problems—'We need a car that [can withstand] a 40 mph crosswind. We need a very low drag. We need so many square feet of solar cells. We need the solar cells broken into panels so a shadow falling on one won't slow down all the others.'" Probably only 20 percent of those who raced in Australia solved those problems, or even understood that they were problems, said Watson.

MacCready's other great insight, Watson maintains, was to keep the number of people on the project so small that "his son Tyler could say, 'Okay, I want you, you and you to help me tomorrow. We are going to make this massive Kevlar lay-up and make it in three hours. We are going to get it all done before the glue dries.'"

WATSON WOULD LATER SAY THAT Alan Cocconi was perhaps the smartest guy at AeroVironment and he didn't even work there. The company had tried to hire him, but Cocconi, an intense, curly-black-haired twenty-nine-year-old loner, didn't want to be tied down. Although he was born in Ithaca, New York, he grew up in Geneva, Switzerland, where his parents, both of whom were physicists, worked at the CERN nuclear laboratory. His father, Giuseppe, had studied under Enrico Fermi and in 1959 co-authored a paper that started the whole search for extraterrestrial intelligence by noting that the 1,420-megahertz hydrogen emission spectra line was the most logical frequency—due to its ability to penetrate interstellar dust—at which to do a radio telescope search for alien signals. Knowing he could never compete with his father in physics, Alan Cocconi threw himself into a field where his father couldn't compete with him: analog electronics, especially those involved in remote-controlled model planes.

As long as he could work on his electronics, Cocconi seemed to have no great interest in money, living in a small tract house in Glendora filled with circuit boards, electronics and model planes hanging from the ceiling, wrote Michael Shnayerson in *The Car That Could.* His living room, decorated in late graduate-student style, had no furniture but a stereo on the floor and two mountain bikes against the wall. He rarely cooked, stopping only to eat a slice of pizza or open a can of sardines. After electronics, an interest at which he worked obsessively, his primary recreations were riding bikes into the San Gabriels and flying a gas-powered model plane with an 8-foot wingspan and an onboard TV camera. On weekends he would drive out to the Mojave Desert and fly the plane by remote control, following its progress on a TV monitor in the back of his black van. Sometimes he would just look at snow-capped peaks, but once when he spotted a car out on a dry lake he sent his plane down to fly circles around it. The occupants kept looking around to see who or what was flying the plane. In the meantime, Cocconi sat in the back of his van, miles away, watching them on the TV monitor and grinning his big toothy grin.

Cocconi's contribution to the Sunraycer was a critical one. Unlike some of the other cars, the Sunraycer wouldn't be using a flat-panel solar array tilted directly toward the sun, but rather one sculpted to the aerodynamic contours of the car. As a result, at any given time some solar cells were receiving less sunlight than others. Because strings of solar cells tend to produce energy at the rate of the lowest-producing cell, Cocconi broke up the entire solar panel into twenty smaller panels. Cocconi's peak-power tracker allowed the solar arrays facing the sun most directly to put out maximum power without being compromised by those arrays on which the radiation was less intense. This permitted the Sunraycer to have a fully aerodynamically efficient shape while still minimizing the power loss. The aerodynamic shape, in turn, let the Sunraycer outrun storm fronts despite gusty winds, a feature which would be a critical advantage in the upcoming race.

TO POWER THE SUNRAYCER, General Motors had built a special rare-earth, 11-pound, 4 hp Magnequench electric motor. "They took it to [the GM test facility in] Phoenix," recalls Bob Boucher, the manufacturer of model airplane motors who built the motor for the Solar Challenger. "And the motor kept blowing up. MacCready calls me up, 'This thing is no good. The goddamned motor blows up every day on this thing. Can't you guys make us a motor that will work?'"

Boucher had earlier developed a motor for a 6-foot-long, air-dropped torpedo. "You dropped it from a helicopter," says Boucher.

> It had a 28-pound warhead and 10,000 feet of fiber optic cable in a spool behind the propeller. The sonar transmitter was in the forward section. Then there is a warhead section. Then there is the propulsion system. We built the whole back end of the torpedo. This motor was 10 horsepower. MacCready only needed 5 horsepower. I cut the motor in half. I sent it to MacCready's boys. They put it in. It worked fine.
>
> Some idiot from Detroit calls me up all bent out of shape: "Where did this motor come from? I didn't order any motor."
>
> I said, "Don't give me any shit. Do you want to use the goddamned motor or don't you?"
>
> MacCready told me he wanted a motor. I built it for him. I charged $5,000 apiece. He kept it. MacCready didn't go through channels. He doesn't work that way. He just calls up. They went [over 60] miles an hour with that thing over in Arizona. It was too fast. They didn't want the competition to know about it.

(For the actual race, says Boucher, the Sunraycer used a Delco motor, although the team brought a couple of his motors to Australia, just in case.)

That was another thing about MacCready: Far more than most engineers, he focused on the ultimate goal—winning the race. With a little more time, his team could have made the Sunraycer perhaps 10 to 20 percent more aerodynamically efficient (and thus faster), but he opted instead for freezing the design early enough in the cycle to devote the rest of the time to reliability testing. He understood that the goal wasn't to make the most efficient car possible. The goal was to build a car that would win the race. And to guarantee that, the car had to be virtually failsafe.

Unlike some teams who were still building their vehicles right up to the moment the race started, the Sunraycer had 4,000 miles of testing beforehand. Test engineers did everything they could think of, running it over homemade cattle grids to judge its handling through the Australian outback and driving it through sprinklers to make sure it wouldn't short out in the rain. Rather than baby the car by flying it from AeroVironment headquarters in southern California to the GM test track in Phoenix, they sent it by truck, figuring that the constant jostling of a long road trip might turn up a weak spot. One thing they did discover when they took it out on public streets: cops didn't like it. "One cop pulled us over because we were going too slow for his tastes," said Watson. "He didn't think we had license, insurance and registration. Another cop didn't think there was any driver inside."

In what turned out to be a lucky break for MacCready, when they did the solar power speed tests in Phoenix, the day was overcast and the Sunraycer only did 35 mph on solar power alone (no batteries). The Ford team was elated at the numbers because their car, in bright sunlight, could do 50 or more.

THIRTY-ONE

Solar Deluge on the Bitumen

WITH THE RACE SCHEDULED to start on November 1, 1987, the Sunraycer team arrived in Darwin in mid-October. A semitropical tourist town on Australia's north coast, Darwin is noteworthy primarily for having been bombed six times by the Japanese in World War II and destroyed by hurricanes both before and since, and for having one of the highest per capita beer consumption rates in the world. Darwin is where the *Crocodile Dundee* movies were shot. Hotels and cafés sell "crocburgers." Closer to Singapore than Sydney, Darwin is gateway to Kakadu National Park, where, in the words of *Sunraycer's Solar Saga* author Bill Tuckey, "thousands of water buffaloes trample lush green waves of grass into swamps, the flights of multi-hued birds block out the sun and huge white waterfalls leap into pink and orange gorges." After October, monsoons hit Darwin every afternoon. The temperature soared to 105, the humidity topped 90 percent and, when the rains stopped, steam rose from the sidewalks.

"We were working in tin buildings with no ventilation," recalls Watson. "And we couldn't drink soft drinks because we would have had to drink 50 or 100 a day. We were wearing shorts, that's all. And a steady stream of water was coming off our chins."

Altogether, twenty-four cars entered the race from countries such as West Germany, Pakistan, Japan, the United States, Denmark, Switzerland and Australia. Some were sponsored by individuals, others by colleges, such as Crowder College of Neosho, Missouri, whose twenty crewmembers had paid their own way, and corporations like GM, Ford of Australia, Nippon and Mitsubishi. One driver packed his car—essentially a tricycle with two solar panels—

in three pieces of luggage. When the plane landed, he unpacked his suitcases, assembled his car and drove away. There was a solar-steam car, the Solar Samba, designed by three Pakistani students and powered by a ten-year-old washing machine motor; and an Australian car, the Team Marsupial, driven by Dick Smith (a passenger in the double-decker bus that Tholstrup used to jump the 25 motorcycles). The designers of two Japanese cars didn't bother fully to enclose the drivers, allowing their heads to stick up through the car tops, which made them look, in Bill Tuckey's words, like World War I fighter planes. Paul Mitchell, president of a hair-care products company and part-owner of a Hawaiian organic fruit farm, drove the Mana La, a large, big-batteried car with a flowing, curved solar array resembling a large hair dryer.

Perhaps the most conventional car was Ford Motors of Australia's Sun-chaser, which had a five-speed chain-drive gearbox and Formula One–type inboard springs. Spirit of Biel, a well-thought-out car from the Swiss watch-making country, was funded by local citizen subscription.

The General Motors team was competing in part with underfunded high school and college kids whose vehicles were in some cases marginally functional, suffering from burned-out motors, overheated solar cells, shorted-out batteries, derailed chains and buckled wheel spokes during the race. Still, the GM team took no chances. It hired a professional racing team from its Australian subsidiary, Holden's Motor Company, to drive the Sunraycer, and Holden's manager of engineering reliability, Ray Borrett, was relentless when it came to testing. Watson said,

> One day we did a test run where we would go along. We had a sched-ule—a guy with a stopwatch would say, "Flat tire! Front tire is flat. Change the tire." We'd run out and change the tire. Then he'd say, "Broken drive shaft. Come in and fix it." And we'd stop, pop the hood and put in a new drive shaft. "Oh, the motor blew up this time. We need a new motor. Get the new motor." Finally, it was Alan Cocconi's electronic controller that was supposed to have blown up—"We're los-ing speed. Get a new controller."
>
> We changed four flats. We beat all our time margins. Everything worked great. We got back. We're having dinner. Some of the other crews had been spying on us. They'd followed us when we had our test run. They were sitting at the other table saying, "I don't think the GM team is going to do so well. They were breaking down every two minutes."

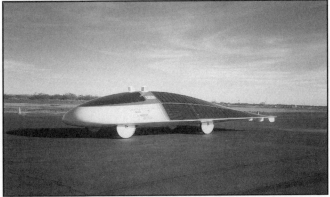

Top, To lower air drag MacCready's Sunraycer was shaped like a "pumpkin seed."
Above, The Sunraycer crossed Australia at 42 mph on one-and-a-third horsepower.

In fact, just to help prevent such breakdowns, a GM survey crew had previously driven the entire route across Australia from north to south, making videos, collecting weather data for each 100-mile section of highway for the previous three years, measuring all 113 cattle grids, determining road gradients, taking soil samples of unpaved sections, noting the coarseness of the pavement and the best places to camp for the night where trees wouldn't shade the solar cells.

Under Tholstrup's rules for the World Solar Challenge, all drivers were ballasted to 85 kilograms, which happened to be Tholstrup's own weight. Racing would start at 8 A.M. each day and end at 5 P.M. Cars were allowed to recharge their batteries with whatever sunlight was available for two hours prior to the start of the racing day and for two hours after it ended. After 7 P.M., the solar panels would be covered to prevent people from using lanterns or floodlights to charge them at night. An official observer would follow each car, staying with it at all times, and sleeping next to the car at night.

To drive the Sunraycer, Borrett picked drivers who, in Bill Tuckey's words, were "socially good mixers" with "tough achiever's minds." In the speed trials the day before the start of the race, the Sunraycer hit 71 mph. The high-powered Mana La, with its hair-dryer solar array, hit 58 mph and Ford of Australia's Sunchaser did 50 mph.

As the Sunraycer and the Mana La were the two fastest cars, on race day they started side by side. Making lane changes in city traffic with as little as two feet to spare, lead driver John Harvey, who had spent months in the United States testing the Sunraycer, took the front position right from the start. "I could see that the crowd was so close there wasn't enough room for us to depart side by side," Harvey later explained, "so I made sure I got the Sunraycer through that hole in the crowd first."

As the Sunraycer proceeded south on the Stuart Highway, the land quickly became dry, barren and exotic. The inland savannas were so flat it was possible to see the curvature of the earth. Off to the sides of the roads were millions of termite mounds, up to fifteen feet tall, looking like everything from "cathedrals" to "piles of melting ice cream," wrote biologist Bill Jordan in the *Smithsonian*. The "deluge" of solar energy was incredible: "The blue sky seems to have liquefied, dripped onto the road and flowed toward us." Then out of the shimmer, Tuckey wrote, would suddenly appear a 130-ton road train, barreling right toward the Sunraycer, trailing black smoke, unable to slow for fear of jackknifing, klaxon playing "Shave and a Haircut" as it roared on by.

As soon as the race began, GM had dispatched a helicopter out ahead both to film a documentary and to note possible road hazards. On the ground an Izuzu Jackeroo scout car preceded the Sunraycer by ten or twelve miles, watching the weather as well as spotting dead cows and water buffaloes lying on the road, or belligerent emus, one of which nearly ran into the Sunraycer ("all I could see were his legs," the driver reported from the low-slung vehicle), and fierce-eyed, wedge-tailed eagles, who stood their ground against the low, silent, vibrationless Sunraycer.

Directly behind the Sunraycer was a Macintosh-equipped motor-home command vehicle with MacCready and the other strategists, followed by a communications vehicle and a traveling workshop truck. The GM convoy also included an air-conditioned press bus, assorted camping vehicles carrying tents and provisions for the catering company and a trailer truck carrying a twelve-foot satellite dish providing instant communications anywhere in the world. At 5 P.M., when by race rules this half-mile-long convoy had to stop for the night (the scout vehicle would help pick the spot with the aid of weather faxes from orbiting weather satellites), the caterers immediately set out cold beer and chilled Australian wine, put up tents and showers and began cooking steaks while the accompanying Hughes communications trailer hooked up with a geosynchronous satellite so crew members and their media entourage could call their editors and wives.

By the end of the first racing day, the Sunraycer had traveled 322 miles. The next-closest car, the Spirit of Biel, was 71 miles behind that. Three or four miles behind Biel was the Ford Sunchaser and 14 miles behind it was Mana La. Despite its big lead, the GM team was still in a state of high anxiety that it might somehow lose the race. The tension was so contagious that MacCready had trouble falling asleep. The race days themselves were completely exhausting. In addition to the nine hours a day allocated to racing, there were two hours of battery charging and debugging before and after each day's racing. Bill Watson was so tired at the end of the day that he'd walk three feet off the road, put down his cot, put his wallet under it and fall asleep in his clothes.

DUE TO THE MANY VARIABLES, racing strategy was mind-bogglingly complicated. Unlike the Mana La team, whose strategy was simply to stay with Sunraycer at all costs, MacCready's team took a far more scientific approach. Hughes' Advanced Systems Design Department had produced a strategy manual for the Sunraycer to deal with road gradient, roughness, acceleration, sun angle and elevation, cloudy skies, dust storms, rain, shattered solar panels and dead batteries. The Sunraycer was sending back ninety channels of telemetry to the computers in the command motor home. Depending on conditions, a Cocconi-devised cruise control could be set for constant speed, current or torque. If there were occasional cumulus clouds, the energy-management protocol called for maintaining constant speed. Under a heavy cloud, the Sunraycer would speed up in order to get to the next sunny spot quicker. Mechanical brakes were never to be used and regenerative braking only sparingly, since it only recovered about half the lost energy. In a head-wind the Sunraycer slowed down by half the wind speed, and in a tailwind it speeded up by half the same amount. In varying winds on flat terrain, the Sunraycer was set to draw a constant current. The basic idea was to start the day with a full battery, draw on it until the sun was high enough to proceed on solar power alone, finish the day's racing with at least 20 percent of a full battery, which would then be replenished by the setting sun during the evening charge period and by the rising sun in the morning.

Initially the GM team was worried about teams with big batteries—some of the cars had five to ten hours worth of battery capacity, compared with the Sunraycer's two or three. But their worries quickly evaporated when by 4 P.M. on the first day, the Mana La team completely exhausted its batteries trying to keep up with the Sunraycer, effectively putting it out of the race (next to a dead, bloated bull). The Sunraycer, in contrast, could cruise at 42 mph on pure solar power with enough energy left over to trickle-charge the battery.

Although Hughes had spent several man-months on the strategy manual and had prepared "pre-set responses for every section of the road," Brooks recalled, "MacCready came in the last minute, did some calculations on the back of the envelope and said, 'Let's try this.'" Brooks didn't like it, but he found it hard to say no. Actually, MacCready would later say, in the long run such errors didn't matter. The only really important call, he told Tuckey, was getting the weather right. If you could do that, you were home free. If you missed it, all the strategy in the world wouldn't help.

Fearful of Mana La and Ford of Australia early in the race (and the traffic problems caused by their large entourages), MacCready had taken a chance the first day, running faster than scheduled on what he believed was the likelihood that solar radiation late in the day would be stronger than forecast. Instead, solar radiation was every bit as low as predicted and the Sunraycer ended that evening charging period with a dangerously low charge.

The next morning, MacCready's famous luck held when the radiation proved so unexpectedly strong that the crew was able to fully charge the battery before the race began. As before, MacCready ran fast, believing optimistically—the forecast not withstanding—that radiation during the recharging periods would be good. Instead, it rained that night, and the next morning a thick cloud cover forced the Sunracyer to start the day's racing with less than a third of a full charge. At this point, most tacticians would not have wanted to risk using up the remaining battery power for fear they'd have none at all. But MacCready boldly decided to run the car full out in hopes of outrunning an approaching storm. If they succeeded, they'd be under sunny skies to the south. If they failed, they'd be stuck with a dead battery in the middle of a driving rain.

MacCready's foresight in insisting on a car able to withstand strong winds now paid off. Because the Sunraycer could shrug off 40 mph side gusts, it didn't have to slow down for the blustery weather. Without high-crosswind capability, all the other racers were caught in drenching rain and gusty winds or forced to navigate newly muddy detours. The Ford team spread their bodies over their car's fragile silicon cells to protect them from one-inch-diameter hailstones coming down in areas where it hadn't rained in three years. A wind gust flipped over the lightweight Crowder College car, badly damaging its solar array. When a flash flood filled a dry wash, the Swiss team began inflating truck inner tubes to float their car to the other side.

Having outrun the storm, the Sunraycer had nothing but clear skies all the way to Adelaide. When the Sunraycer crossed the finish line after five and a half days, no other car was remotely close. The second-place car, Ford of Australia's Sunchaser, didn't cross the finish line for another two and a half days. Officially the race was over five days after the first car finished. At that point only four cars had completed the course: the Sunraycer, Sunchaser, Spirit of Biel and Team Marsupial. (The two slowest cars didn't finish the race for an entire month.)

As the Sunraycer reached the end of the course, General Motors president Robert Stempel was there to offer his congratulations—"You've made all GM people very proud." At a dinner later in the week, Hans Tholstrup announced that the Sunraycer's stunning victory was a triumph of new technology over the old. Generating an average of one and one-third horsepower with its solar array, the Sunraycer had covered the 1,867-mile course in 45 hours of running time at an average speed of 42 mph, which was 50 percent faster than the next-fastest car. The winning margin would have been wider still, but the MacCready team hadn't counted on Adelaide's traffic congestion, which slowed the Sunraycer down so much it couldn't use up its battery power, thus causing it to finish the race with an unduly full charge.

The team's other big mistake, MacCready would later say, was using new tires. If they had used thinner tires or worn tires, there would have been more flats (they had only three, which took no more than two minutes apiece to change), but their lesser rolling resistance would have allowed them to go faster, thereby shaving an hour off their race time.

THIRTY-TWO

Electric Cars and Mental Blocks

AFTER WINNING THE WORLD SOLAR CHALLENGE, General Motors did its best to counter its (well-earned) image as an entrenched dinosaur. It sent the Sunraycer, along with an identical backup, on educational tours all over the country. The company also prepared math and science packets and sent them to every elementary school in the United States. Although another World Solar Challenge was coming up again in 1990, GM decided not to enter the race itself, but rather to sponsor an American Solar Challenge race for college teams and then send the winners to Australia to participate in Tholstrup's World Solar Challenge. Having done all that, GM considered the project over and done.

MacCready, Alec Brooks and Alan Cocconi were not yet through with hyperefficient cars. AeroVironment had been interested in electric cars well before it ever got the contract to build the Sunraycer. Working on improved batteries with some people at Pasadena's Jet Propulsion Laboratory, the company had earlier come to the conclusion that recent developments had now made an electric car feasible. Aerodynamic shapes, lighter weight, different structure, efficient electronics and improved tires could, when pushed to the limit, triple the range of a battery-powered car from 40 to 120 miles.

Electric cars had many advantages: no tailpipe emissions, no spark plugs to change, no heavy transmissions, no wasting fuel while stuck in traffic. About a year before anyone at AeroVironment had even heard of the World Solar Challenge, the company sent a proposal to GM under the project name "Santana" (after the hot, dry Santa Ana winds that sweep southern California every year, giving people the jitters and, in Raymond Chandler's

179

famous phrase, making "meek little wives feel the edge of a carving knife and study their husbands' necks").

On its face the car looked impressive—0 to 60 in eight seconds, a 120-mile range and the power to go 180 mph (though limited electronically to 80 mph). The only thing MacCready's team hadn't figured out how to do was successfully navigate through GM's eight levels of management, and GM turned them down. But that was before the Sunraycer victory made them personal acquaintances of top GM officials. Flushed with that success, in late 1987 Alec Brooks approached Howard Wilson once more to suggest that GM build an electric car. So with Wilson steering through the treacherous GM bureaucracy, AeroVironment put together a proposal that answered all the relevant issues. Then, as Brooks says, they presented it "to ten different groups, up and down the line at GM."

General Motors was wary of electric cars, having been burned in the late 1970s on a project called the Electrovette. On the other hand, GM knew it had to do something to counter pending clean-air legislation. What sold the project was the Santana's acceleration. No overgrown golf cart would sell. It had to be something that would, in GM executive Don Runkle's words, really "throw down the gauntlet." The other thing that convinced GM that the project was doable was Alan Cocconi's inverter (an electronics device for converting DC power from the batteries to the alternating power used by the induction motor). Prior to this time, inverters tended to be huge, heavy devices that sat on factory floors. Cocconi's 60-pound electronics package was far more efficient than the Hughes engineers had even thought was possible. In the fall of 1988, GM allotted $3 million to the project and the problems began immediately. Unlike the arrangement on the Sunraycer project, this time AeroVironment didn't have control. Instead, MacCready's people found themselves working with designers at General Motors Advanced Concepts Center who had no understanding of aerodynamics, and designed a whole line of cars that looked like rockets or barracuda with protruding wheel pods and fighter-plane cockpits, as Mike Shnayerson later wrote in *The Car That Could: The Inside Story of GM's Revolutionary New Vehicle.*

The AeroVironment people were disgusted. But when they drew up their own designs for an efficient vehicle, the GM designers went ballistic. It was "a bloody, unpleasant interaction," MacCready would later say, and the project "almost evaporated" because of it. A thousand phone calls went back and forth until finally GM stepped in and laid down the law—there would be one car or else no cars.

Originally the idea wasn't to build a production car. "It was an engineering exercise to see what could be done to extend the range of electric vehicles," says Howard Wilson, a strong promoter of the project. But when the vehicle was nearly finished, GM management made a last-minute decision to display it at the January 1990 Los Angeles Auto Show.

This was a disappointment to MacCready, who felt that GM should have kept the car secret until it was more technically polished. And it also seemed like a bad idea to some senior managers at GM, who worried that if GM went ahead and displayed the car, harebrained California regulators might actually require them to manufacture it. Although the car, now called the "Impact," looked as if it were ready for a dealer's showroom floor, in fact under the silver paint job the body was fragile fiberglass; the windows didn't go up and down; it had a harsh ride, poor suspension, inadequate motorcycle-caliper brakes and an annoying gear whine. But none of this was apparent to the press or the public, who were responding primarily to the Impact's impressive paint job and the fact that it was smooth, sleek and capable of going from 0 to 60 in eight rubber-burning seconds. The debut was so successful and the fanfare so great that people who normally spent their careers attacking corporations like GM suddenly began talking about the great strides in social responsibility the company had taken.

"The Impact blew away the audience at the auto show," wrote Mark Fischetti in *The Smithsonian.* "Not only was the car novel and exciting, it looked like a million bucks." Some eager buyers mailed checks to GM as down payments. It was the most successful concept car GM had ever shown. Such enthusiasm made the company's CEO, Roger Smith, wonder if perhaps GM should take what had only been meant as a high-efficiency electrically powered demonstration car and turn it into something they could actually sell. By Earth Day in April 1990, Smith had made his decision: GM would manufacture an electric car.

As it turned out, the senior managers under Smith were right to be cynical about the regulators on the California Air Resources Board. Taking GM at its word that it had finally found a way to build a sensible, competitive and high-performing electric vehicle—something no other major auto company had been able to do—CARB issued a new rule in August of 1990: by 1998, 2 percent of an auto company's sales in California had to be "zero-emission" (electrically powered) vehicles.

Although some considered the GM project a great opportunity, Cocconi bailed out of the program at the beginning of 1991 when it was clear that GM wouldn't be using his lightweight conductive battery charger, which allowed the Impact to be recharged by any common electrical outlet. GM, fearful of shocks, had instead opted for what Cocconi regarded as a needless and expensive inductive charger system, which cost $2,000 and had to be installed in the owner's home.

It took GM another six years to bring the car—now called the EV1, for "electric vehicle number one"—to market. Although it was only a two-passenger car, heavier than expected and with the rear wheels closer together than the ones in the front (which caused problems in automatic car washes), it performed pretty much like any sporty production vehicle—with one big exception. The range on a single battery charge was only 75 miles, not the 120 that GM had promised. (GM subsequently introduced a second-generation EV1, which, with improved batteries, increased the range to 100 miles per charge around town and 130 miles on the freeway.) Rather than sell the cars outright, GM also decided only to lease them; otherwise the company would be obligated to support the car for fifteen years. Furthermore, the lease price was $500 a month, which to typical consumers seemed exorbitant, given that one could lease a Mercedes or Lexus for about the same price.

Over the next three years GM produced around a thousand EV1's. But after a series of inverter fires, GM recalled the cars in 2000 and soon quit making them altogether. Except among the ideologically committed and a few Hollywood environmentalists, the cars were neither readily available nor very popular. "People just couldn't accept the idea of a limited range car," says Howard Wilson. One could show them hundreds of charging stations in malls and Costco stores. One could even demonstrate to them, based on the number of miles they drove each day, that they'd never come close to running down their batteries. "But they just couldn't accept it. They had a mental block."

When it became clear that neither GM nor any other major car manufacturer would meet the California Air Resources Board standards for 1998, the deadline was extended. But even if the companies had been able to meet the deadline for zero-emission vehicles, it wouldn't have affected air quality in California. Anyone who thought that, MacCready later said, was leaning on a "rubber crutch." In his opinion the future wasn't pure electric anyway. If there were to be significant alternatives to traditional internal combustion engines, MacCready believed, in the long run they would be hybrid vehicles, with small, efficient, constant-rpm gasoline engines that continuously recharged the onboard batteries, allowing the car to get 60 miles per gallon or more. (And even this change would require a major increase in the price of gas, currently less than that of bottled water.)

On the value of the pure electric car, at least, the auto companies agreed with him. In January 2001, in testimony before the California Air Resources Board, the Alliance of Automobile Manufacturers, which represented GM and twelve other automakers, pronounced its collective judgment on pure electric cars, calling them "an idea whose time has come and gone."

THIRTY-THREE

Day of the Stratospheric Satellite

WHEN I WAS STUDYING JOURNALISM at UC Berkeley, one of my professors, a former *New Yorker* writer, told our class a story about the time he went to turn in a story to the magazine's legendary editor, William Shawn. After handing Shawn his thirty-page manuscript, he found himself feeling very depressed. He had spent three months working on the story, and all he had to show for his efforts was thirty pages. In the same time, construction workers visible from the *New Yorker's* office had put up the framework for a thirty-story office tower.

He had expected that Shawn, who was known for his deep sensitivity to writers' angst, would commiserate, or at least remind him that buildings rust and fall down while a writer's product lasts forever. Instead, Shawn put a finger to his lips. "Ssssh," he said, "don't tell the other writers."

Shawn was just pointing out what most bricklayers, carpenters, plumbers (and engineers) already knew: their contributions stood out for all the world to see and their utility was hard to deny; though paradoxically, that didn't necessarily mean their efforts were always well regarded. When I started working on this book, I was invited to speak to a class of journalism students from Occidental College, a pricey, politically correct school in the northeast corner of Los Angeles near Pasadena. On this occasion we met at the home of another journalist. During a break, I went out on the driveway to enjoy the cool evening air, and ran into a self-assured young man smoking a cigarette. As he blew smoke up into the air, he turned to me and asked, "What are you working on now?"

When I said that I was doing a book about efficient vehicles and the engineers who build them, he looked at me in astonishment. "Why engineers?" he said. He couldn't have been more puzzled if I'd said I was writing about wallpaper.

I began to explain, but it was evident he didn't understand, and even more to the point, didn't care. That was not surprising. Having spent my college education half in humanities and half in engineering, I was used to engineers being regarded as much less interesting than lawyers, activists, artists or college professors. It's hard to deny that many engineers, frankly, are dull, and even the best of them may find it difficult to compete socially with lawyers or businessmen. Success in those professions requires a certain level of dominance, self-assurance and people skills, but little in the way of fidelity to known facts. Back in the seventies, the celebrated Stanford biologist Paul Ehrlich once said that he didn't want to be alive in ten years due to what he expected would be the dreadful quality of life resulting from overpopulation, environmental degradation and economic ruin. Although he was later ridiculed for this pronouncement—and for famously but erroneously asserting that we would soon run out of basic minerals—it didn't so much ruin his career as permanently endear him to the environmental left for saying what they felt needed to be said even when it wasn't true.

Engineers, in contrast, are constrained by physical reality, the laws of nature and demonstrable facts. When they are wrong, there really are observable consequences: wings fall off, transformers explode, buildings collapse. Unlike lawyers, an engineer can't turn a losing issue around with a single clever quip—"If [the glove] doesn't fit, you must acquit." By virtue of constantly having to contend with physical facts, engineers subscribe to what Paul MacCready called a "philosophy of creative reality." Instead of relying on "gods, spirits and the supernatural," they have to operate in "the real material world."

In 1982, a year after relying on the real material world of solar power to propel the Solar Challenger from Paris to London, AeroVironment landed a contract to build a high-altitude, solar-powered plane (HALSOL) for a classified mission involving long-duration flights above 65,000 feet. This time AeroVironment went for pure efficiency, designing a no-compromises 100-foot flying wing with eight electric motors. It had no pilot, no tail, no rudder and, other than the engine nacelles, nothing resembling a fuselage either. It was just a long, flat wing, which was not only the most efficient shape for low-power flight, but also the one that offered the greatest surface area for mounting solar cells. Unfortunately, the HALSOL project suffered from the same problem that Bob Boucher's Sunrise (the first solar-powered plane) did in the mid-seventies—low-efficiency solar cells and no adequate power storage when the sun went down. Although the HALSOL made nine successful low-altitude, battery-powered flights in 1983, reportedly at the secret government air base at Groom Lake, Nevada, it soon became obvious that a solar-powered HALSOL wouldn't be able to carry out the proposed mission, whereupon the project was canceled and the plane put in storage.

Eight years later the Ballistic Missile Defense Office took over President Reagan's Strategic Defense Initiative and began looking into the possibility of using unmanned high-altitude planes for missile defense. The HALSOL was revived and renamed the "Raptor-Talon." The idea this time around was to build a high-altitude, solar-powered plane that could continuously orbit an enemy launch site. If missiles were fired, the Raptor-Talon's infrared detectors could sense the heat bloom, and it would fire kinetic-energy projectiles to destroy the missile while it was still in its boost phase.

NASA, in the meantime, had formed an Environmental Research and Sensor Technology project (ERAST) to develop aircraft for scientific exploration of the upper atmosphere and earth monitoring. In 1995, Raptor-Talon was transferred to NASA and renamed Pathfinder. It subsequently flew to 50,000 feet, setting a world record for propeller-powered aircraft. On June 9, 1996, the Pathfinder, now equipped with lightweight, bi-facial, space-grade solar cells, flew 67,000 feet in Hawaii.

By the summer of 1998 the plane had evolved into the Pathfinder Plus. It had a new center section, a 122-foot optimized airfoil wing, global positioning satellite receivers, new avionics, lightweight computers for semi-autonomous operations, 19 percent efficient solar cells, fixed-pitch propellers and motors with solid state commutation, thus allowing the power train to be simplified to the point where the only moving part was the rotor shaft. "We went from 120 moving parts to one," says Ray Morgan, who was then head of AeroVironment's Design and Development Division in Simi Valley. "It cut maintenance between flights to zero. To replace a motor all you had to do was pull a plug, pull a pin and you could replace a solid state motor and propeller in five minutes."

In flight the Helios's 247-foot wings curve into a Mona Lisa smile.

After the Pathfinder Plus reached 80,000 feet in the summer of 1998, a 206-foot battery-powered version, the Centurion, did a demonstration flight at Edwards Air Force Base, causing otherwise cynical reporters to cheer when it flew overhead. Then in August 2001, the full-size 247-foot version, called the Helios, took off from Barking Sands, Hawaii. Propelled by fourteen 2 hp motors, it reached 96,500 feet, a world altitude record for propeller-powered aircraft. Because this plane lacked fuel cell battery storage, it couldn't stay up at night. But assuming all went well, in the summer of 2003 the plane would make a four-day demonstration flight using power from solar cells during the day and fuel cells at night.

Although MacCready was very proud of the Helios's altitude record—"the world's largest plane flying two miles higher than any plane has ever flown"—he was less confident about the promises that the fuel cell industry was making about their energy storage devices, given that the ratio of hype to substance in fuel cells was, he noted, higher than that of any other field. There were other problems as well. Not only were the Helios's solar cells expensive, their efficiency wasn't yet high enough to allow the plane to provide continuous communications, television or Internet service to such high-latitude cities as Buffalo or Detroit, which in the winter suffered from short days and weak sunlight. Until solar cells became cheaper and much more efficient, the Helios would be limited to developing countries between the Tropic of Cancer and the Tropic of Capricorn that currently didn't have communications infrastructure—either there were no roads or the natives stole the copper line to sell for scrap as soon as it went up.

Still, despite the limitations imposed by the solar cells, Helios had terrific potential. Since in theory it could stay aloft for six months or longer, it could provide continuous scientific monitoring of the earth's surface, track tornadoes and hurricanes, take high-resolution photographs, monitor agriculture, detect algae blooms, scrutinize rain forests and, since it didn't rely on jets or internal combustion engines, provide contamination-free samples of the upper atmosphere. But the biggest application for Helios was as what AeroVironment called a 60,000-foot-high "atmospheric satellite." Because it would be so much closer to the earth than stationary satellites in synchronous orbit, the Helios could use lightweight, lower-powered transmitters, concentrate its signal in a footprint 300 miles in diameter, and free up the same frequency for use in other cities. In this configuration, the Helios would provide high-speed communications links, mobile phone service, television, radio and broadband Internet access to solve what in the communications industry was known as the "final-mile problem"—providing private users what amounted to an inexpensive fiber optic connection to their homes.

THIRTY-FOUR

The Engineer, the Hunter
and the Bear

NOTWITHSTANDING HIS PUBLIC IMAGE as an eccentric genius who succeeded brilliantly at whatever he put a hand to, Paul MacCready had
much the same problems that all pioneers did. Although he thought he could
win the Kremer Prize for man-powered flight in a few weeks, it actually took
him a full year. His *Quetzalcoatlus northropi,* though it performed flawlessly
in front of the IMAX cameras, was only half the size originally planned and
never did gain altitude in flapping flight. MacCready once predicted that
Technalegs (mechanical leg braces that relieve the wearer of the burden of
carrying his own weight) would enable octogenarians to run 90-minute
marathons and people with bad knees to run 3-minute miles. But as the
years passed he forgot about the racing prospects of the legs and concentrated instead on the walking applications: helping soldiers carry 150-pound
backpacks, or allowing people with bad hips and knee joints to walk and
climb stairs. The solar-powered Helios, despite its record-breaking test flight
in the summer of 2001, still had never, after nearly two decades of on-and-
off development (and four different names), stayed up overnight or carried
a useful payload.

Even little projects sometimes fell through. MacCready once tried to
get a class of disadvantaged eighth-graders in a Pomona school to build a
hamster-powered airplane. Initially he called the teacher "fabulous" and
described the kids as being "in a fever of excitement" over doing pioneering
animal research. In theory his idea was a good one. The hamster, by running in a cage, turned a propeller on a big light plane. But in the end, the
hamster-powered plane never got off the ground. The "terminally dumb"

teacher, MacCready said, knew little about physics or aerodynamics. And the hamster wouldn't always run in the same part of the cage, thus causing the center of gravity to shift. Finally, MacCready had to settle for a hamster-powered car towing a hamster in a model plane. Hamsters, he ruefully concluded, were the "couch potatoes" of the rodent world. He wished he'd used a rat.

On the other hand, MacCready made other projects successful long after someone else might have given up on them. "Once he gets an idea in his head, he never gives up," says longtime associate Ray Morgan. "He is stubborn. He stays with it. Many of his ideas are harebrained; they never go anywhere and yet you hear about them for years. He had an idea for something called a Micro-gym. It was like a hand-grip exerciser. It would chirp or buzz or vibrate when you reached a certain force level and he pursued that for years."

His perseverance was a function of his optimism. "They say the average person underestimates by a factor of pi," says Morgan. "MacCready underestimates by two pi. He discounts how tough things will be. He generally is not familiar with what you have to do to get there. That is what drove him into the areas he went into. He doesn't quite grasp how to run an organization."

Although he started three successful companies on his own, MacCready wasn't so much a born businessman as someone with a talent for coming up with interesting ideas and the drive to put teams of creative people together and keep them focused until they succeeded. "And that is the way he works," says Morgan. "He is not a good manager. He will tell you that himself. He would much rather focus on technical details. When I worked in [AeroVironment's] Simi Valley office he came to see me. I was vice president. He would never want to talk about business. He only wanted to talk technical issues or to scrounge some materials to work with or to find a motor, 'this size.'"

The pterodactyl project was not a wise business decision. MacCready did it because he wanted to. Although he often talked about money, and claimed that the only reason he went after the Kremer Prize was for the money, there were times when it seemed he wasn't motivated by financial considerations at all. "If he had been," says Morgan, "there are a thousand better ways he would have gone after that money rather than trying to win the prize for human-powered flight." The truth was that MacCready just liked model planes. All his life he'd been praised and rewarded for it. "In some sense," says MacCready's oldest son, Parker, "the Gossamer Condor was just the next model airplane he decided to build."

In spite of his considerable accomplishments, MacCready was never a leader of men in the traditional sense. Most often he spoke in short bursts in a thin voice devoid of emphasis. Unlike many leaders, he didn't try to whip people into line, give motivational talks or demand deference. When it came to handling all those messy little conflicts that inevitably arise when bright, opinionated people work together, MacCready dealt with them by ignoring them. "People would come to him, asking him to solve some problem," says Taras Kiceniuk, "and he'd say, 'Look, we have to decide, do we want to use 20-thousandths or 25-thousandths wire?'"

It's true that MacCready always seemed to have what Morgan calls "a lot of chaotic creativity going on around him." But it wasn't so much a function of his charisma, which was never his strong point, as the strength of his ideas. "He had a fascinating project," says Kiceniuk. "People were excited and wanted to participate. There was a magic in the group."

In later years MacCready would say he wasn't "trying to stay on top of some pyramid" and he didn't mind working with people smarter than he was. Although this was true enough, it was also true that, despite his image as a modest, mild-mannered, altruistic guy, he had as strong an ego as anyone. That is why he was a soaring champion. "He was fearless," says Morgan.

> He did crazy things. He once won a contest where he flew till after dark and landed on the beach, as far as he could go. He never had a real job [working for someone else]. He came out of school with a Ph.D. in aeronautics and hung out a shingle. [And that's why he succeeds.] He is not afraid of ridicule and not afraid of taking risks.

This didn't mean it was always easy to have a normal give-and-take conversation with him. Morgan recalls,

> You would ask him what time it was, and he would tell you how to make the watch and then he would talk about watchbands and where they come from, the people who build them and how their schools work. He used to call me every Sunday for years like clockwork and give me a brain dump of his current thinking, which was pretty much the same as the week before, which was pretty much the same as the week before that. Then it's like he's through and he's got to go.

MacCready keeps a model plane aloft with air deflected by his hands.

When it came to getting grants or financial support from the top people at places like the Smithsonian, General Motors, Johnson Wax or Dupont, MacCready could do phenomenal things primarily because by the time you got to the top, the people were smart enough to really understand him and sophisticated enough to see the symbolic value of whimsical projects like pterodactyls or the long-term financial impact of a solar-powered plane. On the other hand, said Morgan, "you did not want to have MacCready go with you on a marketing trip to Washington, D.C." MacCready's name was great for getting in the door, but after that, the company would have done better just putting his cardboard cutout in a chair. Morgan would be trying to point out the capabilities of AeroVironment's new battery-powered surveillance plane (the Pointer) to some government official who needed a simple solution to a specific problem, and MacCready off the top of his head would be saying, "Maybe you don't need an airplane; you could do it with a kite."

When MacCready first started doing projects like the Gossamer Condor, the Gossamer Albatross and the Solar Challenger, he was very involved and hands-on. But as the years passed, he became the engineering equivalent of a theoretical physicist. He would come up with an idea. Then, working at home with "crude tools and some duct tape and vises and hacksaws," he'd prove that it worked well enough to turn the idea over to his company. After that he lost interest. The hard nuts and bolts of turning even a great idea into a viable product were to him mere "engineering details." He wasn't interested. He'd already moved on to something else.

Morgan says it always reminded him of the story about the salesman and the engineer who go bear hunting:

> They hunt all day and don't see anything, so the engineer goes back to the cabin and the salesman goes picking berries. He looks up and there's a bear. The bear chases him down the valley, up over the hills. When he gets to the cabin he yells, "Open the door! Open the door!" When the engineer opens the door, the salesman runs in with the bear right behind. As the salesman dives through a window and keeps on running he yells back over his shoulder to the engineer, "You skin that one. I'm going out for another."

And that's how it seemed with Paul. He would come in with these things. We'd say to ourselves, "How in the world are we going to do *that?*" In the meantime he's off thinking about something else.

THIRTY-FIVE

Tao of the Carbon Dragon

IN *The Spirit of St. Louis,* CHARLES LINDBERGH wrote that sometimes when he was flying over a stratus layer at night he lost all sense of the planet.

> You know that down below, beneath that heavenly blanket is the earth, factual and hard. But it's an intellectual knowledge; it's a knowledge tucked away in the mind; not a feeling that penetrates the body. And if at times you renounce experience and mind's heavy logic, it seems that the world has rushed along on its orbit, leaving you alone flying above a forgotten cloud bank, somewhere in the solitude of interstellar space.

The longshoreman-intellectual Eric Hoffer once voiced a similar sentiment, describing our passionate preoccupation with the "sky, the stars and a God somewhere in outer space" as a homing impulse—"We are drawn back to where we came from."

Yet despite the sometimes transcendental experience of aviation's early days, as aviation matured the thrill faded, often in the most mundane ways. After World War II, private aviation was supposed to be the next really big thing. Planes were cheap, airfields were numerous and, because of the war, pilots were everywhere. Anticipating the rise of the family plane, in the fifties and sixties magazines like *Popular Science* regularly featured covers showing the skies over futuristic cities filled with dozens of combination car-planes, as fathers flew home from work and mothers returned from the fly-in supermarket. *Reader's Digest* and *Better Homes and Gardens* ran articles on the difficulties of coping with a flying family.

By the eighties, however, the euphoria about small planes had largely disappeared. Despite all the magazine articles and glowing predictions, there never was any big market for an inexpensive popular plane. And the reason, says Eric Raymond, a San Diego area pilot who flew a long-winged glider across the country in 1990 on batteries and solar power, was that "aviation just hasn't lived up to its promises." Unlike computers and electronics, which make quantum leaps every year, since World War II aviation has, in Raymond's words, been "frozen in time."

This is partly because of a uniquely American curse: ubiquitous, soul-destroying tort litigation. Every time a plane crashes anywhere for any reason, lawyers for the victim's estate sue the airplane manufacturer for faulty design and construction. The plane could be a forty-year-old, poorly maintained hulk. The pilot could have been lost, disoriented or out of gas. He might have flown into turbulence, unexpectedly encountered icing or wind shear, overshot the runway, hit a mountain in clouds or suffered a heart attack in flight, but the result is still the same: the manufacturer gets sued. Whereas computer companies upgrade their line every six months, the private plane industry has little incentive to upgrade components for fear the change will be portrayed in court as an implicit admission that the previous version was (fatally) flawed.

But there's another reason why small private planes in some cases still use fifty-year-old gasoline engine designs instead of modern, vibration-free, brushless electric motors. It's the fuel. Gasoline is just too good. In terns of energy density, nothing comes close to it. Fuel cells are still a distant dream. Batteries aren't even on the chart. In substituting batteries for gasoline, "you take a hundred-to-one hit," says MacCready. "No other inexpensive harnessible energy source comes close to having the energy density of petroleum. If it did, we would have been using it long ago." For people who considered flying not just a commercial enterprise but a source of enlightenment too, there was definitely a need for another approach.

One such approach came from MacCready himself, who at a technical soaring meeting in 1959 had pointed out that a sailplane with a one-foot-per-second sink rate could do what no sailplane had ever done before: fly virtually any day of the year, anywhere in the country, any time of day. With that low a sink rate, a pilot could take advantage of normal, everyday atmospheric turbulence whenever he wanted to. There'd be no need to wait around

The Carbon Dragon flies on nothing more than sideways gusts and burbles in the air.

for it to get hot enough for thermals to form or wind to blow over the ridges. One could fly on winter days when thermals were weak or on cloudy days when they didn't form at all. In short, prolonged motorless flight would be possible using nothing but the normal gusts, burbles and microturbulence of the lower atmosphere.

A decade later, hang-gliding pioneer and aviation writer Richard Miller revisited the same theme. He had long been interested in the transcendental aspects of "personal motorless flight." A sailplane, he wrote in *Without Visible Means of Support*, "makes an aerial excursion, not an incursion. His passage leaves a whisper, not a shriek." Soaring was a "metaphor" for life itself. There was nothing more elemental than the notion of bobbling along in zero sink, at six or seven hundred feet, fighting for your own mortality against "the forces trying to pull you down."

In 1972, Miller summed up his thinking on these matters in a Zen-inspired article for *Soaring* magazine, describing what he called the "Tao" of "supersoarability." As Miller explained it, Tao was the unifying spirit which animated any great project or organization in their quest to solve a problem or achieve a victory. Inherent in Tao, unfortunately, was its ephemerality—it only lasted till the goal was won. After that, the fiercely focused quest for victory always seemed to degenerate into a nervous search for security. "It's the epic of the frontier," wrote Miller. "The pioneer who had to dig for water, fell trees and hunt game to provide for his wants, gives way to the settler who finds his surveyed section lot ready equipped with access road, sewage pipes and utility poles." There was also the matter of complexity. As planes became larger, more expensive and more complicated, they weren't so much thrilling expeditions into the unknown as corporate projects, business propositions beyond the control of a single man. "Thus Tao was diminished," wrote Miller, "and discontent was felt in the hearts of men."

But there was a solution. "Hidden in the folds of the future, obscured by time, are the forms and shapes of things not yet remembered." And one such unremembered shape was the supersoarer. In Miller's vision, as in MacCready's before him, the supersoarer would dispense with the need for tow planes, big expensive gliders and even airports. Instead, this lightweight, foot-launched, low-sink-rate flying wing (Miller called it the "Thistledown") would take off from a small hill in the gentle afternoon breeze, fly softly and silently over fields and flowers, taking advantage of every puff of air and breeze, turn on a dime, out-soar the hawks and vultures, and then set down lightly with the crickets as the sun was going down.

Although to some the notion of flying without thermals seemed impossible—in physics as in life there is no such thing as a free lunch—others noted that albatrosses have always done quite well without thermals, though not everyone could agree exactly why.

When scientists first began studying the albatross, they refused to believe that it could fly without flapping its wings. One observer even managed to convince himself that the albatross flapped its wings after all, but so rapidly that the untrained eye couldn't detect it. The truth, in fact, was both more complex and more interesting. Close to the surface, the wind speed is very low, while at altitude it is generally much higher. Continually swooping back and forth between these two regions of different wind speed, an albatross can extract energy from the air in the same way that a sailboat does when its hull is engulfed in a stationary medium (the water) and the sail is enveloped in the wind.

It isn't only the albatross that can fly without flapping its wings. On windy days, vultures and hawks sometimes fly across the sky without flapping or circling. Sailplane pilot Gary Osoba once shot a video from his driveway of a flock of migrating seagulls. "On this day the winds aloft were 25 to 30 knots," he says. "There was a heavy stratus cloud cover. It was a cool day. I looked at the lapse rate. There was essentially no convection even low down to the ground. Kansas is pretty flat. We don't have a lot of vertical components introduced into the air." Even so, the gulls were flying at an altitude of 200 to 400 feet into the wind, banking off the side gusts so quickly it looked like they were "bouncing off them."

This phenomenon, most commonly known as dynamic soaring, was nothing new. "The birds have been doing it for years," says Taras Kiceniuk, "the albatross being the classic example. But now that we look more closely we see that vultures, seagulls, even the little dinky birds that sort of undulate and bounce from tree to tree seem to be doing a lot of dynamic soaring."

As it turns out, dynamic soaring isn't limited to the atmosphere. If anything, it's easier under water. Fish and some aquatic mammals have done dynamic soaring for eons, as when a salmon swims upstream to spawn. "There tends to be a very turbulent environment in a stream where the undulations in the stream velocity may be equal to the fish's swimming speed," says Kiceniuk. "By working little turbulent eddies off one another, the fish can actually extract energy from the stream, thereby minimizing their own power output." In the ocean dolphins use dynamic soaring to surf three or four feet underwater on the advancing wave fronts. Whales do the same thing, but into the waves, adjusting their pitch frequency to the motion of the oncoming waves, not unlike a sailplane flying through pockets of lift and sink, with the pilot pulling up when he encounters lift and pushing down in sink.

For small, very light sailplanes you don't even necessarily need any lift pockets. Mere sideways gusts will do, especially if one is flying the 145-pound Carbon Dragon, a small, ultralight, high-wing, high-efficiency, carbon fiber sailplane with a minimum sink rate of 1.7 feet per second, a glide ratio of 26:1 and a towed takeoff roll of as little as 5 feet. It's the modern-day equivalent of the Thistledown glider that Miller was proposing in 1972 or the one-foot-per-second sink-rate glider that MacCready was proposing thirteen years before that. "The glider literally leaps off the ground," says Gary Osoba, an academically minded Wichita entrepreneur who has been flying one for years.

Due to the low sink rate, Osoba does what the birds do—take advantage of what he calls the fleeting, elusive, "disorganized burbles, disintegrated thermal fragments, and thin, string-like animals that meander through the sky and often flow into thermals like a winding stream would a lake." Typically Osoba is launched to 600 feet with an auto tow. On crisp, cool Kansas days when the sky is clear and blue, with visibility unlimited and two-foot lengths of corn leaf flying up in the thermals, Osoba is able to fly in any direction without circling, as easily as if he had an engine, but in total silence, staying up all day, out-climbing hawks and vultures.

Once airborne, Osoba maneuvers to take advantage of velocity differences in the atmosphere. Because the Carbon Dragon flies so slowly (25 to 30 mph) and weighs so little, it is responsive to the kind of quarter- or half-second wind gusts that heavier, faster sailplanes (or single-engine planes) wouldn't even notice. In the Carbon Dragon there is so little distinction between the pilot and the plane that at times Osoba flies with his eyes closed, the better to "feel" the air.

Staying aloft in such air is a high-wire routine. His plane is constantly in motion. Even though he never stops to circle, his instantaneous variation from base heading is as much as 10, 20, 30 or 40 degrees. Making dozens of quick banking maneuvers, he can traverse the flat Kansas landscape without an engine, without circling, in more or less a straight line, by bouncing off little bursts of microlift. Flights, which last up to five hours, are as much a function of his bladder capacity as anything else. And when he wants to come down, all he needs is a little patch of level ground and the plane rolls to a stop in as little as 21 feet. It is the closest anyone has yet gotten to realizing man's age-old dream of flying like a bird—slowly and silently, on full intuition, making a partnership with the atmosphere instead of breaking it to your will. It is a mental state so different from that of rational, linear-thinking, competition flying that when Osoba lands, he sometimes finds it hard to drive a car afterward; among other things, he says, he doesn't want to stay on the road.

THIRTY-SIX

Saving the World
10 Percent at a Time

ONCE WHEN I MET PAUL MACCREADY for breakfast at the Atheneum Club at Caltech, he drew a horizontal line in my notebook. This was to represent human intelligence over time. Then, at the point on the curve representing the development of the computer in the mid-twentieth century, he drew a rapidly ascending, near-vertical curve representing silicon processing power. Given the divergence of these curves, he then asked, "Which do you think will be the dominant form of intelligence in two hundred years?"

For someone who is always so congenitally optimistic about his own projects—"I always think my ideas have potential global significance and then revise my estimate downwards as reality intrudes," he says—MacCready tends to be surprisingly pessimistic about the prospects of mankind. The "most important statement of the twentieth century," he once observed, was made by Hal, the IBM 9000 computer in *2001: A Space Odyssey*, when it told the astronaut who wanted to come back inside, "I'm sorry, Dave. I'm afraid I can't do that."

It wasn't only the exponential growth in computer intelligence that worried MacCready. It was the fact that human intelligence, or what passed for it in some people, was in such a sorry state that in order to get elected, politicians had to pander to the public's belief that they had a right to cheap energy. Given the inability of most people to think critically, says MacCready, "a charismatic president intent on war could probably get most of the country behind him in three TV appearances." As the world's only superpower, the United States had in its hands the capacity to decide whether or not civilization survived, and yet 30 percent of the people who picked this country's leaders believed in astrology; 25 percent believed the government had little green men in a freezer on an Air Force base; 30 percent thought it was hotter in the summer because the earth was closer to the sun; and, due to the enduring but dismaying strength of "antiscientific creationist thinking," half the country's population believed that God created the earth six thousand years ago.

In former times, MacCready thought, religion had a purpose: to promote cohesion and keep the tribe together. It satisfied people's needs for "authority, ritual, belonging, tradition, mystery, a forum for thinking about the meaning of life and appreciating life's gifts." But because religion grew out of a much simpler past, it also left people with too narrow a perspective for dealing with what MacCready regarded as the central fact of our existence in the universe—that we were "a magnificent random experiment with no goal." The universe wasn't put here for our benefit and there was no supreme being looking out for us. Human life, and indeed all life, was a wonderful accident, a glorious but meaningless "clumping of particles in our solar system."

Ernest Hemingway once compared life to a baseball game in which they "threw you in and told you the rules and the first time they caught you off base they killed you." And MacCready, it seemed, couldn't agree more. Due to ever-more-powerful technology, exploding population and vanishing resources, MacCready said at a 1991 Caltech future symposium, "the next fifty years are likely to be a new ball game played with rules not yet firmed up, with players not identified and with winning not even defined." If civilization was to survive, humans had to come to grips with their mental failings, blinders, filters and a deep-seated irrationality from their evolutionary heritage; "there is no second chance."

Ten thousand years ago, MacCready often reminds audiences, man and his livestock and pets made up 0.1 percent of the vertebrate mass on the planet. Today, man and his animals make up 97 percent of the vertebrate mass. Man's mind gives him such a huge advantage over the other animals that he has become the modern equivalent to the meteor that killed the dinosaurs. He has wiped out all the "easily obtainable fossil fuels," depleted the rainforest and put so much population pressure on the planet that "250 species of flora and fauna become extinct every day."

Ever since man first appeared on the planet, he has been at war with nature. Now, says MacCready, the war is over and man has won. A quarter-million people are born every day and, given the appalling state of public education, many of them will spend their lives in ignorance and superstition, buying clothes, eating food and watching television. But they won't contribute very much and they won't know how to think. "Things will be quite bleak in forty years," MacCready said in 1990, echoing an equally pessimistic Paul Ehrlich theme of twenty years earlier. And the long-range prospects are far worse. "I estimate the chances of my grandchildren surviving to be my age are about 50–50," MacCready told *California* magazine in 1986. "Man could be finished before the end of the century." Man's accelerating technology, he said, had made us like "three-year-olds with hand grenades." There was no doubt the times were exciting; "but so is a balloon before it pops."

MacCready hadn't started out to be a social critic or a scientific philosopher. His primary concern when he first got his Ph.D. was researching cloud physics and making rain without being sued. But once he won the Kremer Prize, he wasn't just an obscure researcher/rainmaker/environmental consultant anymore. Suddenly fame was thrust upon him. He was asked to give hundreds of speeches following the winning of the £50,000 Kremer Prize for human-powered flight, and everywhere he went, people asked him the same question: how was it that his team won the prize when hundreds of other people, some of whom were quite talented, had tried for eighteen years and failed?

The reason, MacCready knew, wasn't that all the other teams were lacking technical know-how. If anything, the British experts knew more and "got better marks in their engineering classes." Besides, it wasn't as if the plane were all that complicated. "Using linear thinking and the laws of aerodynamics, any aeronautical engineer can figure out the man-powered airplane in three steps and one minute." The reason prior attempts had failed was because everyone involved had taken the exact approach that everyone before them had; they just tried to do it better, an approach MacCready called "digging the same hole deeper."

MacCready, on the other hand, maintains that he wasn't handicapped by expertise because he *had* no expertise in aircraft design. As a result, the "self-organizing" aspect of his mind didn't have the kind of mental blinders that would cause it to dismiss out of hand the simple design that eventually won the prize—"6 sticks and 72 wires."

©2002 PETER MENZEL

"As I look back, boy am I glad I wasn't a football hero type. Now I'd be an over-age football jock. Small, uncoordinated, shy—thank goodness I had that."

MacCready attributed at least some of his success at "out-of-the-box" thinking to an English creativity expert professor named Edward DeBono, an originator of a technique called "lateral thinking." As MacCready explained lateral thinking, when you can't get anywhere attacking a problem head on, you stop the frontal attack and approach the problem from a new direction.

As an example, MacCready told Kenneth Brown in *Inventors at Work*, imagine that you need to move a sofa out of a room, but the door is too small and your only helper is a small child. Under lateral thinking, you abandon the direct-assault approach, and instead pick a word at random. It doesn't matter what the word is; it could be absurd and have no connection to the problem at hand—say, "xylophone." But when you meditate on "xylophone" for a while, MacCready said, pretty soon you find yourself thinking about keys and rails and sticks, and all of a sudden you realize you're looking at the problem from directions you never would have imagined before. You still might not solve it—not all problems have solutions; but at least you are no longer in the same old rut, trying the same thing over and over, except harder.

After MacCready told me about DeBono I immediately checked out some of his books and audiotapes from the local library. I must say they never struck me as powerfully as they apparently did MacCready. It seemed to me that DeBono was saying some rather obvious things and holding them out as major insights. Later, Bert Pearlman, an educator on creativity who once worked with MacCready on education issues, did come up with one DeBono insight that was actually rather clever (perhaps too clever). There was a London property management firm, said Pearlman, which was losing major tenants because the elevators in one of its skyscrapers were too slow. The linear solution in such a case would have been to rip out the slow elevators and replace them with faster ones. But that was expensive and would take a lot of time. DeBono's lateral-thinking solution was to line the lobby walls with mirrors. That way, people could look at themselves and each other while waiting for the elevators and, as a result, those formerly long waits now seemed a lot shorter.

Perhaps because MacCready himself is not a dominant figure in personal encounters, one of his insights does strike me as precisely right: There are many people in the world who are very bright and articulate and "great at winning the debate," yet lousy at solving the problem. And the reason is that as soon as people start defending their positions, they quit being open to new ideas. The schools don't help. They put an unwarranted premium on raw intelligence, not because that is what children need to succeed in life but because that is what they need to get good grades in school. But even if one's IQ is in the top one percent, says MacCready, that means there could still be "60 million people on earth brighter than you."

Besides, he argues, pure intelligence is no guarantee of success. Bright people who slide through school without having to push themselves never develop the discipline to overcome life's problems. Not only is a high IQ a poor predictor of success in life, it is sometimes an outright disadvantage, given the difficulties the superbright have in finding peers, establishing relationships and coping with depression and suicide. "I read an article in *Esquire,*" MacCready recently told a group of sailplane builders. "The smartest man in America is a bouncer in a nightclub."

In the long run, says MacCready, the important thing is getting the job done, not how you do it. "If you get it done by some great intuitive leap that is typically called creativity, that's fine. But who cares if you get it done that way?" If you had to grind it out through sheer drudgery, there was nothing wrong with that. If you got it done by calling a "friend in Tampa" who knew how to do it, that was fine too.

Recently MacCready was inducted into an organization that every year invited about thirty or forty famous and accomplished people—Wayne Gretzky, Barbra Streisand, a Noble Prize winner, the Librarian of Congress—to spend three days interacting with four hundred high school valedictorians. The students got to have lunch with Whoopi Goldberg or hang out with the chairman of the Joint Chiefs of Staff. But the interesting thing to MacCready was that when the newly inducted adults gave talks about how they created a $3 billion business, ran an airline or created some great work of art, it turned out that "over half of them did poorly in school, not because they were bored but because they just couldn't do well in school."

In many ways, educators are like generals in that they are always fighting the last war, but nowadays, argues MacCready, the world is changing too fast. "Whatever you were trained in, it's the wrong field twenty years from now." What the schools should be teaching is not what is needed to succeed in school, but what is needed to succeed in life: "motivation, breadth, rationality, questioning, creativity, problem solving, critical thinking, seeing various sides, avoiding gullibility, considering consequences and goals, personal interaction, integrity, respect, empathy, optimism, excitement, enjoyment, even edging toward wisdom—in other words, effectiveness, passion and satisfaction in life."

When MacCready was on the board of directors of the National Educational Corporation he asked the board to put a course in thinking skills into the curriculum. "I couldn't make the slightest impact," says MacCready. "There is no public demand for thinking. There is only a public demand for learning."

Jack Lambie would later say that MacCready was "nuts" to crusade for thinking skills—"He's not charismatic that way."

BECAUSE MACCREADY HAS WON numerous awards, prizes and honorary degrees over the years, people tend to assume, he notes, that he's both super-creative and superbright. Actually, he maintains, when it comes to his own abilities there's "a lot less than meets the eye." His big advantage, he recently told a group of college students, was being lucky enough to have been born a dyslexic, which freed him from what he calls the "grunt work" of being concerned with details. "Thank God there are people with great memories who remember lots of details," he said. "Of course they will be replaced by computers in a little while," just as people who were good at adding long rows of numbers were replaced by adding machines.

It isn't that dyslexics don't have their problems. MacCready, for one, is "lousy at names and faces." On the other hand, he never gets hung up on details, a trait which allows him to see connections and relationships, synthesize ideas and keep the big picture in mind. It was this ability to see connections, said MacCready, that enabled him to succeed with the Gossamer Condor when so many others failed. His mind, he said, was like a smooth, sandy beach where no running rivulets have left channels to confine his thinking to traditional paths.

In fact, says Ray Morgan, after working for MacCready for two decades it was clear to him that MacCready has just as many prejudices as everyone else. "His are just different. If you look at [Morton Grosser's book] *The Gossamer Odyssey,* there are pictures of the [big wire-braced] indoor flying models he used to fly as a kid and, if you blow them up, they are [similar to] the original design of the Gossamer Condor, his first human-powered plane." In the 1970s, MacCready was introduced to huge wire-braced hang gliders, and then "all he did was combine the two."

This is not to say that MacCready isn't exceptionally bright or creative, says Morgan.

But as for coming up with new ideas, I don't see him as any different from anyone else who has worked there at AeroVironment. Maybe he's 10 or 20 percent different. But he's not ten times better than anyone else. He tinkers and pursues things, some of which turn into big things for the company. To be honest, some of the airplanes he's won prizes with he's never seen until they were finished. The Pathfinder he saw fly on videotape for the first time in 1993 and we'd flown it ten years before that. He hadn't been involved in it at all. But as chairman of the company he gets credit [because] it happened on his watch.

Not that there's anything wrong with that. Leonardo da Vinci didn't personally do everything he's credited with either, points out Morgan. "Most great scientists are the same way. They get the credit because they own the shop."

THIRTY-SEVEN

Doctoral Thesis Immortality

A**FTER MACCREADY BECAME FAMOUS** for human-powered flight he increasingly found himself having to address two issues: why did he build such aircraft and what good were they?

As to the matter of building the Gossamer Condor, MacCready has always replied the same way: he was $100,000 in debt and he needed the Kremer Prize money to repay the bank. As for the utility of his famous aircraft, that was harder to explain. It certainly wasn't a practical machine. Only superathletes had the strength to pedal one for more than a few minutes, and even to do that, one still needed a hangar, a ground crew and a willingness to get up at 3 A.M. to fly in the still air of dawn. Finally, they were infamously fragile (an MIT-built plane, the Daedalus, flew 74 miles from Crete to the island of Santorini in 1988, only to snap in two in sharp turbulence 30 feet from shore).

This wasn't to say that such aircraft weren't worth building. According to James Burke, the Jet Propulsion Lab official who worked with MacCready on the Condor and the Albatross, the best projects are always those "for which it is hard to articulate a justification." And as MacCready himself was fond of pointing out, Charles Lindbergh, when he flew from New York to Paris, did not discover any new territory, build a better airplane or establish any new principles of aerodynamics. He did something much more important: he raised man's horizons. In the same fashion, says MacCready, the justification for human-powered aircraft is that they nourish "the spirit, not the stomach."

I once asked MacCready what, if anything, his name would be remembered for, and he replied that he wasn't sure his name would be remembered at all. "Any person's existence is like a stone dropped in a lake and the ripples go out in all directions."

His modesty notwithstanding, it's clear that MacCready's work has had major, if indirect, effects. The Gossamer Condor led to the Gossamer Albatross, which led to the Solar Challenger, which led to the Sunraycer, which in turn led to GM's abortive electric-powered car, the EV1. And although that car had too short a range and too high a cost to have any direct impact, GM's mere decision to build such a car led the California Air Resources Board to adopt zero-emission standards, which, says MacCready, advanced the schedule for alternative fuel vehicles "by ten years." In the meantime, it helped inspire superefficient hybrid cars like the Toyota Prius and the Honda EV Plus.

In winning the first World Solar Challenge so convincingly, Mac-Cready's Sunraycer led Australian adventurer-turned-environmentalist Hans Tholstrup to institutionalize the World Solar Challenge and General Motors to help sponsor an American version. As a result, engineering schools all across the country regularly participate in an American solar challenge race in which they learn to meet deadlines, raise money, deal with legal issues and safety concerns and, perhaps most importantly of all, work together. "Car companies have learned it isn't even worth their time interviewing people coming out of universities who haven't had this experience making hybrid cars or solar cars or things like that," MacCready recently said. "The ones who do it turn out to be good employees."

Partly for reasons such as these, says MacCready, accreditation agencies for engineering schools have changed their grading criteria to focus on the capabilities and characteristics that are desirable in graduating students, such as problem solving, working with people, communicating effectively, understanding global issues, voting rationally and running a good family. "It's been a complete change, and very much related to this hands-on stuff that gives people the abilities that count as opposed to getting A's in their computer courses but not being able to think."

MacCready often notes in speeches that he spends 10 percent of his time "trying to save the world." Once such effort was a two-week summer program that he taught in 2000 at Occidental College in Los Angeles for a small group of very bright youngsters from all over the country. In Mac-Cready's view, life was far harder for the superbright than most people ever imagined. "The kids are so gifted they should be in graduate school, not the eighth grade." Under the aegis of the Pasadena-based Institute for Educational

Advancement, MacCready's program not only sought to give these students a chance to bond with their peers, it tried to teach them about nature, creativity, aerodynamics, electronics, birds and model planes—in short, everything that MacCready had been fascinated with all his life.

As a way of understanding the interface between nature and technology, MacCready took the students out to Simi Valley to watch a flock of vultures leave their roosts each morning to soar on rising thermals. In hopes of inoculating the kids against the world's Uri Gellers and their spoon-bending performances, he took the group to Hollywood's Magic Castle where they would see, he hoped, that "psychic powers" were nothing but distraction, tricks and sleight of hand. To help them experience the joy of being in touch with nature, he took them all for sailplane rides and helped them build model planes equipped with TV cameras that could soar with the birds while they sent images back to the ground.

In the process the students had to face many of the problems that engineers face in the real world: models that land in trees or are carried away by thermals; critical parts that don't arrive on time; wiring that doesn't work and lenses that don't fit. "It was a very demanding project," said MacCready. "They spent two weeks on flight skills, wiring, building. And they are to take it back with them and continue on and try to infect some of their friends and where it will all lead I don't know."

Bert Pearlman—a former administrator with the Institute for Educational Advancement who worked with MacCready on the summer education project and is currently in the Peace Corps teaching creativity to teachers in the Ukraine—told me that MacCready's summer program may lead more places than MacCready ever realized.

> He's an enormously courageous man and I don't just mean physical things. He's courageous about ideas. That is a very special kind of courage. He stands up under criticism. MacCready holds on to ideas and he pulls them off. And he does it, not by luck, not by political charisma and not by being a Daddy Warbucks, but by the strength of his ideas. The first time I heard him speak in public I was afraid the audience wouldn't appreciate who he is and what he's done. He doesn't make your blood race or your heart pound. He engages your mind.

But Pearlman need not have worried. Within a few sentences, he said, everyone realized they were in the presence of a "gifted visionary."

As for MacCready's students, says Pearlman, "he focused them, taught them, and gave them a powerful guidance system for their flight through life. When they are in their thirties, forties and fifties they're going to realize they were touched by a gift. His name will live on in doctoral theses forever."

THIRTY-EIGHT

Exploding Biomimicry

ALTHOUGH NATURE HAS BEEN SOLVING engineering problems for the last 4 billion years, often in ingenious and efficient ways, until recently most engineers paid scant attention to natural solutions. One reason: almost none of the country's three hundred engineering programs ever required students to take a single class in the biological sciences. But in the last decade, a lot has changed. With powerful new instruments and an explosion in biological knowledge, engineers are studying things they previously would never have thought of—the propulsion system of worms, the swimming techniques of tuna, the walking patterns of cockroaches, geckos and lobsters, the construction of abalone shells, the structure of rat teeth, and the flying methods of insects and birds.

For many engineers this new field—called biomimicry, for imitation of life—is terrifically exciting. For MacCready, it's what he's been doing his entire life. When he began to fly sailplanes, he studied hawks and vultures, first using them to spot thermals and then trying to extract the secrets of their flight. It was his simultaneous study of the lift coefficients and power expenditure of soaring birds and hang gliders that gave him the insight to build a human-powered plane. He won the Kremer Prize using wing warping and a tilting canard—the same things, he likes to say, that birds have been doing with their tail feathers for 50 million years. Before building a flying pterodactyl his team went down to the *Queen Mary* to watch birds in the lee vortex, how they yaw and pop their wingtip feathers in flight. When MacCready talked about "mother nature, the engineer," he meant it quite literally. Once on a trip to Kenya he found a vulture feather and when he returned he gave a talk in "hushed tones" about its ingenious solutions to unsteady state aerodynamics, rectangular-cross-section spar, variable camber and "Velcro" hooks for maintaining the airfoil. "If you tried to do a research study on this feather, it would literally be a million-dollar project," MacCready told a Caltech audience. "It would take a good Ph.D. thesis just to understand the aerodynamics."

Man has made a lot of progress in aerodynamics in recent decades, but nature's been working at the same task for 100 million years. "Through evolution birds have achieved solutions to fluid mechanics questions that we haven't even asked yet," says MacCready. And they do many things that engineers and pilots have managed to do, but only in recent decades and with great effort—flying above 30,000 feet, staying aloft for days at a time, refueling in midair, hovering, flying in formation, staging dogfights, doing somersaults and slow rolls, spiraling up in thermals and flopping down like old rags.

With global positioning satellites a pilot can now accurately determine his place anywhere on the planet, but for eons migrating birds have been flying thousands of miles to specific destinations using the sun and stars, sky polarization and magnetic fields. "A homing bird can be taken away from its home in a black box, released and will come back to where it started," says MacCready. A monarch butterfly, hatched in the United States and three generations removed from an ancestor that migrated from Mexico, carries enough genetic information in its "tiny" brain to find its way back to its winter quarters in a specific tree in Mexico.

MacCready has looked to the birds since he first began flying sailplanes. And even after six decades he still hasn't given up on the old dream of building a small, slow, silent, low-powered plane that would enable him to circle with hawks in thermals, fly "low over a lake shore," "operate like a bird, land in a tiny space, drift along a river and go between houses."

THIRTY-NINE

Why Blind People Don't Sky Dive

T HE TWO DECADES FROM THE MID-SEVENTIES to the mid-nineties were a
Golden Age for Paul MacCready. Whimsical, cutting-edge, icon-like aircraft and vehicles, all of which did far more with less than anyone thought
possible, were coming out of his workshops every few years, winning prizes,
garnering him (and his project associates) worldwide publicity, not to mention awards, medals and honorary degrees. But as MacCready's role in the
projects changed over the years from all-MacCready-all-the-time to "the lead
guy who was pulling everything together" to someone who wasn't even "the
chief protagonist" anymore, many of the people who had worked on, con-
tributed to, paved the way or even run MacCready's projects drifted away
to pursue their individual destinies.

In 2000, after more than twenty intense years at AeroVironment, Ray
Morgan left the company to do consulting and write a book on management. He was tired, he said, of reporting to other people, and wanted to be
in charge before he was too old to change careers. He'd spent thirty years in
aerospace, the first ten of which he was "terrified" that he wouldn't remember how to use the Bessel Function to solve a differential equation. It was
only after he had proved himself as an engineer that it dawned on him that
such deep attention to detail was not only not needed, but downright coun-
terproductive. It was knowing how to plan and estimate that made or broke
companies, not academic brilliance. Although brains and creativity never
hurt, they were also overrated. When he speaks at schools, says Morgan,
teachers often ask him what, if anything, he would change about education.
"I say: Well, number one, I would make every test open-book and I would

encourage people to cooperate because that is the way the real world works. The hardest thing for people to learn in the real world is to work together." That was also why, as a manager, he was opposed to employee evaluations. Not only were they highly subjective, they were invariably divisive. Only a few people got top grades and everyone else went away with their feelings hurt.

The other thing he used to tell his engineers, says Morgan, was "never integrate an equation, never differentiate data and never subtract two big numbers to get a small one."

Why?

A small difference in two big numbers is meaningless, he says. "It's like weighing the cat by holding it in your arms and standing on a scale. You find out the cat weighs nothing."

Bob Boucher, who always felt underemployed when he made model airplane motors, found a more fitting outlet for his formidable gifts during the early nineties, which he spent battling Willie Brown and the California legislature over what he felt were desperately needed changes to the workman's compensation laws. He suddenly became interested in the subject when a former employee filed a workman's compensation claim against him. "Mental stress," says Boucher. "Everyone is having mental stress. I had four people with mental stress. It cost me $300,000."

In response, Boucher closed his plant and went to Sacramento to complain to Governor Pete Wilson, testify before committees, leaflet members of the state assembly and, along with members of the a workman's compensation reform organization, picket Willie Brown's birthday party at Beverly Wilshire Hotel.

We thought we would get some coverage on one of the television stations. Nothing, not on TV, not in the newspaper, not a word about us anywhere. They weren't going to say a word against Willie. That's how it works.

This went on for six months. Finally I said at one of the meetings [of the California Small Manufacturers Association], "We aren't going to get anywhere this way. We need to get up a million dollars and give it to Willie. That's the only thing that's going to work."

Somebody said, "He's against us."

I said, "Bullshit, the guy who gives him the most is his friend. The lawyers always give him more."

So the group decided to have a "Willie for the Assembly" fundraising luncheon at the Burbank Hilton for five hundred people, at $500 a plate. The ballroom was full, Boucher recalls. "Willie said, 'I'm glad I'm here. I'm glad you people finally understand politics. From now on your voice will be heard.' He took the money and left. But he changed the law."

After leaving General Motors' ill-fated battery-powered electric car project, Alan Cocconi took off a couple of months to calm his mind and ride his bicycle. But pretty soon he was wondering what could be done with electric cars if one could be built with no compromises. Pulling $250,000 out of his savings, he started a company called AC Propulsion and began mounting home-built AC power trains in converted Honda Civics. His 120 hp Honda CR-X could do 0 to 60 in 9 seconds. The 150 hp model could do it in 6.2 seconds and it set a distance record of 146 miles on a single charge, far better than the GM EV1 was able to do years later. In 1997, with the aid of Alec Brooks, who had left AeroVironment to join him, he designed and built the "tZero," a high-performance battery-powered sports car capable of 0 to 60 in 4.9 seconds.

Although the tZero was a dramatic demonstration of what cutting-edge electric power could do, it didn't pay the bills. To support themselves, they built 200 hp electric vehicle power trains for public agencies or corporations that wanted to promote an environmentally progressive image. "The company is profitable," says Cocconi, "if we don't pay ourselves too much."

More recently AC Propulsion has gotten a contract to use Internet-controlled electric vehicles as power regulators for what Cocconi calls the "second-to-second fluctuations that happen in any power grid." Rather than fire up or turn off big generators, the power companies can, through Internet control, store or withdraw power from hundreds of thousands of electric cars, thus keeping the grid's frequency and voltage stable. When blackouts occur, electric vehicles can serve as emergency power supplies.

After leaving AeroVironment in 1980, Peter Lissaman, who designed the airfoil for the Gossamer Condor, Gossamer Albatross and Solar Challenger, returned to teaching at the University of Southern California and at the Art Center College of Design in Pasadena. In the summer of 2000 he traveled to Italy to visit Vinci, birthplace of Leonardo da Vinci. When he returned he wrote a comedic screenplay about Leonardo da Vinci, an early flying machine and the Mona Lisa. He's currently teaching design and composite materials at USC, consulting for the aerospace industry and doing development work on flying disks (Frisbees).

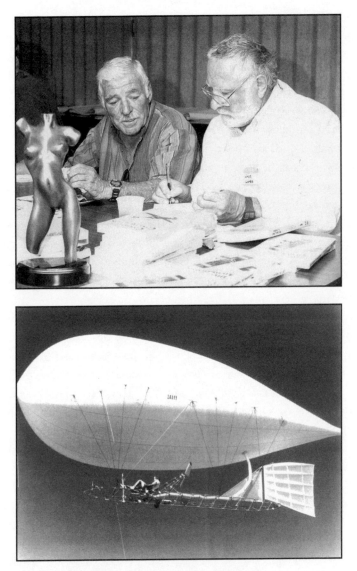

Top, Jack Lambie signing books while his brother Bill looks on.
Above, Pedaling the White Dwarf was so smooth and effortless it was "like walking up invisible stairs."

Taras Kiceniuk, who had been the project engineer on the Gossamer Albatross, overseeing construction and supervising flight testing, was asked by MacCready to be a part of the Solar Challenger project, but, he says, he asked for more than MacCready wanted to pay. "I had too much money in my pocket at the time," says Kiceniuk. Later Kiceniuk started his own firm, Icarus Engineering. He has also worked on some cutting-edge scientific projects: the earth-flip hypothesis, dynamic soaring, and more recently, the possibility of building a rotating space-based interferometer with a long baseline that would allow astronomers to see physical images of planets in other star systems. At the same time, he's a consultant to some of MacCready's longer-range projects, such as mechanically assisted leg struts ("Technalegs"), battery-assisted bikes, and walking canes with attached foot stirrups (as a replacement for crutches).

After the Sunraycer project, Bill Watson went into the toy design business. To force himself to think outside the box, he wrote a computer program to combine words randomly from three lists and generate a catalogue of possible toys—blinking fuzzy shoes, bubbling plastic yo-yos, hopping paper pencils. Watson had four people in his shop working on toys for two years, but took too long to get up to speed. It didn't pay as much as project engineering, and, he says, "I was ripped off by an agent."

In 1984, Watson built the "White Dwarf," a 47-foot pedal-powered blimp for Gallagher, the comedian, who at the time, says Watson, was in dire need of a tax write-off. To reassure the insurance company, Watson gave the balloon a Jules Verne sort of look and made the propeller out of Styrofoam. Gallagher wore two seat belts and Watson kept the blimp on a tether at all times. When Watson flew it out in Palm Springs he found it closer to his vision of pure flight than anything he'd ever tried before.

Whereas flying Taras Kiceniuk's ground-effect machine had been like "pedaling a hydrofoil" and flying the Gossamer Condor had been like pedaling a "big shaky bag," pedaling the White Dwarf was quiet, effortless, dreamy, "like walking up invisible stairs." Watson would pedal over to a house, stop twenty feet away, bump into a tree, look at a bird, back up and pedal somewhere else. Motorists would pull over and get out of their cars, and Watson would fly over and talk to them. Because the White Dwarf was so readily visible from the ground, when he flew near residential areas dozens of dogs would be barking at it in any moment. Of course, there wasn't a big market for such a plane and it was expensive to keep it filled with helium. Currently, Watson supports himself by building radio-controlled models for the film industry and one-of-a-kind working prototypes for aerospace.

After such great success flying the Gossamer Condor, the Gossamer Albatross and the Bionic Bat—a plane built for a triangular-course Kremer Prize—Bryan Allen tried out for one of the pilot slots on the MIT Daedalus project to fly 76 miles across the ocean from Crete to Santorini. But the team leaders were trying to create a completely egalitarian pool of pilots and were afraid, he says, that his "notoriety" from the previous ventures would upset team unity. Allen later joined the Jet Propulsion Laboratory, where he maintains the Unix system for the Mars Lander program. On weekends he paddles around southern California waters in a sea kayak.

After the end of the Solar Challenger project, Janice Brown returned to teaching and Steve Ptacek went on to become a United Airlines Airbus captain, flying out of Denver.

HANG-GLIDING PIONEER RICHARD MILLER spent the thirty years following the Otto Lilienthal Meet in what he calls "one of the great intellectual adventures of his life." In 1972, having previously committed himself to "Sadhana"—the renunciation of self-indulgence and acceptance of austerity as a way of life—he was living in a small wooden barracks in Vista, California, enjoying a redemptive love affair with an artist named Miriam who played viola in a string quartet and kept her diary in Greek. One winter morning, Miller and Miriam visited the beach at Oceanside at a time when the wind was blowing over the dunes and the seagulls were soaring, and out of the blue Miriam said, "You should investigate the way the air flows around a gull's wing."

Because Miriam had no scientific inclinations at all, it seemed to Miller that for her to make such a comment she had to be acting as "a pure channel." That night, he was lying on the bed reading when a light flashed in his head and a loud, clear, "suprahuman" voice spoke to him. "When Miriam spoke to you this morning it was on our behalf," it said in a totally assured tone. "If you follow through with this project you will be richly rewarded." In two minutes, Miller had a tablet and a pencil in his hand and thus began "a grand intellectual adventure" which he has pursued with "persistence and industry" for nearly three decades. His mission: to investigate the mechanism by which an airplane's wings produce lift.

Miller had long known that many aerodynamicists and engineers regarded the explanations given for lift in basic aeronautical or physics texts as clearly wrong. Setting out to do something about it, he began with first principles, going back to the "great unknown, unheralded, unread, unacknowledged" second book of Isaac Newton's *Principia Mathematica,* which deals with fluid mechanics.

Because scientists either never knew about or avoided the "bastard child" that was Newton's *Book II,* says Miller, they treated air molecules impinging on an inclined plane as if they were billiard balls obliquely banking off the side of a billiard table. In the process, they totally ignored the field effect, Miller maintains.

> The initial framing of the house of physics was a one-story building dominated by Newtonian mechanics. In 1819 Faraday and Maxwell introduced the concept of the field. The field was the second floor. Einstein went up to the second floor, looked around and liked what he saw. Einstein said, "The field is the most important concept to come around in years." But when Einstein closed up shop, no one else went up there anymore.

Despite his best efforts, according to Miller, they still haven't. He worked on lift for thirty years, and in all that time he never succeeded in changing "the mentality of a single individual, credentialed or not, away from the Newtonian-mechanical concept of lift."

And with good reason, says Peter Lissaman. Among aerodynamicists, "there is not the slightest debate about it." (The subject of lift has been fully and completely understood "since 1918," notes MacCready.)

Miller first met Paul MacCready when they were both teenage model builders. During the next sixty years, he says, he has tracked their parallel lives with a kind of "amused attitude" when things were good and "bitterness and depression and fatigue and penury" when they were not. Year after year he waited for the spiritual rewards of the austere life, and year after year nothing changed. "There were times when I was convinced, by singular concatenations of events, that the day and the hour were at hand, got up on tippy toes waiting to be kissed, got the rug pulled out from under me. Back to the grind. Same old shit. No good deed goes unpunished. *Thou shalt not operate at a higher frequency than the one assigned to you.*" At age seventy-seven and still in his VW van, his only consolation, he says, is that he's been at "bottom dead center" so long there's nowhere to go but up.

JACK LAMBIE'S CAREER WENT DOWNHILL after Gossamer Condor and Gossamer Albatross. Karen, his fourth wife, was tired of the swinging life. Even so, she says, leaving Jack was the hardest thing she'd ever done. When she broke up with him, he sat in the middle of their living room floor, holding his socks while tears ran down his face.

He had written several technical books on aviation, but sales were meager. In hopes of improving his writing skills, he ordered books on making fictional dialogue come alive. In the meantime he supported himself by making marble sculptures of naked women. He'd go to a swingers' convention and talk a couple into buying a sculpture of the woman's torso.

As someone who presented himself as being thirty-nine well into his fifties, Lambie didn't grow old gracefully. He had badly damaged his knee in a bike accident in Australia (he always claimed he'd hit a kangaroo), which caused him to walk with a rolling gait. Years of drinking beer and eating cashews had given him an alarming pot belly. Whereas he used to be able to have any woman he wanted, now even older women were turning him down.

In 1997, at the twentieth reunion of the winning of the Kremer Prize at Sam Duran's home in Bakersfield, Lambie showed up with what Bryan Allen describes as his "kinda weird and scary" younger brother, Bill, and some "not necessarily tasteful metal sculptures of nude females." Lambie astounded Allen by telling him that his new goal was just to make it through the next ten or fifteen years, by which time, he said, science would have conquered death. "Other people were saying, 'What are you talking about?'" recalls Allen. "And Jack was saying, 'I want to live to be a thousand years old.' He was quite outspoken about it."

Lambie's death stunned everyone who knew him. At the time, he and Bill had been living in a couple of small houses near Morongo, a lightly populated, high desert area northwest of Palm Springs. He had planned to do his sculpture in the back yard, but the fierce winds blowing through the San Gorgonio Pass made it difficult to work. In addition, he and Bill, a hard-drinking former ship captain, didn't really get along, given their dramatically different personalities. If Bill needed more power out to a remote location, he'd run Romex, put up a board and install circuit breakers, whereas Jack would just throw an extension cord on the ground. As time passed, drinking and desert living began to take its toll on Bill. Repeated burglaries made him paranoid. He patrolled the fence line with a loaded gun.

In June of 1999, Jack came back from a weekend trip with a side panel missing from a small trailer they kept around the compound. Although Jack was not someone who easily lost his temper—"I never heard him raise his voice," says Charlie Webber, an old friend of both brothers since Jack's Flabob Airport days—an argument started when Bill called Jack a "mechanical moron." It escalated when Jack discovered that Martha, his housekeeper and friend, had spent the weekend with Bill, drinking and watching auto races on TV.

What happened after that, the police never determined with any certainty. The only two witnesses were Bill, whose story "changed every few minutes," complained San Bernardino County deputy district attorney Camelia Mesrobian, and Martha, who was so drunk and distraught, Bill's attorney would later say, that she sat on the porch "babbling."

According to William Sasnett, the Joshua Tree attorney who represented Bill at his murder trial, when Jack refused to leave the house, Bill took out a 9 mm Makarov semi-automatic pistol, which he kept hidden between the sofa cushions, pointed it at Jack and ordered him to get out.

Jack, who had been a college wrestler and in any case was far bigger than Bill, just laughed at him and took the gun away. What happened then was never clear. Bill claimed he'd been "pistol whipped," but Mesrobian dismissed the notion, saying that Bill's few scratches and bruises were nothing that couldn't be fixed with a little "Neosporin and a Band-Aid." In contrast, she pointed out, Jack had a "skull fracture" and "gushing" head wound where Bill had hit him with a carpenter's level. Dazed and bleeding, Jack had sat down at the table while Martha tried to stop the blood-flow. Bill kept asking "Where's the gun?" and Jack, who was sitting on it, said, "I have the gun. And I might just shoot you with it." In response Bill went into the rear bedroom, loaded a Ruger .22 caliber target pistol, came back and fired one round, hitting Jack squarely between the eyes. Jack was dead before he hit the floor.

Although Bill claimed he had fired in self-defense, the fact that Jack had been sitting on the Makarov (as shown by the gun's imprint in the Naugahyde chair cushion) weighed heavily on the jury, as did the fact that Bill had gone into the rear bedroom to retrieve (and load) a second gun. In the end, the jury convicted Bill of second-degree murder and the judge sentenced him to forty years in prison, where, against all odds, he seemed rather content.

"You know why blind people don't go sky diving?" he recently wrote in a letter to Webber. "It scares the shit out of their dogs."

FORTY

The Johnny Appleseed
of Ornithopters

IN RECENT YEARS, PAUL MACCREADY has attributed at least some of his success to his ability to surmount obstacles, such as those caused by dyslexia. But the one difficulty he has never overcome is finding enough time. Whereas in the heady days following the victories of Gossamer Condor and Albatross he gave a dozen speeches a month or more, he now says he's trying to hold the number down to one. He hears the ticking of the clock. He complains constantly that the need to respond to phone calls, letters and e-mails keeps him from doing what he really wants to do, which is to think, to work, to fill yellow legal pads in his cramped hand, develop new projects, oversee old ones, attend conferences, phone colleagues, network, bring people together, read magazines (as many as five a day, he says) and order books "in batches" from Amazon.com.

In the tradition of Henry Kremer, whose "creativity" prize he so much admired, he has initiated two creativity prizes of his own. The $25,000 Dempsey-MacCready Prize, offered jointly with Santa Ana businessman and racer Ed Dempsey, goes to the first person to travel 90 kilometers in one hour in a human-powered vehicle. The second prize is for the first person to create an animal-powered plane, using any animal from a roach to a goldfish to a dog.

Meanwhile, MacCready is attempting, as he says, to "reinvent the wheel" by creating cars with mechanical legs.

I think I have a way to make a car run on legs perfectly smoothly. It travels over rough terrain or a beach with only a tenth of the power required with a regular car. The reason is it doesn't have rolling friction. Almost a third of the gas you buy, which comes all the way from the Middle East, is squandered in heating your tires. A legged device doesn't have that. You can double the weight of the car and there still is no rolling friction.

MacCready has described another project as an attempt to "do for the human body what the computer does for the mind." Technalegs are a set of ingenious leg, foot and hip braces that lock when your foot is in contact with the ground, thus bearing most of the weight themselves. But when you lift your foot, they unlock, thus allowing you to wriggle your foot around, "kick the dog" or "carry your spouse on your back all day if only she would quit talking."

All his life MacCready has been talking about building a small, quiet, lightweight plane to fly over the fields and streams, drift lightly over houses and soar with the birds. And although that dream has never died, he has meanwhile developed a kind of virtual-reality substitute: a battery-powered model plane with a lightweight TV camera, which enables the plane to fly among birds without frightening them and transmit live in-flight pictures back to the ground. To make the sense of flying more realistic to the operator, the computer also generates a virtual image that gives the operator the feeling of viewing the scene from the back of a hawk or vulture or pterodactyl. The end goal, says MacCready, would be an autonomously flying model sailplane with the ability to soar with birds or even accompany them in actual migrations.

Although MacCready makes far fewer personal appearances than he did in the past, when he does he always talks about the future of the planet, a sustainable population, resource depletion, species extinction, climate modification, thinking skills and the need for balance between nature and technology. His role, he believes, is to show how technology can be used to work with nature, not overpower it. Other than that, there are no limits. "My field is anything I want to get into," he says.

When MacCready makes a public appearance he sometimes brings along a small, super-lightweight, rubber-band-powered, ten-inch flapping-wing ornithopter. They're delightful little four-wing fliers and so unexpectedly full of life and whimsy that birds sometimes follow them down to the grass as if to aid a fallen comrade. For MacCready, the ornithopters are a kind of concrete metaphor for more with less. In the video made of Jack

Lambie's memorial service, there's a shot of MacCready sitting in a chair, holding one of these little thin-film fliers. As the other guests look on in awe and delight, he launches it with a gentle push, whereupon the ornithopter genially flaps up toward the ceiling in half a dozen leisurely circles. Then, having reached the top of its spiral arc, it slowly descends, coming to rest on a coffee table in front of the chair where MacCready confidently waits— as he has ever since he figured out the secret of man-powered flight—with a small, knowing smile.

Acknowledgments

I would like to thank the following people for permission to reprint their photographs or to use quotes from their books or magazine articles.

Paul MacCready for the cover photo, as well as the photographs of him as a boy with a big model, p. 3; the Screamin' Wiener, p. 13; Orlik over the Sierras, p. 27; Breguet with open cockpit, p. 35; Gossamer Albatross over the Channel, p. 111; Solar Challenger over the Channel, p. 137; *Quetzalcoatlus northropi* in flight, p. 151; MacCready with QN head, p. 151; MacCready in front of the Sunraycer, p. 174; MacCready with pusher plane, p. 193.

George Uvegas for the photograph of Richard Miller in the Bamboo Butterfly, p. 49; Jack Lambie in the Hang Loose, p. 64; Richard Miller in the Conduit Condor, p. 64; Jack Lambie with raven, p. 75.

Taras Kiceniuk Jr. for the photograph of him in the Icarus, p. 56.

Joe Mastropaolo for the photo of the Gossamer Condor, p. 97.

NASA Dryden Flight Research Center for the photograph of Janice Brown in the Gossamer Penguin, p. 137; the Helios in flight, p. 187.

Dan Winters for the photo of Alan Cocconi on p. 163.

Alec Brooks for the Sunraycer photograph, p. 174.

Gary Osoba for the photo of the Carbon Dragon in flight, p. 198.

Peter Menzel for the photo of Paul MacCready on p. 205.

Bill Watson for the photo of the White Dwarf on p. 219.

I also want to thank Paul E. Teague for permission to use the opening paragraphs from his copyrighted March 1, 1999, story in *Design News,* "Model Pioneer."

Finally, I want to thank my wife, Holly, for her extraordinary patience over the many months it took me to write this book.

Notes

CHAPTER 1: FROM RODENT-POWERED AIRCRAFT TO STRATOSPHERIC SATELLITES

page

1 One freezing dawn ...: Bob Jones, "Legacy of the Albatross," *Los Angeles Times,* 22 November 1998, p. B1.

1 Gradually it rose ...: Ibid.

1 As the wing passed over ...: Ibid.

2 Once in commercial ...: Author interview with Ray Morgan, May 2000.

2 With the propeller shaft ...: Ibid.

CHAPTER 2: THE MORAL CASE FOR EFFICIENCY

6 As MacCready himself ...: Paul MacCready talk, "Natural and Artificial Flying Machines," California Institute of Technology, Caltech Institute Archives audiotape, 12 January 1985.

6 "Once it gets to ten ...": Paul MacCready talk, Skeptics Society Festschrift in Honor of Stephen Jay Gould, Beckman Auditorium, Caltech, 7 October 2000.

6 A smaller relation ...: Susan Abram, "Albatrosses around the Net," *Los Angeles Times,* 7 May 1998.

6 Even so, harvester ants ...: Author interview with John Lighton, June 2000.

6 As biologist Bernd ...: Bernd Heinrich, *Racing the Antelope* (New York: Cliff Street Books, HarperCollins, 2001), p. 178.

7 On the chase ...: Ibid.

7   "Other things being equal ...": Ibid.

7   When it came to calories ...: Chris Ellison, "Cyclists' Energy Efficiency," Cyber Cyclery, http://cycling.org/lists/eurobike/eurobike-archive-hyper/eurobike.199809/0160.html, 25 September 1998.

7   When the Navajos ...: Heinrich, *Racing the Antelope,* p. 128.

7   It may also be why ...: Paul MacCready, "The Value and Future of Human Powered Vehicles," in *Human Powered Vehicles,* ed. Allan Abbott and David Wilson (Human Kinetics, 1995), p. 266.

8   Einstein wrote his initial ...: Tim Ferris, *Coming of Age in the Milky Way* (New York: Morrow, 1988), p. 189.

8   Quoting the American historian ...: Ibid.

8   "Under existing theory ...": Ibid.

8   "I just wanted to minimize ...": Paul Ciotti, "Revenge of the Nerds," *California,* July 1982, p. 75.

CHAPTER 3: ALPHA MALES AND THE TWILIGHT CLUB

10   He's been called ...: Author interview with Chuck Mahony, 2000.

10   He's a ubiquitous lecturer ...: Santa Barbara Speakers Bureau, http://www.sbsb.net/index.html, January 2001.

10   Still, for someone hailed ...: Phil Patton, "The Esquire Twenty-One," *Esquire,* November 1999, p. 125.

11   Although in his seventies ...: Karen Kaplan, "They've Got Connections," *Los Angeles Times,* 19 October 2000.

11   "In person, Paul MacCready ...": Josh Hammer, "Driven to Extremes," *Los Angeles Times,* 25 October 1987, p. 22.

11   "He's always been ...": Author interview with Henry Jex, June 2000.

11   He has climbed ...: Paul MacCready, "The Excitement and Value of Engineering," The Ralph Coats Roe Lecture, ASME International Mechanical Engineering Congress & Exposition, Anaheim, 19 November 1998.

12   "He's got a new idea ...": Author interview with Chet Kyle, April 2000.

CHAPTER 4: THE CASE AGAINST ELEGANT ENGINEERING

15   "There are thousands ...": Author interview with Paul MacCready, July 2000.

16   He has never suffered ...: Ray Morgan interview, May 2000.

16   There was no level ...: Ibid.

16   "If you're not making ...": Linda Hales, "Movers and Shapers:

Smithsonian Debuts National Design Awards," *Washington Post,*
16 November 2000, p. C1.

CHAPTER 5: FROM KING BLADUD TO THE WRIGHT BROTHERS

17 Bladud, the ninth king . . . : E. Charles Vivian, *A History of Aeronautics,*
Project Gutenberg Etext, http://sailor.gutenberg.org/index/by-
author/vii.html, April 1997.

17 In Rome in A.D. 67 . . . : Ibid.

17 In 1178, the "Saracen . . . " : Ibid.

17 The heart constitutes only . . . : Anthony B. Wright, *Daedalus: The Long
Odyssey from Myth to Reality,* Yale–New Haven Teachers Institute,
http://www.yale.edu/ynhti/curriculum/units/1988/6/88.06.10.x.html,
2001.

17 Furthermore, unlike a sparrow's . . . : Ibid.

18 In Lucca, an artist . . . : Vivian, *A History of Aeronautics.*

18 In 1853, Sir George Cayley . . . : Michael A. Markowski, *The Hang Glider's
Bible* (Blue Ridge Summit, Pennsylvania: Tab Books, 1977), p. 28.

18 Despite his stunning success . . . : Don Dedera, *Hang Gliding: The Flyingest Flying* (Flagstaff, Arizona: Northland Press, 1975), p. 27.

18 Two years later, a French . . . : Vivian, *A History of Aeronautics.*

18 In the 1890s, Otto Lilienthal . . . : Ibid.

18 When the wind . . . : Ibid.

18 Crickets would climb . . . : Tom Crouch, *A Dream of Wings* (Washington, D.C.: Smithsonian Institution Press, 1989), p. 160.

18 Glowing accounts . . . : Jim Wilson, "A Century of Science," *Popular
Mechanics,* January 2000, p. 64.

19 Right from the start . . . : Author interview with Peter Lissaman, June
2000.

19 In the rush . . . : Paul MacCready, Caltech Y. talk, Caltech Archives
audiotape, November 1978.

19 The only attention . . . : Paul MacCready, "Natural and Artificial Flying Machines," audiotape, Caltech Institute Archives, 12 January 1985.

19 The SST's engine exhaust . . . : T. A. Heppenheimer, *Turbulent Skies*
(New York: John Wiley & Sons, 1995), pp. 228–29.

20 Most important perhaps . . . : Ibid., p. 229.

20 As aviation writer T. A. Heppenheimer . . . : Ibid., p. 227.

20 Initial public reaction . . . : Ibid., pp. 227–28.

20 Forty-nine hundred . . . : Ibid., p. 228.

20 Despite anguished cries ...: Ibid., p. 229.

20 In 2000, the big European ...: The Website for the Aerospace Indus-
    try, "Airbus Industrie 380," http://www.aerospace-technology.com/
    projects/a380/index.html, January 2001.

21 In short, an economic ...: Heppenheimer, *Turbulent Skies,* p. 259.

21 But the problem ...: K. W. Kelley in The Home Planet, http://www.
    earth.com/quotes.html, 1988.

23 In a weightless environment ...: Jerome Groopman, "Medicine on
    Mars," *New Yorker,* 14 February 2000, p. 36; AP, "NASA to Study Why
    Heart Shrinks," *Los Vegas Sun,* 30 November 2001.

23 Once astronauts leave ...: Groopman, "Medicine on Mars."

23 If NASA were to follow ...: Ibid.

23 "After World War II ..." : Maralys Wills, *Manbirds* (Englewood Cliffs,
    New Jersey: Prentice-Hall, 1981), pp. 32–42.

24 Where, he asked, was the intense awareness ...: Jack Lambie, "The
    Natural Philosophy of Soaring," *Soaring,* May 1960, p. 10.

CHAPTER 6: BUILDING SELF-CONFIDENCE

25 "I had two sisters ..." : Paul MacCready dyslexia talk, Art Center Col-
    lege of Design, 29 July 2000.

25 "We found one ..." : Ibid.

25 "At puberty ..." : Ibid.

25 He didn't just build ...: Morton Grosser, *Gossamer Odyssey* (New York:
    Dover Publications, 1981), p. 53.

25 He kept flies ...: MacCready dyslexia talk.

26 "My father was ..." : Kenneth A. Brown, *Inventors at Work* (Redmond,
    Washington: Tempus Books, Microsoft Press, 1988).

26 When he was fourteen ..." : Grosser, *Gossamer Odyssey,* p. 54.

26 The following year ...: Ibid., p. 87.

26 As he saw it ...: Brown, *Inventors at Work.*

26 At other times ...: John Hurst and James Pavlick, "Dr. Paul MacCready
    Interview," Academy of Achievement, http://209.146.26.198/ teach-
    ers/icdv2i2s/SITES/ACHIEVE/mainmenu.htm, 1995–1998.

26 "In high school ..." : MacCready dyslexia talk.

28 That first flight ...: Paul MacCready, "Soaring: Addictions and Per-
    spectives," presentation at SAA Soaring Convention in Knoxville, Ten-
    nessee, 27 February 1999, AeroVironment (Monrovia, California).

28 He had thought the farmer ...: Ibid.

29 "I just followed him around ...": Hurst and Pavlick, "Dr. Paul Mac-Cready Interview," 1995–1998.

29 "It looks like ...": Scholer Bangs, "Date with a Cloud," *Interavia,* April 1949, p. 215.

29 As MacCready explained ...: Ibid.

29 This was known ...: Ibid., p. 212.

29 Although Moazagotl clouds ...: Robert Whelan, *Exploring the Monster* (Niceville, Florida: Wind Canyon Books, 2000), pp. 30–38.

30 Symons, a former employee ...: Ibid., p. 34.

30 Once, as he was returning ...: Scholer Bangs, "To the Stratosphere in a Glider," *Saturday Evening Post,* 23 August 1951, p. 94.

30 But if you wanted ...: Bangs, "Date with a Cloud," p. 212.

30 One moment the rotor ...: Whelan, *Exploring the Monster,* p. 47.

30 "Taut" was the word ...: Ibid., p. 60.

31 If he were to take off ...: Bangs, "Date with a Cloud," p. 215.

31 Because darkness would ...: MacCready interview, October 2001.

31 MacCready prepared carefully ...: Bangs, "Date with a Cloud," pp. 213–14.

31 "You feel all alone ...": Bangs, "To the Stratosphere in a Glider," p. 94.

31 It reminded him again ...: MacCready dyslexia talk.

31 "I very quickly ...": Bangs, "Date with a Cloud," p. 214.

31 Although his head ...: Whelan, *Exploring the Monster,* p. 48.

32 MacCready had gone up ...: MacCready, "Soaring: Addictions and Perspectives," p. 4.

32 But that wasn't so much ...: MacCready interview, October 2001.

CHAPTER 7: THE CONTEST AT ST. YAN

33 In 1947, while daydreaming ...: Paul MacCready, "Soaring: Addictions and Perspectives," presentation at SAA Soaring Convention in Knoxville, Tennessee, 27 February 1999, AeroVironment (Monrovia, California), p. 5.

33 The advantage of the speed ...: Ibid., p. 6.

33 MacCready's strategy for winning ...: Paul MacCready, "Flying in the 1956 Internationals," *Soaring,* November/December 1956, p. 2.

34 He almost preferred ...: MacCready, "Soaring: Addictions and Perspectives," p. 3.

34 If that required him ...: MacCready, "Flying in the 1956 Internationals," p. 3.

34   As the afternoon ... : Barney Wiggin, *Soaring,* September/October 1956, p. 9.

34   Finally, nine hours ... : Ibid.

34   The French were so impressed ... : *The National Soaring Museum's Historical Journal,* vol. 16, no. 2 (1994), p. 13.

36   As MacCready described ... : MacCready, "Flying in the 1956 Internationals," p. 5.

36   In the wind shear ... : Ibid.

36   "The first thing ... " : E. Charles Vivian, *A History of Aeronautics,* Project Gutenberg Etext, http://sailor.gutenberg.org/index/by-author/vii.html, April 1997.

37   As he lay dying ... : Michael A. Markowski, *The Hang Glider's Bible* (Blue Ridge Summit, Pennsylvania: Tab Books, 1977), p. 40.

37   Alone in the Haute Alps ... : MacCready, "Flying in the 1956 Internationals," p. 5.

37   Furious for getting ... : Ibid.

37   He was nearly sick ... : Ibid.

37   It was pure luck ... : MacCready, "Soaring: Addictions and Perspectives," p. 7.

37   Life was too short ... : Ibid.

CHAPTER 8: MIDLIFE CRISIS

38   He knew he didn't ... : Mark Wheeler, "Paul MacCready's Flying Circus," *Discover,* 1 September 1999, p. 78.

38   He had no natural ... " : Kenneth A. Brown, *Inventors at Work* (Redmond, Washington: Tempus Books, Microsoft Press, 1988).

38   "When it worked ... " : Wheeler, "Paul MacCready's Flying Circus," p. 78.

38   "The people who paid ... " : Author interview with Henry Jex, June 2000.

38   "You find yourself in the position ... " : MacCready interview, October 2001.

38   MacCready flew Cessna 180s ... : MacCready talk, "Natural and Artificial Flying Machines," audiotape, Caltech Institute Archives, 12 January 1985.

39   "[The sixties] should have been ... " : Morton Grosser, *Gossamer Odyssey* (New York: Dover Publications,1981), p. 62.

39   In 1969 his brother-in-law ... : Ibid., pp. 63–65.

39 The company failed ...: MacCready dyslexia talk, Art Center College of Design, 29 July 2000.

39 His "most important ...": MacCready, "Soaring: Addictions and Perspectives," 27 February 1999, p. 3.

40 During World War II ...: Paul MacCready, "Soaring Bird Aerodynamics," *Groundskimmer,* October 1976, p. 17.

40 Basically, he had discovered ...: Ibid., p. 18.

40 "I thought this ...": Brown, *Inventors at Work.*

40 It was an "elegant" ...: Paul MacCready, "Soaring Bird Aerodynamics," p. 18; Brown, *Inventors at Work.*

40 As he drove through Arizona ...: Grosser, *Gossamer Odyssey,* p. 69.

40 MacCready's oldest son ...: Ibid., p. 67.

40 Charles Darwin had nothing ...: Sy Montgomery, "Heavenly Scavengers," *Animals,* March 2000, p. 26.

41 Unlike European vultures ...: Bill Kohlmoos, "Turkey Buzzard Page," First State Bank, Canisteo, New York, http://www.fsbcanisteo.com/turkey_buzzard_page.htm, 2000.

41 They have such a keen ...: Barbara Samuelson, "Turkey Vulture," http://barbarascamera.com/turkeyvulture.html, 1999.

41 Eventually one vulture ...": Paul MacCready, Sailplane Homebuilders Workshop, Tehachapi, California, September 2000.

41 The vulture is an atmospheric ...: Bill Kohlmoos, "Some Interesting Information about the Turkey Vulture," http://www.accutek.com/vulture/facts.htm.

42 All he really had ...: MacCready interview, January 2000.

42 Pretty soon he ...: MacCready, "Soaring Bird Aerodynamics," pp. 17–19.

42 To his surprise ...: Paul MacCready talk, "The Gossamer Condor," Guggenheim Aeronautical Laboratory at the California Institute of Technology—The First Fifty Years, 1983, Caltech Institute Archives, p. 34.

CHAPTER 9: MAN'S INNATE DESIRE TO FLY

44 A mouse on the ground ...: MacCready dyslexia talk, July 2000.

44 As for birds ...: Ken McCall, "A Man for All Reasonings," *California,* November 1986, p. 98.

44 Naturalist John Burroughs ...: Laurence Goldstein, "Look! Up in the Sky! It's a Bird! It's a Plane! It's Envious Man!" *Los Angeles Times,* 26 June 1986, p. 5.

44   "I may be flying . . . " : Charles Lindbergh, *The Spirit of St. Louis,* Great Aviation Quotes, http://www.skygod.com/quotes/quotes.html.

45   "When you fly really high . . ." : Author interview with Ken deRussy, June 2000.

46   In hang-gliding's . . . : Author interview with Joe Greblo, August 2000.

CHAPTER 10: HANG-GLIDING IN SOUTHERN CALIFORNIA

47   The year 2000 . . . : Author interview with Richard Miller, June 2000.

52   "I went farther . . . " : Maralys Wills, *Manbirds* (Englewood Cliffs, New Jersey: Prentice-Hall, 1981), p. 126.

52   When Miller sent photos . . . : Miller interview, June 2000.

CHAPTER 11: THE EARTH-FLIP HYPOTHESIS

56   As he explained to me . . . : Taras Kiceniuk, "Planetary Heat Engine Theory," 2 December 2001, http://www.icarusengineering.com/Plan-Heat-Eng.htm.

CHAPTER 12: THE OTTO LILIENTHAL MEET

61   It was during that time . . . : Jack Lambie, "Downhill Racer," *Soaring,* December 1970, pp. 16–17.

61   As with all of Lambie's . . . : Ibid., p. 16.

62   Always on the lookout . . . : Author interview with Karen Hoiland, July 2000.

62   To his amazement . . . : Author interview with Mark Lambie, June 2000.

62   In recent years, hang-gliding . . . : Mark Woodhams, "Who Really Invented the Flex Wing Hang Glider?" *Sky Wings Magazine,* September 1996.

62   In 1969, Bennett flew . . . : Don Dedera, *Hang Gliding: The Flyingest Flying* (Flagstaff, Arizona: Northland Press, 1975), p. 46.

64   Although not opposed . . . : Mark Lambie interview, June 2000.

64   As he later explained . . . : Wills, *Manbirds.*

65   As the gliders were visible . . . : Mark Lambie interview, June 2000.

65   Joe Faust, who . . . : Joe Faust, "The Great Universal Hang Glider Championships," *Soaring,* July 1971, p. 32.

66   Amiable and good-natured . . . : Mark Lambie interview, June 2000.

66   "What good is it? . . . " : Wills, *Manbirds,* p. 42.

CHAPTER 13: TARAS KICENIUK AND ICARUS GROUND EFFECT I

69 The best they could do ... : Author interview with Joe Greblo, August 2000.

69 Finally in 1975 ... : Author interview with Taras Kiceniuk Jr., March 2000.

CHAPTER 14: HOW HENRY KREMER CHANGED PAUL MACCREADY'S LIFE

70 A German professor ... : Patrick Cooke, "The Man Who Launched a Dinosaur," *Science '86,* April 1986, p. 26; Coles Phinzy, "On a Clear Day You Can Fly Forever," *Sports Illustrated,* 16 February 1981, p. 36.

70 "They [the British] had ... ": MacCready dyslexia talk, Art Center College of Design, 29 July 2000.

70 The first was a news item ... : Leon Jaroff, "He Gives Wings to Dreams," *Time,* 11 June 1990, p. 52.

70 Suddenly, says MacCready ... : "Flying Free," *Scientific American Frontiers,* Chedd-Angier Production Company, PBS Home Video, 1990–2000.

71 "If you keep the weight ... ": MacCready dyslexia talk, July 2000.

71 "It was just a big ... ": MacCready, "Natural and Artificial Flying Machines," audiotape, Caltech Institute Archives, 12 January 1985; *Children of Icarus,* NOVA Adventures in Science (Addison-Wesley, 1983), p. 198.

72 Since MacCready's design ... : Author interview with Bryan Allen, July 2001.

72 He decided to call ... : Paul MacCready, "Gossamer Albatross—Son of Gossamer Condor," audiotape, Caltech Institute Archives, 5 December 1978.

72 To help him ... : MacCready interview, October 2001.

CHAPTER 15: LAMBIE LUCK

73 "If it's worth doing ... ": Mark Lambie interview, June 2000.

74 "He loved the feeling ... ": Author interview with Charlie Webber, August 2000.

74 He would take his trailer truck ... : Mark Lambie interview, June 2000.

76 For personal use ... : Author interview with Sue Currier, June 2000.

77 He thought that people ... : Author interview with Edmund Burke, July 2000.

79 "It's okay," he would . . . : Mark Lambie interview, June 2000.

80 MacCready offered to pay . . . : Morton Grosser, *Gossamer Odyssey* (New York: Dover Publications, 1981), p. 78.

80 To keep MacCready's design a secret . . . : Ibid., p. 79.

81 Despite the rain . . . : Ibid., p. 82; Jack Lambie, "The Gossamer Condor," *Air Progress,* (month unknown) 1978, p. 71.

CHAPTER 16: A HUMAN TEST STAND

82 "He was at the brown bag stage . . . " : Author interview with Joe Mastropaolo, March 2000.

CHAPTER 17: TALES OF THE MOJAVE

86 On one side of the highway . . . : Alec Wilkinson, "Extraterrestrials: The Flying Rutan Brothers of Mojave, California," *Esquire,* June 1998, p. 86.

86 Because MacCready had insisted . . . : Grosser, *Gossamer Odyssey,* p. 90.

86 In turbulence, the ultrathin . . . : J. D. Burke, "The Gossamer Condor and Albatross: A Case Study in Aircraft Design," AIAA Professional Study Series, AeroVironment (Monrovia, California), Report No. AV-R-80/540, 16 June 1980, p. 5-3.

87 "The landing gear was laughable . . . " : Ibid., p. 4-4.

87 With MacCready's 108-pound son . . . : MacCready, "Natural and Artificial Flying Machines," audiotape, Caltech Institute Archives, 12 January 1985.

87 "We had all kinds . . . " : Author interview with J. D. Burke, July 2000.

88 Even a 2 mph . . . : Paul MacCready talk, "The Gossamer Condor," Caltech Institute Archives, p. 37.

88 Mojave was "a cold beautiful . . . " : MacCready, "Natural and Artificial Flying Machines."

CHAPTER 18: THE SHAFTER CONNECTION

89 Glenn Miller once . . . : P. F. Kluge, "A Modern Icarus Reaches to the Sun for Power to Fly," *Smithsonian,* February 1981, p. 75.

90 "He had a remarkable . . . " : Author interview with Bryan Allen, July 2001.

91 "If someone wanted . . . " : Burke, "The Gossamer Condor and Albatross: A Case Study," p. 2-5.

91 "And always," wrote Jim Burke . . . : Ibid.

CHAPTER 19: REINVENTING THE WRIGHT BROTHERS

92   There were some successes . . . : Grosser, *Gossamer Odyssey,* pp. 96, 102.

92   "It is sort of horrifying . . . : Paul MacCready, "Gossamer Albatross—Son of Gossamer Condor," audiotape, Caltech Institute Archives, 5 December 1978.

93   The problem, it soon became clear . . . : Ibid.

94   "Anyone who showed up . . . " : Author interview with Bill Watson, June 2000.

CHAPTER 20: A TURN FOR THE BETTER

95   Within a month . . . : Grosser, *Gossamer Odyssey,* p. 116.

98   Equally important, he was currently . . . : Bryan Allen interview, July 2001.

98   Pedaling the Gossamer Condor . . . : Grosser, *Gossamer Odyssey,* p. 123.

99   It flew so well . . . : Paul MacCready, "Natural and Artificial Flying Machines," audiotape, Caltech Institute Archives, 12 January 1985.

100 MacCready was "discouraged . . . " : Grosser, *Gossamer Odyssey,* p. 140.

CHAPTER 21: THE CASE FOR APPARENT ALTRUISM

103 In this vein, *Soaring* . . . : *The National Soaring Museum's Historical Journal,* vol. 16, no. 2 (1994), p. 13.

103 The accompanying text . . . : "The Esquire Twenty-one," *Esquire,* p. 125.

103 "He once told me . . . " : Author interview with Bob Boucher, March 2000.

105 "The tiny, rocky outcrop . . . " : Paul E. Teague, "Model Pioneer," *Design News,* 1 March 1999.

CHAPTER 22: THE CHANNEL CROSSING

106 "All inventions are obvious . . . " : Kenneth A. Brown, *Inventors at Work* (Redmond, Washington: Tempus Books, Microsoft Press, 1988), p. 12.

106 Because it had taken . . . : MacCready, "The Gossamer Condor," Caltech Institute Archives, p. 39.

107 Compared to wood . . . : Amy C. Edmondson, *A Fuller Explanation,* ch. 15, "From Geodesics to Tensegrity: The Invisible Made Visible," online edition, http://www.angelfire.com/mt/marksomers/41.html, January 2000, pp. 245–49.

108 Although the press . . . : Ibid.

108 When he spotted the Albatross ... : Jack Lambie, "The Triumph of Paul MacCready's Gossamer Albatross," *Soaring,* August 1979, p. 19.

CHAPTER 23: VIKINGS VERSUS THE EMERALD ISLE

109 Their troops were needed ... : R. J. White, *The Horizon Concise History of England* (New York: American Heritage Publishing Co., 1971), p. 9.

110 With what Winston Churchill ... : Winston Churchill, *Birth of Britain* (New York: Dodd, Mead & Co., 1956), p. 93.

112 For MacCready, the toughest part ... : Paul MacCready, "Perspectives on Gossamer Aircraft: Doing More with Less," Watson Lecture, audiotape, Caltech Institute Archives, 18 February 1981.

112 "It was like running ... " : MacCready interview, January 2000.

114 For his part, Allen ... : Grosser, *Gossamer Odyssey,* p. 192; Bryan Allen interview, July 2001.

114 "I was telling him ... " : Allen interview, July 2001.

115 Ground school was five minutes ... : Mastropaolo interview, March 2000.

117 "I think I know what ..." : Allen interview, July 2001.

117 "If it had been high tide ... " : Mark Wheeler, "Paul MacCready's Flying Circus," *Discover,* 1 September 1999, p. 76.

CHAPTER 24: WHY THE BRITISH DIDN'T WIN

118 Just for turning down ... : Allen interview, July 2001.

CHAPTER 26: HOW THE OIL CRISIS CHANGED THE COUNTRY

122 To set an example ... : Arthur Allen, "Prodigal Sun," *Mojo Wire,* March/April 2000.

122 In fact, as William Tucker ... : William Tucker, "The Energy Crisis Is Over," *Harper's,* November 1981.

123 OPEC subsequently raised prices ... : Ibid.

CHAPTER 27: BOB BOUCHER AND THE ETERNAL PLANE

126 At that altitude ... : Author interview with Bob Boucher, March 2000.

126 "There's no goddamned sun ... " : Ibid.

127 They named their plane ... : Bob Boucher, "The Quiet Revolution," Astro Flight, 1979.

128 By 1972, they had ... : Ibid.

128 That led to a government . . . : Bob Boucher, "History of Solar Flight," AIAA/SAE/ASME 20th Joint Propulsion Conference, Paper #AIAA-84-1429, Cincinnati, Ohio, 11–13 June 1984, p. 1.

128 To prove how quiet . . . : Ibid.

128 Even so, John Foster . . . : Ibid.

128 It was at this point . . . : Ibid.

128 If they built . . . : Boucher interview, March 2000.

129 "We were basically just . . . " : Ibid.

129 The Sunrise was to be powered . . . : Bob Boucher, "Project Sunrise," AIAA/SAE/ASME 15th Joint Propulsion Conference, Las Vegas, Nevada, 18–20 June 1979, p. 1.

129 With its 32-foot wingspan . . . : Boucher, "History of Solar Flight," p. 2.

130 The Sunrise II made its first . . . : Boucher, "Project Sunrise," p. 3.

131 "Great," said MacCready . . . : Boucher interview, March 2000.

133 Although Morgan half-expected . . . : David Holzman, "Masterful Tinkering of Genius," *Insight,* 25 June 1990, p. 12.

133 As it turned out, Dupont's chairman . . . : MacCready interview, July 2000.

134 "Paul called me on the phone . . ." : Author interview with Janice Brown, June 2001.

CHAPTER 28: FROM POINTOISE TO "A RIGHT PROPER PISS-UP"

136 The electric motor . . . : Boucher, "History of Solar Flight," p. 11.

136 This was gear-reduced . . . : Boucher, "History of Solar Flight," p. 11.

136 The samarium-cobalt motor . . . : Boucher interview, March 2000.

140 "I barely graduated . . . " : Author interview with Ray Morgan, May 2000.

141 "They laid off . . . " : Ibid.

143 Dupont was so proprietary . . . : Brown interview, June 2001.

143 To keep the press . . . : Boucher interview, March 2000.

144 The Dupont public relations representative . . . : Ibid.

144 By the time Dupont's PR . . . : Ibid.

145 As the day grew hotter . . . : Steve Ptacek, "From France to England Aboard the Solar Challenger," *Soaring,* December 1981, p. 27.

145 At 11:28, on Ptacek's eighth . . . : Ibid.

145 At first the thermal . . . : Ibid.

145 But on successive . . . : Ibid.

145 By the time Ptacek . . . : Ibid., p. 28.

146 To protect the Solar Challenger . . . : Author interview with Steve Ptacek, October 2000.

146 Then suddenly Ptacek . . . : Ibid.

146 The craft was twisted . . . : Ptacek, "From France to England," p. 29.

146 He put the plane back . . . : Ibid.

146 They in turn contacted . . . : Ibid.

146 The twin cobalt motors . . . : Ibid., p. 28.

146 It felt as if he were . . . : Ibid.

146 "I was thinking . . . " : Ptacek interview, March 2000.

146 "The colonel is inviting . . . " : Boucher interview, March 2000.

CHAPTER 29: "A BIG DAMN BIRD CAME OUT OF THE SKY"

148 He built the Solar Challenger . . . : MacCready interview, January 2000.

148 If they could just see . . . : MacCready interview, July 2000.

149 "Everybody loves ugly extinct . . . " : MacCready interview, January 2000.

150 The members of the Caltech workshop . . . : Paul MacCready, "The Great Pterodactyl Project," *Engineering & Science,* November 1985, p. 21.

150 It was as if one had combined . . . : Ibid.

150 Sixteen years after . . . : Author interview with Jim Cunningham, November 2001.

150 The QN had an 8.5-foot . . . : Ibid.

152 To get into the air . . . : Ibid.

152 Cunningham and Langston eventually . . . : Ibid.

152 To feed, it most likely . . . : Ibid.

152 It stayed aloft . . . : Ibid.

152 When the local lakes . . . : Ibid.

152 Since there wasn't much information . . . : Author interview with Henry Jex, June 2000.

152 They concluded that QN's . . . : Ibid.

153 Because the paleontologists . . . : Cunningham interview, November 2001.

153 If MacCready had known . . . : Ibid.

153 When the replica flapped . . . : Morgan interview, May 2000.

153 "Nature did it . . . " : Author interview with Alec Brooks, September 2000.

154 Even then, the pterodactyl crashed . . . : Morgan interview, May 2000.

154 "If you make a car . . . " : Brooks interview, September 2000.

155 Instead, says Morgan . . . : Paul MacCready talk, "Soaring—The Catalyst

for Invention," National Soaring Museum's 25th Anniversary Address at the Third Annual Community Soaring Day, Elmira, New York, p. 16.

157 "Then Friday morning . . . ": MacCready interview, July 2000.

159 To the newspapers . . . : Ken McCall, "A Man for All Reasonings," *California,* November 1986, p. 98.

159 *Miami Herald* humor columnist . . . : Dave Barry, "Dave Barry's Concise History of 1986," *Miami Herald,* 4 January 1987.

159 Although MacCready was . . . : MacCready interview, October 2001; McCall, "A Man for All Reasonings," p. 98.

159 MacCready, who not only . . . : Author interview with Bill Watson, March 2000.

159 Then, assuming all went well . . . : Patrick Cooke, "The Man Who Launched a Dinosaur," *Science '86,* April 1986, p. 26.

CHAPTER 30: BIKING THROUGH THE GENE POOL

160 To supply their needs . . . : "Interview with David Rosner: Portrait of an Unhealthy City: New York in the 1880s," Development Lab, The Living City, http://wap.google.com/search?q=%22Interview+with+David+Rosner%22&btnG=Google+Search, 2002.

160 In 1892, Rudyard Kipling . . . : David B. Perry, *Bike Cult* (New York/London: Four Walls Eight Windows, 1995), p. 242.

161 Bicycles allowed farm workers . . . : *Kith & Kin,* vol. 8, no. 3 (September/October 1991).

161 Its "sheer humanity" . . . : S. S. Wilson, "Bicycle Technology," *Scientific American,* March 1973.

161 The bicycle was the "perfect transducer . . . ": Ibid.; Ivan Illich, *Towards a History of Needs* (Berkeley: Heydey Books, 1977).

161 In running, too much . . . : Paul MacCready talk to Pasadena Twilight Club, June 2000.

161 Whereas a typical man . . . : Perry, *Bike Cult,* p. 189.

161 Whereas in a bike, 95 percent . . . : Thomas A. Bass, "By Land and by Sea and Even by Air, Pedal Power Wins," *Smithsonian,* January 1985, p. 90; James Flannigan, "To Cleaner Air and Good Jobs Please Step on It," *Los Angeles Times,* 26 April 1992, p. 1.

161 If a rider could find a place . . . : Bass, "By Land and by Sea and Even by Air," p. 90.

164 He had circumnavigated . . . : "History of the World Solar Challenge," World Solar Challenge, http://www.wsc.org.au/About/history.solar,

Solar Odyssey 2001, 26 January 2002; Henry Kingman, "Front Seat of the Race Bus," Great Australian Bike Challenge, http://milly.org/hkingman/oz/oz2.htm, 1992.

164 If MacCready could ...: "History of the World Solar Challenge."

164 As the rules posted by Tholstrup ...: Howard Wilson, Paul MacCready and Chester Kyle, "Lessons of the Sunraycer," *Scientific American,* March 1989, p. 92.

165 Although such a design ...: Ibid.

165 GM agreed to put up ...: Bill Moore, "Paul MacCready—EV Soul Man," *EV World,* http://www.evworld.com/archives/interviews/maccready.html, 1997–1998.

165 As if to emphasize ...: Brooks interview, September 2000.

166 The driver's Plexiglas ...: Floyd Tuckey, *Sunraycer's Solar Saga* (Australia: Berghouse, Floyd Tuckey Publishing Group, 1988), p. 15.

167 To save the batteries ...: Ibid., p. 104.

167 For power, the Sunraycer ...: Wilson, MacCready, Kyle, "Lessons of the Sunraycer," p. 92.

168 As long as he could ...: Michael Shnayerson, *The Car That Could* (New York: Random House, 1996), p. 17.

168 His living room ...: Ibid., p. 23.

168 He rarely cooked ...: Ibid.

168 Sometimes he would just ...: Author interview with Alan Cocconi, September 2000.

170 Test engineers did everything ...: Tuckey, *Sunraycer's Solar Saga.*

170 Rather than baby the car ...: Ibid.

170 The Ford team was elated ...: Ibid.

CHAPTER 31: SOLAR DELUGE ON THE BITUMEN

171 A semitropical tourist town ...: Tuckey, *Sunraycer's Solar Saga,* pp. 18–19.

171 Hotels and cafés ...: Ibid., p. 18.

171 After October, monsoons ...: Ibid., p. 14.

171 The temperature soared ...: Stuart F. Brown, "Chasing Sunraycer across Australia," *Popular Science,* February 1988, p. 64.

171 One driver packed his car ...: William H. Jordan Jr., "Racing with the Sun," *Smithsonian,* February 1988, p. 48.

172 The designers of two Japanese ...: Tuckey, *Sunraycer's Solar Saga,* p. 21.

172 Paul Mitchell, president ...: Jordan, "Racing with the Sun, p. 48.

172 Perhaps the most conventional ...: Tuckey, *Sunraycer's Solar Saga,* p. 19.

172 The General Motors team ...: Jordan, "Racing with the Sun," p. 48; Tuckey, *Sunraycer's Solar Saga,* pp. 35–36.

174 In fact, just to help prevent ...: Jordan, "Racing with the Sun," p. 48.

174 To drive the Sunraycer ...: Tuckey, *Sunraycer's Solar Saga,* p. 52.

174 In the speed trials ...: Ibid., p. 22.

174 "I could see that the crowd ..." : Brown, "Chasing Sunraycer across Australia," p. 64.

174 The inland savannas ...: Tuckey, *Sunraycer's Solar Saga,* p. 147.

174 Off to the sides ...: Jordan, "Racing with the Sun," p. 48.

174 Then out of the shimmer ...: Tuckey, *Sunraycer's Solar Saga,* p. 124.

175 On the ground ...: Ibid., p. 150.

175 At 5 P.M., when by race ...: Brown, "Chasing Sunraycer across Australia," p. 64.

175 Unlike the Mana La ...: Brooks interview, September 2000.

176 The Sunraycer was sending ...: Watson interview, June 2000.

176 Fearful of Mana La ...: Paul MacCready, "Sunraycer Odyssey," *Engineering & Science,* Winter 1988, p. 11.

177 The next morning ...: Ibid.

177 But MacCready boldly ...: Ibid.

177 The Ford team spread ...: Brown, "Chasing Sunraycer across Australia," p. 64.

177 A wind gust ...: Jordan, "Racing with the Sun," p. 48.

177 When a flash flood ...: Ibid.

177 When the Sunraycer crossed ...: Tuckey, *Sunraycer's Solar Saga,* p. 177.

178 If they had used ...: Author interview with Chet Kyle, April 2000.

CHAPTER 32: ELECTRIC CARS AND MENTAL BLOCKS

179 Working on improved batteries ...: Bill Moore, "Paul MacCready—EV Soul Man," *EV World,* http://www.evworld.com/archives/interviews/maccready.html, 1997–1998.

180 On its face ...: MacCready interview, October 2001.

180 General Motors was wary ...: Shnayerson, *The Car That Could,* p. 7.

180 Cocconi's 60-pound ...: William J. Cook, "The Soul of a New Machine: Risk and Innovation," *U.S. News & World Report,* 26 August 1991, p. 80.

180 Instead, MacCready's people ...: Shnayerson, *The Car That Could,* p. 22.

180 It was "a bloody, unpleasant ..." : Moore, "Paul MacCready—EV Soul Man."

180 A thousand phone calls . . . : Cook, "The Soul of a New Machine."

181 And it also seemed . . . : Shnayerson, *The Car That Could,* p. 24.

181 Although the car . . . : Ibid., pp. 24–25.

181 "The Impact blew away . . . " : Mark Fischetti, "Here Comes the Electric Car," *Smithsonian,* April 1992, p. 34.

181 Taking GM at its word . . . : Ibid.

182 GM, fearful of shocks . . . : Glenn Zorpette, "Electric Cars and Petrosaurs Are My Business," *Scientific American,* May 1997.

182 The range on . . . : Will Nixon, "Back to the Future," *Amicus Journal,* New York, Fall 1999.

182 Furthermore, the lease . . . : Author interview with Howard Wilson, December 2001.

182 Anyone who thought . . . : Dick Ackerman, "The Folly of the AQMD's Subsidized Electric Vehicle," *Business Forum,* Los Angeles, Winter 1997.

182 If there were to be . . . : Paul MacCready talk, "Soaring—The Catalyst for Innovation," The National Soaring Museum's 25th Anniversary Address at the Third Annual Community Soaring Day.

183 In January 2001 . . . : Scott Memmer, "California Holds the Line on Zero Emissions Vehicles," http://www.edmunds.com/news/feature/general/45399/article.html, 17 April 2001.

CHAPTER 33: DAY OF THE STRATOSPHERIC SATELLITE

185 By virtue of constantly . . . : Paul MacCready, "The Excitement and Value of Engineering," The Ralph Coats Roe Lecture, ASME International Mechanical Engineering Congress & Exposition, Anaheim, 19 November 1998, p. 1.

186 Although the HALSOL . . . : Seth Dunn, "The Electric Car Arrives Again," *World-Watch,* March/April 1997.

186 If missiles were fired . . . : Ibid.

186 It had a new center . . . : Ray Morgan interview, May 2000.

188 Until solar cells became cheaper . . . : Ibid.

CHAPTER 34: THE ENGINEER, THE HUNTER AND THE BEAR

191 Hamsters, he ruefully concluded . . . : Paul MacCready talk, Skeptics Society Festschrift in Honor of Stephen Jay Gould, Beckman Auditorium, Caltech, 7 October 2000.

194 Then, working at home . . . : Leon Jaroff, "Dream Makers: Great Ideas Spring from Many Sources in Many Different Ways," *Time,* 4 December 2000, p. 102.

194 The hard nuts and bolts . . . : Ken McCall, "A Man for All Reasonings," *California,* November 1986, p. 102.

CHAPTER 35: TAO OF THE CARBON DRAGON

196 In substituting batteries . . . : Paul MacCready, 1991 Annual Conference for Inventors and Entrepreneurs, Caltech Institute Archives, 1991.

196 "No other inexpensive . . . " : Lyle McCarty, "Lessons from an Aeronautical Master," *Design News,* 26 August 1991, p. 141.

196 One such approach . . . : Author interview with Bruce Carmichael, December 2001.

198 He had long been . . . : Mark Woodhams, "Who Really Invented the Flex Wing Hang Glider?" *Sky Wings Magazine,* September 1996.

198 A sailplane, he wrote . . . : Richard Miller, *Without Visible Means of Support* (Los Angeles: Parker, 1967), p. 1.

198 In 1972, Miller . . . : Richard Miller, "The New Era in Soaring," *Soaring,* March 1972, p. 27.

198 "Thus Tao was diminished . . . " : Ibid., p. 28.

198 But there was a solution . . . : Richard Miller, "The Shape of Things to Come," *Soaring,* May 1978, p. 18.

199 Sailplane pilot Gary Osoba . . . : Gary Osoba talk on dynamic soaring, Sailplane Homebuilders Workshop, September 2000.

200 "The glider literally leaps . . . " : Author interview with Gary Osoba, September 2001.

CHAPTER 36: SAVING THE WORLD 10 PERCENT AT A TIME

202 The "most important statement . . . " : MacCready talk, Stephen Jay Gould Festschrift, 7 October 2000.

202 Given the inability . . . : Kenneth A. Brown, *Inventors at Work* (Redmond, Washington: Tempus Books, Microsoft Press, 1988), p. 14.

202 As the world's only . . . : MacCready talk, Sailplane Homebuilders Workshop, September 2000.

203 In former times . . . : Paul MacCready, "An Evolutionary Perspective," *Free Inquiry,* Spring 1987, p. 20.

203 Due to ever-more-powerful technology . . . : Paul MacCready, "Visions of a Sustainable World," Future Symposium, Caltech Institute Archives, 29 October 1991.

203 If civilization was to survive . . . : Paul MacCready, "Soaring on Gossamer Wings," *Education Network News,* January/February 1984, p. 2.

203 Man's mind gives him . . . : McCall, "A Man for All Reasonings," p. 103.

203 He has wiped out ...: MacCready, "Soaring on Gossamer Wings," p. 1; Lori Mammen, "Interview with Paul MacCready," *Think,* December 1993, p. 8.

203 Now, says MacCready, the war ...: Paul MacCready, "Unleashing Creativity," Keynote Presentation, Conferences and Symposia, The Inventor and the Innovative Society, 10 November 1995.

203 A quarter-million people ...: MacCready talk, Stephen Jay Gould Festschrift; Brown, *Inventors at Work,* p. 16.

204 "I estimate the chances ..." : McCall, "A Man for All Reasonings," p. 103.

204 He was asked to give ...: Paul MacCready, "An Ambivalent Luddite at a Technological Feast," AeroVironment paper, 15 October 1998, p. 2.

204 If anything, the British experts ...: Paul MacCready, "Careers in Science," National Energy Conference, audiotape, Caltech Institute Archives, 5 November 1983.

204 "Using linear thinking ..." : Brown, *Inventors at Work,* p. 12.

206 MacCready attributed at least ...: MacCready interview, January 2000.

206 As an example, MacCready told ...: Brown, *Inventors at Work,* p. 11.

207 Not only is a high IQ ...: MacCready, "Potential and Achievement, Categorization of Genius," *Skeptic,* vol. 2, no. 1 (1993), p. 44.

207 "Whatever you were trained in ..." : John Hurst and James Pavlick, "Dr. Paul MacCready Interview," Academy of Achievement, http://209.146.26.198/teachers/icdv2i2s/SITES/ACHIEVE/mainmenu.htm, 1995–1998.

208 Jack Lambie would later say ...: David Holzman, "Masterful Tinkering of Genius," *Insight,* 25 June 1990, p. 17.

208 Actually, he maintains ...: Brown, *Inventors at Work,* p. 4.

208 His big advantage ...: MacCready dyslexia talk, Art Center College of Design, 29 July 2000.

CHAPTER 37: DOCTORAL THESIS IMMORTALITY

210 And as MacCready himself ...: Chee Pearlman, "Inventing Efficiency," *International Design,* November/December 1990, p.35.

210 In the same fashion ...: MacCready, "The Gossamer Condor," Caltech Institute Archives, p. 39.

211 And although that car ...: MacCready interview, October 2001.

211 "The kids are so gifted ..." : Paul MacCready talk, Sailplane Homebuilders Workshop, Tehachapi, California, September 2000.

212 "It was a very demanding project . . ." : Ibid.

CHAPTER 38: EXPLODING BIOMIMICRY

214 Although nature has . . . : George Bugliarello, "Biomimesis: The Road Less Traveled," *The Bridge,* Fall 1997.

214 One reason: almost none . . . : Ibid.

214 He won the Kremer Prize . . . : MacCready talk, "The Gossamer Condor," Caltech Institute Archives, p. 39.

214 When MacCready talked . . . : Stefi Weisburd, "Learning How to Fly, Reptile Style," *Science News,* 19 October 1985, p. 247.

214 Once on a trip to Kenya . . . : McCall, "A Man for All Reasonings," p. 98.

215 "If you tried to do . . ." : MacCready talk, "Natural and Artificial Flying Machines," audiotape, Caltech Institute Archives, 12 January 1985.

215 "Through evolution birds have achieved . . ." : Ibid.

215 And they do many things . . . : Ibid.

215 "A homing bird can . . ." : Ibid.

215 A monarch butterfly . . . : Ibid.

215 And even after six decades . . . : Paul Dean, "It's a Bird . . . It's a Plane; It's Weird, but It Can Fly," *Los Angeles Times,* 16 February 1986, p. 1.

CHAPTER 39: WHY BLIND PEOPLE DON'T SKY DIVE

218 "The company is profitable . . ." : Glenn Zorpette, "Electric Cars and Petrosaurs Are My Business," *Scientific American,* May 1997.

224 According to William Sasnett . . . : Author interview with William Sasnett, December 2001.

224 "You know why blind people . . ." : Author interview with Charlie Webber, August 2000.

CHAPTER 40: THE JOHNNY APPLESEED OF ORNITHOPTERS

225 He complains constantly . . . : MacCready dyslexia talk, July 2000.

225 In the tradition . . . : Leon Jaroff, "He Gives Wings to Dreams," *Time,* 11 June 1990, p. 52.

227 As the other guests . . . : "Jack Lambie Memorial," AeroVironment videotape, 24 July 1999.

Index